The World's Classics

CXVI

SOPHOCLES

THE SEVEN PLAYS IN ENGLISH VERSE

CAMPBELL

OXFORD: HORACE HART
PRINTER TO THE UNIVERSITY

SOPHOCLES

SOPHOCLES

THE SEVEN PLAYS

TRANSLATED INTO
ENGLISH VERSE

BY

LEWIS CAMPBELL

HENRY FROWDE
OXFORD UNIVERSITY PRESS
LONDON, NEW YORK AND TORONTO.

SOPHOCLES

THE

SEVEN PLAYS IN ENGLISH VERSE

BY

LEWIS CAMPBELL, M.A.

HON. LL.D., HON. D.LITT.

EMERITUS PROFESSOR OF GREEK IN THE UNIVERSITY OF ST. ANDREWS
HON. FELLOW OF BALLIOL COLLEGE, OXFORD

NEW EDITION, REVISED

HENRY FROWDE

OXFORD UNIVERSITY PRESS

LONDON, NEW YORK AND TORONTO

SOPHOCLES

Born at Colonos . . . probably 495 B.C.
Died . . . . . 406 B.C.

*The present translation was first published in 'The
World's Classics' in* 1906.

Sie hören nicht die folgenden Gesänge,
Die Seelen, denen ich die ersten sang.

CONTENTS

PREFACE

In 1869, having read the Antigone with a pupil who at the time had a passion for the stage, I was led to attempt a metrical version of the *Antigone*, and, by and by, of the Electra and Trachiniae.[1] I had the satisfaction of seeing this last very beautifully produced by an amateur company in Scotland in 1877; when Mrs. Fleeming Jenkin may be said to have 'created' the part of Dêanira. Thus encouraged, I completed the translation of the seven plays, which was published by Kegan Paul in 1883 and again by Murray in 1896. I have now to thank Mr. Murray for consenting to this cheaper issue.

The seven extant plays of Sophocles have been variously arranged. In the order most frequently adopted by English editors, the three plays of the Theban cycle, Oedipus Tyrannus, Oedipus Coloneus, and Antigone, have been placed foremost.

In one respect this is obviously convenient, as appearing to present continuously a connected story. But on a closer view, it is in two ways illusory.

1. The Antigone is generally admitted to be, comparatively speaking, an early play, while the Oedipus Coloneus belongs to the dramatist's latest manner; the first Oedipus coming in somewhere between the two. The effect is therefore analogous to that produced on readers of Shakespeare by the habit of placing Henry VI after Henry IV and V. But tragedies and 'histories' or chronicle plays are not *in pari materia*.

2. The error has been aggravated by a loose way of speaking of 'the Theban Trilogy', a term which could only be properly applicable if the three dramas had been produced in the same year. I have therefore now

[1] *Three Plays of Sophocles:* Blackwood, 1873.

arranged the seven plays in an order corresponding to the most probable dates of their production, viz. Antigone, Aias, King Oedipus, Electra, Trachiniae, Philoctetes, and Oedipus at Colonos. A credible tradition refers the Antigone to 445 B.C. The Aias appears to be not much later—it may even be earlier—than the Antigone. The Philoctetes was produced in 408 B.C., when the poet was considerably over eighty. The Oedipus at Colonos has always been believed to be a composition of Sophocles' old age. It is said to have been produced after his death, though it may have been composed some years earlier. The tragedy of King Oedipus, in which the poet's art attained its maturity, is plausibly assigned to an early year of the Peloponnesian war (say 427 B.C.), the Trachiniae to about 420 B.C. The time of the Electra is doubtful; but Professor Jebb has shown that, on metrical grounds, it should be placed after, rather than before, King Oedipus. Even the English reader, taking the plays as they are grouped in this volume, may be aware of a gradual change of manner, not unlike what is perceptible in passing from Richard II to Macbeth, and from Macbeth to The Winter's Tale or Cymbeline. For although the supposed date of the Antigone was long subsequent to the poet's first tragic victory, the forty years over which the seven plays are spread saw many changes of taste in art and literature.

PREFATORY NOTE TO THE EDITION OF 1883

I. THE Hellenic spirit has been repeatedly characterized as simple Nature-worship. Even the Higher Paganism has been described as 'in other words the purified worship of natural forms.'[1] One might suppose, in reading some modern writers, that the Nymphs and Fauns, the River-Gods and Pan, were at least as prominent in all Greek poetry as Zeus, Apollo, and Athena, or that Apollo was only the sweet singer and not also the prophet of retribution.

The fresh and unimpaired enjoyment of the Beautiful is certainly the aspect of ancient life and literature which most attracted the humanists of the sixteenth century, and still most impresses those amongst ourselves who for various reasons desire to point the contrast between Paganism and Judaism. The two great groups of forces vaguely known as the Renaissance and the Revolution have both contributed to this result. Men who were weary of conventionality and of the weight of custom 'heavy as frost and deep almost as life,' have longed for the vision of 'Oread or Dryad glancing through the shade,' or to 'hear old Triton blow his wreathèd horn.' Meanwhile, that in which the Greeks most resembled us, 'the human heart by which we live,' for the very reason that it lies so near to us, is too apt to be lost from our conception of them. Another cause of this one-sided view is the illusion produced by the contemplation of statuary, together with the unapproachable perfection of form which every relic of Greek antiquity indisputably possesses.

[1] [Sir John Seeley's] *Natural Religion*, p. 79.

But on turning from the forms of Greek art to the substance of Greek literature, we find that Beauty, although everywhere an important element, is by no means the sole or even the chief attribute of the greatest writings, nor is the Hellenic consciousness confined within the life of Nature, unless this term is allowed to comprehend man with all his thoughts and aspirations. It was in this latter sense that Hegel recognized the union of depth with brightness in Greek culture : ' If the first paradise was the paradise of nature, this is the second, the higher paradise of the human spirit, which in its fair naturalness, freedom, depth and brightness here comes forth like a bride out of her chamber. The first wild majesty of the rise of spiritual life in the East is here circumscribed by the dignity of form, and softened into beauty. Its depth shows itself no longer in confusion, obscurity, and inflation, but lies open before us in simple clearness. Its brightness (Heiterkeit) is not a childish play, but covers a sadness which knows the hardness of fate but is not by that knowledge driven out of freedom and measure.' Hegel's Werke, vol. xvi. p. 139 (translated by Prof. Caird). The simplicity of Herodotus, for example, does not exclude far-reaching thoughts on the political advantages of liberty, nor such reflections on experience as are implied in the saying of Artabanus, that the transitoriness of human life is the least of its evils. And in what modern writing is more of the wisdom of life condensed than in the History of Thucydides ? It is surely more true to say of Greek literature that it contains types of all things human, stamped with the freshness, simplicity, and directness which belong to first impressions, and to the first impressions of genius.

Now the ' thoughts and aspirations,' which are nowhere absent from Greek literature, and make a centre of growing warmth and light in its Periclean period— when the conception of human nature for the first time takes definite shape—have no less of Religion in them than underlay the ' creed outworn.' To think otherwise would be an error of the same kind as that ' abuse

of the word Atheism ' against which the author of the
work above alluded to protests so forcibly.

Religion, in the sense here indicated, is the main-
spring and vital principle of Tragedy. The efforts of
Aeschylus and Sophocles were sustained by it, and its
inevitable decay through the scepticism which preceded
Socrates was the chief hindrance to the tragic genius of
Euripides. Yet the inequality of which we have con-
sequently to complain in him is redeemed by pregnant
hints of something yet ' more deeply interfused,' which
in him, as in his two great predecessors, is sometimes
felt as ' modern,' because it is not of an age but for all
time. The most valuable part of every literature is
something which transcends the period and nation out
of which it springs.

On the other hand, much that at first sight seems
primitive in Greek tragedy belongs more to the subject
than to the mode of handling. The age of Pericles was
in advance of that in which the legends were first
Hellenized and humanized, just as this must have been
already far removed from the earliest stages of mytho-
poeic imagination. The reader of Aeschylus or Sophocles should therefore be warned against attributing to
the poet's invention that which is given in the fable.

An educated student of Italian painting knows how
to discriminate—say in an Assumption by Botticelli—
between the traditional conventions, the contemporary
ideas, and the refinements of the artist's own fancy.
The same indulgence must be extended to dramatic art.
The tragedy of King Lear is not rude or primitive,
although the subject belongs to prehistoric times in
Britain. Nor is Goethe's Faust mediaeval in spirit as
in theme. So neither is the Oedipus Rex the product
of ' lawless and uncertain thoughts,' notwithstanding
the unspeakable horror of the story; but is penetrated
by the most profound estimate of all in human life that
is saddest, and all that is most precious.

Far from being naïve naturalists after the Keats

fashion, the Greek tragic poets had succeeded to a pessimistic reaction from simple Pagan enjoyment; they were surrounded with gloomy questionings about human destiny and Divine Justice, and they replied by looking steadily at the facts of life and asserting the supreme worth of innocence, equity, and mercy.

They were not philosophers, for they spoke the language of feeling ; but the civilization of which they were the strongest outcome was already tinged with influences derived from early philosophy—especially from the gnomic wisdom of the sixth century and from the spirit of theosophic speculation, which in Aeschylus goes far even to recast mythology. The latter influence was probably reinforced, through channels no longer traceable, by the Eleusinian worship, in which the mystery of life and death and of human sorrow had replaced the primitive wonder at the phenomena of the year.

And whatever elements of philosophic theory or mystic exaltation the drama may have reflected, it was still more emphatically the repository of some of the most precious traditions of civilized humanity—traditions which philosophy has sometimes tended to extenuate, if not to destroy.

Plato's Gorgias contains one of the most eloquent vindications of the transcendent value of righteousness and faithfulness as such. But when we ask, 'Righteousness in what relation ? '—' Faithfulness to whom ? '— the Gorgias is silent ; and when the vacant outline is filled up in the Republic, we are presented with an ideal of man's social relations, which, although it may be regarded as the ultimate development of existing tendencies, yet has no immediate bearing on any actual condition of the world.

The ideal of the tragic poet may be less perfect ; or rather he does not attempt to set before us abstractedly any single ideal. But the grand types of character which he presents to the world are not merely imaginary. They are creatures of flesh and blood, men and women, to whom the unsullied purity of their homes, the free-

dom and power of their country, the respect and love
of their fellow-citizens, are inestimably dear.   From a
Platonic, and still more from a Christian point of view,
the best morality of the age of Pericles is no doubt
defective.   Such counsels of perfection as ' Love your
enemies', or ' A good man can harm no one, not even
an enemy ',—are beyond the horizon of tragedy, unless
dimly seen in the person of Antigone.   The co-existence
of savage vindictiveness with the most affectionate tenderness is characteristic of heroes and heroines alike, and
produces some of the most moving contrasts.   But the
tenderness is no less deep and real for this, and while
the chief persons are thus passionate, the Greek lesson
of moderation and reasonableness is taught by the
event, whether expressed or not by the mouth of sage
or prophet or of the ' ideal bystander '.

Greek tragedy, then, is a religious art, not merely
because associated with the festival of Dionysus, nor
because the life which it represented was that of men
who believed, with all the Hellenes, in Zeus, Apollo,
and Athena, or in the power of Moira and the Erinyes,—
not merely because it represented

' the dread strife
Of poor humanity's afflicted will
Struggling in vain with ruthless destiny,'

but much more because it awakened in the Athenian
spectator emotions of wonder concerning human life,
and of admiration for nobleness in the unfortunate—
a sense of the infinite value of personal uprightness and
of domestic purity—which in the most universal sense
of the word were truly religious ;—because it expressed
a consciousness of depths which Plato never fathomed,
and an ideal of character which, if less complete than
Shakespeare's, is not less noble.   It is indeed a ' rough '
generalization that ranks the Agamemnon with the
Adoniazusae as a religious composition.

II. This spiritual side of tragic poetry deserves to be
emphasized both as the most essential aspect of it, and
as giving it the most permanent claim to lasting recog-

nition. And yet, apart from this, merely as dramas, the works of Aeschylus, Sophocles, and Euripides will never cease to be admired. These poets are teachers, but they teach through art. To ask simply, as Carlyle once did, 'What did they think ?' is not the way to understand or learn from them.

Considered simply as works of art, the plays of Sophocles stand alone amongst dramatic writings in their degree of concentration and complex unity.

1. The interest of a Sophoclean drama is always intensely personal, and is almost always centred in an individual destiny. In other words, it is not historical or mythical, but ethical. Single persons stand out magnificently in Aeschylus. But the action is always larger than any single life. Each tragedy or trilogy resembles the fragment of a sublime Epic poem. Mighty issues revolve about the scene, whether this is laid on Earth or amongst the Gods, issues far transcending the fate of Orestes or even of Prometheus. In the perspective painting of Sophocles, these vast surroundings fall into the background, and the feelings of the spectator are absorbed in sympathy with the chief figure on the stage, round whom the other characters—the members of the chorus being included—are grouped with the minutest care.

2. In this grouping of the persons, as well as in the conduct of the action, Sophocles is masterly in his use of pathetic contrast. This motive must of course enter into all tragedy—nothing can be finer than the contrast of Cassandra to Clytemnestra in the Agamemnon,—but in Sophocles it is all-pervading, and some of the minor effects of it are so subtle that although inevitably felt by the spectator they are often lost upon the mere reader or student. And every touch, however transient, is made to contribute to the main effect.

To recur once more to the much-abused analogy of statuary :—the work of Aeschylus may be compared to a colossal frieze, while that of Sophocles resembles the pediment of a smaller temple. Or if, as in considering the Orestean trilogy, the arrangement of the pediment affords the more fitting parallel even for Aeschylus, yet the forms are so gigantic that minute touches of characterization and of contrast are omitted as superfluous. Whereas in Sophocles, it is at once the finish of the chief figure and the studied harmony of the whole, which have led his work to be compared with that of his contemporary Phidias. Such comparison, however, is useful by way of illustration merely. It must never be forgotten that, as Lessing pointed out to some who thought the Philoctetes too sensational, analogies between the arts are limited by essential differences of material and of scope. All poetry represents successive moments. Its figures are never in repose. And although the action of Tragedy is concentrated and revolves around a single point, yet it is a dull vision that confounds rapidity of motion with rest.

3. Sophocles found the subjects of his dramas already embodied not only in previous tragedies but in Epic and Lyric poetry. And there were some fables, such as that of the death of Oedipus at Colonos, which seem to have been known to him only through oral tradition. For some reason which is not clearly apparent, both he and Aeschylus drew more largely from the Cyclic poets than from ' our Homer '. The inferior and more recent Epics, which are now lost, were probably more episodical, and thus presented a more inviting repertory of legends than the Iliad and Odyssey.

Arctinus of Lesbos had treated at great length the story of the House of Thebes. The legend of Orestes, to which there are several allusions, not always consistent with each other, in the Homeric poems, had been a favourite and fruitful subject of tradition and of poetical treatment in the intervening period. Passages of the Tale of Troy, in which other heroes than Achilles had the pre-eminence, had been elaborated by Lesches and other Epic writers of the Post-Homeric time. The voyage of the Argonauts, another favourite heroic theme, supplied the subjects of many dramas which have disappeared. Lastly, the taking of Oechalia by

b 2

Heracles, and the events which followed it, had been narrated in a long poem, in which one version of that hero's multiform legend was fully set forth.

The subjects of the King Oedipus, Oedipus at Colonos, and Antigone, are taken from the Tale of Thebes ; the Aias and the Philoctetes are founded on incidents between the end of the Iliad and the taking of Troy ; the Electra represents the vengeance of Orestes, the crowning event in the tale of 'Pelops' line ' ; the Trachiniae recounts the last crisis in the life of Heracles.

4. Of the three Theban plays, the Antigone was first composed, although its subject is the latest. Aeschylus in the Seven against Thebes had already represented the young heroine as defying the victorious citizens who forbade the burial of her brother, the rebel Polynices. He allowed her to be supported in her action by a band of sympathizing friends. But in the play of Sophocles she stands alone, and the power which she defies is not that of the citizens generally, but of Creon, whose will is absolute in the State. Thus the struggle is intensified, and both her strength and her desolation become more impressive, while the opposing claims of civic authority and domestic piety are more vividly realized, because either is separately embodied in an individual will. By the same means the situation is humanized to the last degree, and the heart of the spectator, although strained to the uttermost with pity for the heroic maiden whose life when full of brightest hopes was sacrificed to affection and piety, has still some feeling left for the living desolation of the man, whose patriotic zeal, degenerating into tyranny, brought his city to the brink of ruin, and cost him the lives of his two sons and of his wife, whose dying curse, as well as that of Haemon, is denounced upon him.

In the Oedipus Tyrannus, Sophocles goes back to the central crisis of the Theban story. And again he fixes our attention, not so much on the fortunes of the city, or of the reigning house, as on the man Oedipus, his glory and his fall : —

' O mirror of our fickle state
Since man on earth unparalleled !
The rarer thy example stands,
By how much from the top of wondrous glory,
Strongest of mortal men,
To lowest pitch of abject fortune thou art fallen [1].

The horror and the pity of it are both enhanced by
the character of Oedipus—his essential innocence, his
affectionateness, his uncalculating benevolence and
public spirit ;—while his impetuosity and passionate-
ness make the sequel less incredible.

The essential innocence of Oedipus, which survives
the ruin of his hopes in this world, supplies the chief
motive of the Oedipus at Colonos. This drama, which
Sophocles is said to have written late in life, is in many
ways contrasted with the former Oedipus. It begins
with pity and horror, and ends with peace. It is only
in part founded on Epic tradition, the main incident
belonging apparently to the local mythology of the
poet's birthplace. It also implies a later stage of ethical
reflection, and in this respect resembles the Philoctetes ;
it depends more on lyrical and melodramatic effects,
and allows more room for collateral and subsidiary
motives than any other of the seven. Yet in its prin-
cipal theme, the vindication or redemption of an essen-
tially noble spirit from the consequences of error, it
repeats a note which had been struck much earlier in the
Aias with great force, although with some crudities of
treatment which are absent from the later drama.

5. In one of the Epic poems which narrated the fall of
Troy, the figure of Aias was more prominent than in the
Iliad. He alone and unassisted was there said to have
repulsed Hector from the ships, and he had the chief
share, although in this he was aided by Odysseus, in
rescuing the dead body of Achilles. Yet Achilles'
arms were awarded by the votes of the chieftains, as the
prize of valour, not to Aias, but to Odysseus. This, no
doubt, meant that wisdom is better than strength. But

[1] Milton, *Samson Agonistes*, 164-169.

the wisdom of Odysseus in these later Epics was often less nobly esteemed than in the Iliad and Odyssey, and was represented as alloyed with cunning.

Aias has withdrawn with his Salaminians, in a rage, from the fight, and after long brooding by the ships his wrath has broken forth into a blaze which would have endangered the lives of Odysseus and the Atridae, had not Athena in her care for them changed his anger into madness. Hence, instead of slaying the generals, he makes havoc amongst the flocks and herds, which as the result of various forays were the common property of the whole army. The truth is discovered by Odysseus with the help of Athena, and from being next to Achilles in renown, Aias becomes the object of universal scorn and hatred. The sequel of this hour of his downfall is the subject of the Aias of Sophocles. After lamenting his fate, the hero eludes the vigilance of his captive bride Tecmessa, and of his Salaminian mariners, and, in complete solitude, falls upon his sword. He is found by Tecmessa and by his half-brother Teucer, who has returned too late from a raid in the Mysian highlands. The Atridae would prohibit Aias' funeral; but Odysseus, who has been specially enlightened by Athena, advises generous forbearance, and his counsel prevails. The part representing the disgrace and death of Aias is more affecting to modern readers than the remainder of the drama. But we should bear in mind that the vindication of Aias after death, and his burial with undiminished honours, had an absorbing interest for the Athenian and Salaminian spectator.

Philoctetes also is rejected by man and accepted by Destiny. The Argives in his case, as the Thebans in the case of Oedipus, are blind to the real intentions of the Gods.

The Philoctetes, like the Oedipus at Colonos, was a work of Sophocles' old age; and while it can hardly be said that the fire of tragic feeling is abated in either of these plays, dramatic effect is modified in both of them by the influence of the poet's contemplative mood. The interest of the action in the Philoctetes is more inward

and psychological than in any other ancient drama.
The change of mind in Neoptolemus, the stubborn fixity
of will in Philoctetes, contrasted with the confiding
tenderness of his nature, form the elements of a dramatic movement at once extremely simple and wonder-
fully sustained. No purer ideal of virtuous youth has
been imagined than the son of Achilles, who in this play,
though sorely tempted, sets faithfulness before ambition.

6. In the Electra, which, though much earlier than the
Philoctetes, is still a work of his mature genius, our poet
appears at first sight to be in unequal competition with
Aeschylus. If the Theban trilogy of the elder poet had
remained entire, a similar impression might have been
produced by the Oedipus Tyrannus. It is best to lay
such comparisons aside, and to consider the work of
Sophocles simply on its own merits. The subject, as
he has chosen to treat it, is the heroic endurance of a
woman who devotes her life to the vindication of intolerable wrongs done to her father, and the restoration
of her young brother to his hereditary rights. Hers is
the human agency which for this purpose works together with Apollo. But the divine intention is concealed from her. She suffers countless indignities from
her father's enemies, of whom her own mother is the
chief. And, at length, all her hopes are shattered by
the false tidings that Orestes is no more. Even then
she does not relinquish her resolve. And the revulsion
from her deep sorrow to extremity of joy, when she finds
Orestes at her side and ready to perform the act of
vengeance in his own person, is irresistably affecting,
even when the play is only read.

Sophocles is especially great in the delineation of ideal
female characters. The heroic ardour of Antigone, and
the no less heroic persistence and endurance of Electra,
are both founded on the strength of their affection.
And the affection in both cases is what some moderns
too have called the purest of human feelings, the love of
a sister for a brother. Another aspect of that world-old
marvel, 'the love of women,' was presented in Aias'
captive bride, Tecmessa. This softer type also attains

to heroic grandeur in Dêanira, the wronged wife of Heracles, whose fatal error is caused by the innocent working of her wounded love.

It is strange that so acute a critic as A. W. Schlegel should have doubted the Sophoclean authorship of the Trachiniae. If its religious and moral lessons are even less obtrusive than those of either Oedipus and of the Antigone, there is no play which more directly pierces to the very heart of humanity. And it is a superficial judgement which complains that here at all events our sympathies are distracted between the two chief persons, Dêanira and Heracles. To one passion of his, to one fond mistake of hers, the ruin of them both is due. Her love has made their fates inseparable. And the spectator, in sharing Hyllus' grief, is afflicted for them both at once. We may well recognize in this treatment of the death of Heracles the hand of him who wrote—

$$\sigma\grave{\upsilon}\ \kappa\alpha\grave{\iota}\ \delta\iota\kappa\alpha\acute{\iota}\omega\nu\ \grave{\alpha}\delta\acute{\iota}\kappa\sigma\upsilon\varsigma$$
$$\varphi\rho\acute{\epsilon}\nu\alpha\varsigma\ \pi\alpha\rho\alpha\sigma\pi\grave{\alpha}\varsigma\ \grave{\epsilon}\pi\grave{\iota}\ \lambda\acute{\omega}\beta\alpha,$$

$$\mathring{\alpha}\mu\alpha\chi\sigma\varsigma\ \gamma\grave{\alpha}\rho\ \grave{\epsilon}\mu\pi\alpha\acute{\iota}\zeta\epsilon\iota\ \theta\epsilon\grave{\sigma}\varsigma\ \,\text{'A}\varphi\rho\sigma\delta\acute{\iota}\tau\alpha\,[1].$$

7. It is unnecessary to expatiate here on the merits of construction in which these seven plays are generally acknowledged to be unrivalled; the natural way in which the main situation is explained, the suddenness and inevitableness of the complications, the steadily sustained climax of emotion until the action culminates, the preservation of the fitting mood until the end, the subtlety and effectiveness of the minor contrasts of situation and character [2].

But it may not be irrelevant to observe that the ' acting qualities ' of Sophocles, as of Shakespeare, are

---

[1]   ' Thou drawest awry
      Just minds to wrong and ruin. . . .
      . . . . With resistless charm
      Great Aphrodite mocks the might of men.'
                                        Antigone.

[2] Cf. *Sophocles* in Green's ' Classical Writers.' Macmillan & Co.

best known to those who have seen him acted, whether
in Greek, as by the students at Harvard [1] and Toronto [2],
and more recently at Cambridge [3], or in English long
ago by Miss Helen Faucit (since Lady Martin [4]), or still
earlier and repeatedly in Germany, or in the French
version of the Antigone by MM. Maurice and Vac-
querie (1845) or of King Oedipus by M. Lacroix, in
which the part of Œdipe Roi was finely sustained by
M. Geoffroy in 1861, and by M. Mounet Sully in 1881 [5].
With reference to the latter performance, which was
continued throughout the autumn season, M. Francisque
Sarcey wrote an article for the *Temps* newspaper of
August 15, 1881, which is full of just and vivid appre-
ciation. At the risk of seeming absurdly ' modern ',
I will quote from this article some of the more striking
passages.

' Ce troisième et ce quatrième actes, les plus émou-
vants qui se soient jamais produits sur aucune scène,
se composent d'une suite de narrations, qui viennent
l'une après l'autre frapper au cœur d'Œdipe, et qui ont
leur contrecoup dans l'âme des spectateurs. Je ne sais
qu'une pièce au monde qui soit construite de la sorte,
c'est l'*École des Femmes*. Ce rapprochement vous paraî-

---

[1] Oed. Tyr., 1881.   [2] Antigone, 1882.
[3] Ajax, Nov. 1882.   [4] Antigone, 1845.
[5] The performance of Greek plays (as of the Agamemnon
at Oxford in 1880) is not altogether a new thing in England.
The author of Ion, Mr. Serjeant Talfourd, in his Notice
prefixed to that drama in 1836, mentions, amongst other
reasons for having intended to dedicate it to Dr. Valpy,
' the exquisite representations of Greek Tragedy, which he
superintended,' and which ' made his images vital.' At
a still earlier time, ' the great Dr. Parr ' had encouraged
his pupils at Stanmore to recite the dialogue of Greek
tragedies before an audience and in costume. It would
be ungrateful to omit all reference here to some perfor-
mances of the Trachiniae in English in Edinburgh and
St. Andrews in 1877, which, though not of a public nature,
are still remembered with delight by those who were
present at them, and were really the first of a series.

tra singulier, sans doute. . . . Mais. . . . c'est dans
le vieux drame grec comme dans la comédie du maître
français une trouvaille de génie. . . . .

'Sophocle a voulu, après des émotions si terribles,
après des angoisses si sèches, ouvrir la source des larmes :
il a écrit un cinquième acte. . . . .

'Les yeux crevés d'Œdipe ne sont qu'un accident, ou,
si vous aimez mieux, un accessoire. Le poète, sans
s'arrêter à ce détail, a mis sur les lèvres de son héros
toute la gamme des sentiments douloureux qu'excite
une si prodigieuse infortune. . . . .

'À la lecture, elle est un peu longue cette scène de
lamentations. Au théâtre, on n'a pas le temps de la
trouver telle : on pleure de toute son âme et de tous ses
yeux. C'est qu'après avoir eu le cœur si longtemps
serré comme dans un étau, on épreuve comme un sou-
lagement à sentir en soi jaillir la source des larmes.
Sophocle, qui semble avoir été le plus malin des drama-
turges, comme il est le plus parfait des écrivains drama-
tiques, a cherché là un effet de contraste dont l'effet est
immanquant sur le public.'

These and other like remarks of one of the best-known
critics of the Parisian stage show that the dramatic art
of Sophocles is still a living power.

I am well aware how feeble and inadequate the present
attempted reproduction must appear to any reader who
knows the Greek original. There is much to be said for
the view of an eminent scholar who once declared that
he would never think of translating a Greek poet. But
the end of translating is not to satisfy fastidious
scholars, but to make the classics partially accessible to
those whose acquaintance with them would otherwise
be still more defective. Part of this version of Sophocles was printed several years ago in an imperfect form.
The present volume contains the seven extant plays
entire. As the object has been to give the effect of
each drama as a whole, rather than to dwell on particular
'beauties' (which only a poet can render), the fragments have not been included. But the reader should

bear in mind that the seven plays are less than a tithe of the work produced by the poet in his lifetime.

It may very possibly be asked why verse has been employed at all. Why not have listened to Carlyle's rough demand, 'Tell us what they thought; none of your silly poetry'? The present translator can only reply that he began with prose, but soon found that, for tragic dialogue in English, blank verse appeared a more natural and effective vehicle than any prose style which he could hope to frame. And with the dialogue in verse, it was impossible to have the lyric parts in any sort of prose, simply because the reader would then have felt an intolerable incongruity. These parts have therefore been turned into such familiar lyric measures as seemed at once possible and not unsuitable. And where this method was found impracticable, as sometimes in the *Commoi*, blank metres have again been used,—with such liberties as seemed appropriate to the special purpose. The writer's hope throughout has been, not indeed fully to transfuse the poetry of Sophocles into another tongue, but to make the poet's dramatic intention to be understood and felt by English readers. One more such endeavour may possibly find acceptance at a time when many causes have combined to awaken a fresh interest at once in dramatic literature and in Hellenic studies.

The reader who is hitherto unacquainted with the Greek drama, should be warned that the parts assigned to the 'Chorus' were often distributed among its several members, who spoke or chanted, singly or in groups, alternately or in succession. In some cases, but not in all, *Ch.* 1, *Ch.* 2, &c., have been prefixed, to indicate such an arrangement.

ANTIGONE

THE PERSONS

ANTIGONE, } *Daughters of Oedipus and Sisters of Poly-*
ISMENE,   }   *nices and Eteocles.*
CHORUS *of Theban Elders.*
CREON, *King of Thebes.*
A Watchman.
HAEMON, *Son of Creon, betrothed to Antigone.*
TIRESIAS, *the blind Prophet.*
A Messenger.
EURYDICE, *the Wife of Creon.*
Another Messenger.

SCENE.   Before the Cadmean Palace at Thebes.

Note.   The town of Thebes is often personified as Thebè.

ANTIGONE

THE PERSONS

POLYNICES, son and heir to the unfortunate Oedipus, having been supplanted by his younger brother Eteocles, brought an army of Argives against his native city, Thebes. The army was defeated, and the two brothers slew each other in single combat. On this Creon, the brother-in-law of Oedipus, succeeding to the chief power, forbade the burial of Polynices. But Antigone, sister of the dead, placing the dues of affection and piety before her obligation to the magistrate, disobeyed the edict at the sacrifice of her life. Creon carried out his will, but lost his son Haemon and his wife Eurydice, and received their curses on his head. His other son, Megareus, had previously been devoted as a victim to the good of the state.

ANTIGONE

ANTIGONE. ISMENE.

ANTIGONE. Own sister of my blood, one life with me,
Ismenè, have the tidings caught thine ear?
Say, hath not Heaven decreed to execute
On thee and me, while yet we are alive,
All the evil Oedipus bequeathed? All horror,
All pain, all outrage, falls on us! And now
The General's proclamation of to-day—
Hast thou not heard?—Art thou so slow to hear
When harm from foes threatens the souls we love?

ISMENE. No word of those we love, Antigone,
Painful or glad, hath reached me, since we two
Were utterly deprived of our two brothers,
Cut off with mutual stroke, both in one day.
And since the Argive host this now-past night
Is vanished, I know nought beside to make me
Nearer to happiness or more in woe.

ANT. I knew it well, and therefore led thee forth
The palace gate, that thou alone mightst hear.

ISM. Speak on! Thy troubled look bodes some dark
            news.

ANT. Why, hath not Creon, in the burial-rite,
Of our two brethren honoured one, and wrought
On one foul wrong? Eteocles, they tell,
With lawful consecration he lays out,
And after covers him in earth, adorned
With amplest honours in the world below.
But Polynices, miserably slain,
They say 'tis publicly proclaimed that none
Must cover in a grave, nor mourn for him;
But leave him tombless and unwept, a store
Of sweet provision for the carrion fowl
That eye him greedily. Such righteous law
Good Creon hath pronounced for thy behoof—

Ay, and for mine! I am not left out!—And now
He moves this way to promulgate his will
To such as have not heard, nor lightly holds
The thing he bids, but, whoso disobeys,
The citizens shall stone him to the death.
This is the matter, and thou wilt quickly show
If thou art noble, or fallen below thy birth.

Ism. Unhappy one! But what can I herein
Avail to do or undo?

Ant.   Wilt thou share
The danger and the labour? Make thy choice.

Ism. Of what wild enterprise? What canst thou
        mean?

Ant. Wilt thou join hand with mine to lift the
        dead?

Ism. To bury him, when all have been forbidden?
Is that thy thought?

Ant.   To bury my own brother
And thine, even though thou wilt not do thy part.
I will not be a traitress to my kin.

Ism. Fool-hardy girl! against the word of Creon?

Ant. He hath no right to bar me from mine own.

Ism. Ah, sister, think but how our father fell,
Hated of all and lost to fair renown,
Through self-detected crimes—with his own hand,
Self-wreaking, how he dashed out both his eyes:
Then how the mother-wife, sad two-fold name!
With twisted halter bruised her life away;
Last, how in one dire moment our two brothers
With internecine conflict at a blow
Wrought out by fratricide their mutual doom.
Now, left alone, O think how beyond all
Most piteously we twain shall be destroyed,
If in defiance of authority
We traverse the commandment of the King!
We needs must bear in mind we are but women,
Never created to contend with men;
Nay more, made victims of resistless power,
To obey behests more harsh than this to-day.
I, then, imploring those beneath to grant

Indulgence, seeing I am enforced in this,
Will yield submission to the powers that rule.
Small wisdom were it to overpass the bound.

    ANT. I will not urge you! no! nor if now you
       list
To help me, will your help afford me joy.
Be what you choose to be! This single hand
Shall bury our lost brother. Glorious
For me to take this labour and to die!
Dear to him will my soul be as we rest
In death, when I have dared this holy crime.
My time for pleasing men will soon be over;
Not so my duty toward the Dead! My home
Yonder will have no end. You, if you will,
May pour contempt on laws revered on High.

    ISM. Not from irreverence. But I have no strength
To strive against the citizens' resolve.

    ANT. Thou, make excuses! I will go my way
To raise a burial-mound to my dear brother.

    ISM. Oh, hapless maiden, how I fear for thee!

    ANT. Waste not your fears on me! Guide your own
       fortune.

    ISM. Ah! yet divulge thine enterprise to none,
But keep the secret close, and so will I.

    ANT. O Heavens! Nay, tell! I hate your silence
       worse;
I had rather you proclaimed it to the world.

    ISM. You are ardent in a chilling enterprise.

    ANT. I know that I please those whom I would
       please.

    ISM. Yes, if you thrive; but your desire is boot-
       less.

    ANT. Well, when I fail I shall be stopt, I trow!

    ISM. One should not start upon a hopeless quest.

    ANT. Speak in that vein if you would earn my hate
And aye be hated of our lost one. Peace!
Leave my unwisdom to endure this peril;
Fate cannot rob me of a noble death.

    ISM. Go, if you must—Not to be checked in folly,
But sure unparalleled in faithful love!　　　　[*Exeunt*

CHORUS (*entering*).

Beam of the mounting Sun!   I 1
O brightest, fairest ray
Seven-gated Thebè yet hath seen!
Over the vale where Dircè's fountains run
At length thou appearedst, eye of golden Day,
And with incitement of thy radiance keen
  Spurredst to faster flight
The man of Argos hurrying from the fight.
Armed at all points the warrior came,
But driven before thy rising flame
He rode, reverting his pale shield,
Headlong from yonder battlefield.

      [*Half-Chorus*
In snow-white panoply, on eagle wing,
He rose, dire ruin on our land to bring,
  Roused by the fierce debate
  Of Polynices' hate,
Shrilling sharp menace from his breast,
Sheathed all in steel from crown to heel,
  With many a plumèd crest.

Then stooped above the domes,   I 2
With lust of carnage fired,
And opening teeth of serried spears
Yawned wide around the gates that guard our
  homes;
But went, or e'er his hungry jaws had tired
On Theban flesh,—or e'er the Fire-god fierce
  Seizing our sacred town
Besmirched and rent her battlemented crown.
Such noise of battle as he fled
About his back the War-god spread;
So writhed to hard-fought victory
The serpent struggling to be free.

      [*Half-Chorus*
High Zeus beheld their stream that proudly rolled
Idly caparisoned with clanking gold:

Zeus hates the boastful tongue:
He with hurled fire down flung
One who in haste had mounted high,
And that same hour from topmost tower
Upraised the exulting cry.

Swung rudely to the hard repellent earth   II 1
Amidst his furious mirth
He fell, who then with flaring brand
Held in his fiery hand
Came breathing madness at the gate
In eager blasts of hate.
And doubtful swayed the varying fight
Through the turmoil of the night,
As turning now on these and now on those
Ares hurtled 'midst our foes,
Self-harnessed helper on our right.

[Half-Chorus

Seven matched with seven, at each gate one,
Their captains, when the day was done,
Left for our Zeus who turned the scale,
The brazen tribute in full tale:—
All save the horror-burdened pair,
Dire children of despair,
Who from one sire, one mother, drawing breath,
Each with conquering lance in rest
Against a true-born brother's breast,
Found equal lots in death.

But with blithe greeting to glad Thebè came   II 2
She of the glorious name,
Victory,—smiling on our chariot throng
With eyes that waken song.
Then let those battle-memories cease,
Silenced by thoughts of peace.
With holy dances of delight
Lasting through the livelong night
Visit we every shrine, in solemn round,
Led by him who shakes the ground,
Our Bacchus, Thebè's child of light.

LEADER OF CHORUS.

But look ! where Creon in his new-made power,
Moved by the fortune of the recent hour,
Comes with fresh counsel. What intelligence
Intends he for our private conference,
That he hath sent his herald to us all,
Gathering the elders with a general call ?

Enter CREON.

CREON. My friends, the noble vessel of our State,
After sore shaking her, the Gods have sped
On a smooth course once more. I have called you hither,
By special messengers selecting you
From all the city, first, because I knew you
Aye loyal to the throne of Laïus ;
Then, both while Oedipus gave prosperous days,
And since his fall, I still beheld you firm
In sound allegiance to the royal issue.
Now since the pair have perished in an hour,
Twinned in misfortune, by a mutual stroke
Staining our land with fratricidal blood,
All rule and potency of sovereign sway,
In virtue of next kin to the deceased,
Devolves on me. But hard it is to learn
The mind of any mortal or the heart,
Till he be tried in chief authority.
Power shows the man. For he who when supreme
Withholds his hand or voice from the best cause,
Being thwarted by some fear, that man to me
Appears, and ever hath appeared, most vile.
He too hath no high place in mine esteem,
Who sets his friend before his fatherland.
Let Zeus whose eye sees all eternally
Be here my witness. I will ne'er keep silence
When danger lours upon my citizens
Who looked for safety, nor make him my friend
Who doth not love my country. For I know
Our country carries us, and whilst her helm
Is held aright we gain good friends and true.

Following such courses 'tis my steadfast will
To foster Thebè's greatness, and therewith
In brotherly accord is my decree
Touching the sons of Oedipus. The man—
Eteocles I mean—who died for Thebes
Fighting with eminent prowess on her side,
Shall be entombed with every sacred rite
That follows to the grave the lordliest dead.
But for his brother, who, a banished man,
Returned to devastate and burn with fire
The land of his nativity, the shrines
Of his ancestral gods, to feed him fat
With Theban carnage, and make captive all
That should escape the sword—for Polynices,
This law hath been proclaimed concerning him:
He shall have no lament, no funeral,
But lie unburied, for the carrion fowl
And dogs to eat his corse, a sight of shame.

Such are the motions of this mind and will.
Never from me shall villains reap renown
Before the just. But whoso loves the State,
I will exalt him both in life and death.

CH. Son of Menoeceus, we have heard thy mind
Toward him who loves, and him who hates our city.
And sure, 'tis thine to enforce what law thou wilt
Both on the dead and all of us who live.

CR. Then be ye watchful to maintain my word.

CH. Young strength for such a burden were more
    meet.

CR. Already there be watchers of the dead.

CH. What charge then wouldst thou further lay on
    us?

CR. Not to give place to those that disobey.

CH. Who is so fond, to be in love with death?

CR. Such, truly, is the meed. But hope of gain
Full oft ere now hath been the ruin of men.

WATCHMAN (entering). My lord, I am out of breath,
    but not with speed.
I will not say my foot was fleet. My thoughts
Cried halt unto me ever as I came

And wheeled me to return. My mind discoursed
Most volubly within my breast, and said—
Fond wretch! why go where thou wilt find thy bane?
Unhappy wight! say, wilt thou bide aloof?
Then if the king shall hear this from another,
How shalt thou 'scape for't? Winding thus about
I hasted, but I could not speed, and so
Made a long journey of a little way.
At last 'yes' carried it, that I should come
To thee; and tell thee I must needs, and shall,
Though it be nothing that I have to tell.
For I came hither, holding fast by this—
Nought that is not my fate can happen to me.

CR. Speak forth thy cause of fear. What is the
                matter?

WATCH. First of mine own part in the business. For
I did it not, nor saw the man who did,
And 'twere not right that I should come to harm.

CR. You fence your ground, and keep well out of
                danger;
I see you have some strange thing to declare.

WATCH. A man will shrink who carries words of fear.

CR. Let us have done with you. Tell your tale, and
                go.

WATCH. Well, here it is. The corse hath burial
From some one who is stolen away and gone,
But first hath strown dry dust upon the skin,
And added what religious rites require.

CR. Ha!
What man hath been so daring in revolt?

WATCH. I cannot tell. There was no mark to show—
No dint of spade, or mattock-loosened sod,—
Only the hard bare ground, untilled and trackless.
Whoe'er he was, the doer left no trace.
And, when the scout of our first daylight watch
Showed us the thing, we marvelled in dismay.
The Prince was out of sight; not in a grave,
But a thin dust was o'er him, as if thrown
By one who shunned the dead man's curse. No sign
Appeared of any hound or beast o' the field

Having come near, or pulled at the dead body.
Then rose high words among us sentinels
With bickering noise accusing each his mate,
And it seemed like to come to blows, with none
To hinder. For the hand that thus had wrought
Was any of ours, and none ; the guilty man
Escaped all knowledge. And we were prepared
To lift hot iron with our bare palms ; to walk
Through fire, and swear by all the Gods at once
That we were guiltless, ay, and ignorant
Of who had plotted or performed this thing.

When further search seemed bootless, at the last
One spake, whose words bowed all our heads to the earth
With fear. We knew not what to answer him,
Nor how to do it and prosper. He advised
So grave a matter must not be concealed,
But instantly reported to the King.

Well, this prevailed, and the lot fell on me,
Unlucky man ! to be the ministrant
Of this fair service. So I am present here,
Against my will and yours, I am sure of that.
None love the bringer of unwelcome news.

CH. My lord, a thought keeps whispering in my
    breast,
Some Power divine hath interposed in this.

CR. Cease, ere thou quite enrage me, and appear
Foolish as thou art old. Talk not to me
Of Gods who have taken thought for this dead man !
Say, was it for his benefits to them
They hid his corse, and honoured him so highly,
Who came to set on fire their pillared shrines,
With all the riches of their offerings,
And to make nothing of their land and laws ?
Or, hast thou seen them honouring villany ?
That cannot be. Long time the cause of this
Hath come to me in secret murmurings
From malcontents of Thebes, who under yoke
Turned restive, and would not accept my sway.
Well know I, these have bribed the watchmen here
To do this for some fee. For nought hath grown

Current among mankind so mischievous
As money. This brings cities to their fall:
This drives men homeless, and moves honest minds
To base contrivings. This hath taught mankind
The use of wickedness, and how to give
An impious turn to every kind of act.
But whosoe'er hath done this for reward
Hath found his way at length to punishment.
If Zeus have still my worship, be assured
Of that which here on oath I say to thee—
Unless ye find the man who made this grave
And bring him bodily before mine eye,
Death shall not be enough, till ye have hung
Alive for an example of your guilt,
That henceforth in your rapine ye may know
Whence gain is to be gotten, and may learn
Pelf from all quarters is not to be loved.
For in base getting, 'tis a common proof,
More find disaster than deliverance.

    Watch. Am I to speak ? or must I turn and go ?
    Cr. What ? know you not your speech offends even
          now ?
    Watch. Doth the mind smart withal, or only the ear ?
    Cr. Art thou to probe the seat of mine annoy ?
    Watch. If I offend, 'tis in your ear alone,
The malefactor wounds ye to the soul.
    Cr. Out on thee ! thou art nothing but a tongue.
    Watch. Then was I ne'er the doer of this deed.
    Cr. Yea, verily : self-hired to crime for gold.
    Watch. Pity so clear a mind should clearly err !
    Cr. Gloze now on clearness ! But unless ye bring
The burier, without glozing ye shall tell,
Craven advantage clearly worketh bane.
    Watch. By all means let the man be found ; one thing
I know right well :—caught or not caught, howe'er
Fate rules his fortune, me you ne'er will see
Standing in presence here. Even now I owe
Deep thanks to Heaven for mine escape, so far
Beyond my hope and highest expectancy.

                           [Exeunt severally

Chorus.

Many a wonder lives and moves, but the wonder of all is
    man,   I. 1
That courseth over the grey ocean, carried of Southern
    gale,
Faring amidst high-swelling seas that rudely surge
    around,
And Earth, supreme of mighty Gods, eldest, imperish-
    able,
Eternal, he with patient furrow wears and wears away
     As year by year the plough-shares turn and
     turn,—
Subduing her unwearied strength with children of the
    steed.

And wound in woven coils of nets he seizeth for his
    prey   I. 2
The aëry tribe of birds and wilding armies of the
    chase,
And sea-born millions of the deep—man is so crafty-
    wise.
And now with engine of his wit he tameth to his will
The mountain-ranging beast whose lair is in the country
    wild ;
     And now his yoke hath passed upon the mane
Of horse with proudly crested neck and tireless moun-
    tain bull.

Wise utterance and wind-swift thought, and city-
     moulding mind,   II. 1
And shelter from the clear-eyed power of biting frost,
He hath taught him, and to shun the sharp, roof-pene-
    trating rain,—
Full of resource, without device he meets no coming
    time ;
     From Death alone he shall not find reprieve ;
No league may gain him that relief ; but even for fell
    disease,
That long hath baffled wisest leech, he hath contrived a
    cure.

Inventive beyond wildest hope, endowed with bound-
     less skill,   II 2
One while he moves toward evil, and one while toward
     good,
According as he loves his land and fears the Gods above.
Weaving the laws into his life and steadfast oath of
     Heaven,
     High in the State he moves: but outcast he,
Who hugs dishonour to his heart and follows paths of
     crime.
Ne'er may he come beneath my roof, nor think like
     thoughts with me.

LEADER OF CHORUS.

What portent from the Gods is here?
My mind is mazed with doubt and fear.
How can I gainsay what I see?
I know the girl Antigone.
O hapless child of hapless sire!
Didst thou, then, recklessly aspire
To brave kings' laws, and now art brought
In madness of transgression caught?

Enter Watchman, *bringing in* ANTIGONE.

WATCH. Here is the doer of the deed: this maid.
We found her burying him. Where is the King?
  CH. Look, he comes forth again to meet thy call.

Enter CREON.

  CR. What call so nearly times with mine approach?
  WATCH. My lord, no mortal should deny on oath;
Judgement is still belied by after-thought.
When quailing 'neath the tempest of your threats,
Methought no force would drive me to this place.
But joy unlook'd for and surpassing hope
Is out of bound the best of all delight,
And so I am here again,—though I had sworn
I ne'er would come,—and in my charge this maid,
Caught in the act of caring for the dead.
Here was no lot-throwing; this hap was mine

Without dispute. And now, my sovereign lord,
According to thy pleasure, thine own self
Examine and convict her. For my part
I have good right to be away and free
From the bad business I am come upon.
  CR. This maiden!
How came she in thy charge? Where didst thou find
      her?
  WATCH. Burying the prince. One word hath told
      thee all.
  CR. Hast thou thy wits, and knowest thou what thou
      sayest?
  WATCH. I saw her burying him whom you forbade
To bury. Is that, now, clearly spoken, or no?
  CR. And how was she detected, caught, and taken?
  WATCH. It fell in this wise. We were come to the
      spot,
Bearing the dreadful burden of thy threats;
And first with care we swept the dust away
From round the corse, and laid the dank limbs bare:
Then sate below the hill-top, out o' the wind,
Where no bad odour from the dead might strike us,
Stirring each other on with interchange
Of loud revilings on the negligent
In 'tendance on this duty. So we stayed
Till in mid heaven the sun's resplendent orb
Stood high, and the heat strengthened. Suddenly,
The Storm-god raised a whirlwind from the ground,
Vexing heaven's concave, and filled all the plain,
Rending the locks of all the orchard groves,
Till the great sky was choked withal. We closed
Our lips and eyes, and bore the God-sent evil.
When after a long while this ceased, the maid
Was seen, and wailed in high and bitter key,
Like some despairing bird that hath espied
Her nest all desolate, the nestlings gone.
So, when she saw the body bare, she mourned
Loudly, and cursed the authors of this deed.
Then nimbly with her hands she brought dry dust,
And holding high a shapely brazen cruse,

Poured three libations, honouring the dead.
We, when we saw, ran in, and straightway seized
Our quarry, nought dismayed, and charged her with
The former crime and this. And she denied
Nothing;—to my delight, and to my grief.
One's self to escape disaster is great joy;
Yet to have drawn a friend into distress
Is painful. But mine own security
To me is of more value than aught else.
  CR. Thou, with thine eyes down-fastened to the
    earth !
Dost thou confess to have done this, or deny it ?
  ANT. I deny nothing. I avow the deed.
  CR. (to Watchman). Thou may'st betake thyself
    whither thou wilt,
Acquitted of the grievous charge, and free.
(To ANTIGONE) And thou,—no prating talk, but briefly
    tell,
Knew'st thou our edict that forbade this thing ?
  ANT. I could not fail to know. You made it plain.
  CR. How durst thou then transgress the published
    law ?
  ANT. I heard it not from Heaven, nor came it forth
From Justice, where she reigns with Gods below.
They too have published to mankind a law.
Nor thought I thy commandment of such might
That one who is mortal thus could overbear
The infallible, unwritten laws of Heaven.
Not now or yesterday they have their being,
But everlastingly, and none can tell
The hour that saw their birth. I would not, I,
For any terror of a man's resolve,
Incur the God-inflicted penalty
Of doing them wrong. That death would come, I knew
Without thine edict ;—if before the time,
I count it gain. Who does not gain by death,
That lives, as I do, amid boundless woe ?
Slight is the sorrow of such doom to me.
But had I suffered my own mother's child,
Fallen in blood, to be without a grave,

That were indeed a sorrow. This is none.
And if thou deem'st me foolish for my deed,
I am foolish in the judgement of a fool.
   CH. Fierce shows the maiden's vein from her fierce
            sire ;
Calamity doth not subdue her will.
   CR. Ay, but the stubborn spirit first doth fall.
Oft ye shall see the strongest bar of steel,
That fire hath hardened to extremity,
Shattered to pieces. A small bit controls
The fiery steed. Pride may not be endured
In one whose life is subject to command.
This maiden hath been conversant with crime
Since first she trampled on the public law ;
And now she adds to crime this insolence,
To laugh at her offence, and glory in it.
Truly, if she that hath usurped this power
Shall rest unpunished, she then is a man,
And I am none. Be she my sister's child,
Or of yet nearer blood to me than all
That take protection from my hearth, the pair
Shall not escape the worst of deaths. For know,
I count the younger of the twain no less
Copartner in this plotted funeral :
And now I bid you call her. Late I saw her
Within the house, beyond herself, and frantic.
—Full oft when one is darkly scheming wrong,
The disturbed spirit hath betrayed itself
Before the act it hides. —But not less hateful
Seems it to me, when one that hath been caught
In wickedness would give it a brave show.
   ANT. Wouldst thou aught more of me than merely
            death ?
   CR. No more. 'Tis all I claim. Death closes all.
   ANT. Why then delay ? No talk of thine can charm
            me,
Forbid it Heaven ! And my discourse no less
Must evermore sound noisome to thine ear.
Yet where could I have found a fairer fame
Than giving burial to my own true brother ?

c. s.   c

All here would tell thee they approve my deed,
Were they not tongue-tied to authority.
But kingship hath much profit; this in chief,
That it may do and say whate'er it will.

CR. No Theban sees the matter with thine eye.

ANT. They see, but curb their voices to thy sway.

CR. And art thou not ashamed, acting alone?

ANT. A sister's piety hath no touch of shame.

CR. Was not Eteocles thy brother too?

ANT. My own true brother from both parents' blood.

CR. This duty was impiety to him.

ANT. He that is dead will not confirm that word.

CR. If you impart his honours to the vile.

ANT. It was his brother, not a slave, who fell.

CR. But laying waste the land for which he
        fought.

ANT. Death knows no difference, but demands his
        due.

CR. Yet not equality 'twixt good and bad.

ANT. Both may be equal yonder; who can tell?

CR. An enemy is hated even in death.

ANT. Love, and not hatred, is the part for me.

CR. Down then to death! and, if you must, there
        love
The dead. No woman rules me while I live.

CH. Now comes Ismenè forth. Ah, see,
From clouds above her brow
The sister-loving tear
Is falling wet on her fair cheek,
Distaining all her passion-crimson'd face!

Enter ISMENE.

CR. And thou, that like a serpent coiled i' the house
Hast secretly been draining my life-blood,—
Little aware that I was cherishing
Two curses and subverters of my throne,—
Tell us, wilt thou avouch thy share in this
Entombment, or forswear all knowledge of it?

ISM. If her voice go therewith, I did the deed,
And bear my part and burden of the blame.

ANT. Nay, justice will not suffer that. You would not,
And I refused to make you mine ally.

ISM. But now in thy misfortune I would fain
Embark with thee in thy calamity.

ANT. Who did the deed, the powers beneath can tell.
I care not for lip-kindness from my kin.

ISM. Ah! scorn me not so far as to forbid me
To die with thee, and honour our lost brother.

ANT. Die not with me, nor make your own a deed
You never touched! My dying is enough.

ISM. What joy have I in life when thou art gone?
ANT. Ask Creon there. He hath your care and duty.
ISM. What can it profit thee to vex me so?
ANT. My heart is pained, though my lip laughs at thee.
ISM. What can I do for thee now, even now?
ANT. Save your own life. I grudge not your escape.
ISM. Alas! and must I be debarred thy fate?
ANT. Life was the choice you made. Mine was to die.
ISM. I warned thee——
ANT.   Yes, your prudence is admired
On earth. My wisdom is approved below.

ISM. Yet truly we are both alike in fault.
ANT. Fear not; you live. My life hath long been given
To death, to be of service to the dead.

CR. Of these two girls, the one hath lost her wits:
The other hath had none since she was born.

ISM. My lord, in misery, the mind one hath
Is wont to be dislodged, and will not stay.

CR. You have ta'en leave of yours at any rate,
When you cast in your portion with the vile.

ISM. What can life profit me without my sister?
CR. Say not 'my sister'; she is nothing now.
ISM. What? wilt thou kill thy son's espousal too?
CR. He may find other fields to plough upon.
ISM. Not so as love was plighted 'twixt them twain.
CR. I hate a wicked consort for my son.
ANT. O dearest Haemon! how thy father wrongs
                thee!

CR. Thou and thy marriage are a torment to me.
CH. And wilt thou sever her from thine own son?

CR. 'Tis death must come between him and his joy.
CH. All doubt is then resolved : the maid must die.
CR. I am resolved ; and so, 'twould seem, are you.
In with her, slaves ! No more delay ! Henceforth
These maids must have but woman's liberty
And be mewed up ; for even the bold will fly
When they see Death nearing the house of life.

    [ANTIGONE *and* ISMENE *are led into the palace.*

CHORUS.

Blest is the life that never tasted woe.   I 1
      When once the blow
Hath fallen upon a house with Heaven-sent doom,
Trouble descends in ever-widening gloom
Through all the number of the tribe to flow ;
      As when the briny surge
      That Thrace-born tempests urge
(The big wave ever gathering more and more)
Runs o'er the darkness of the deep,
      And with far-searching sweep
Uprolls the storm-heap'd tangle on the shore,
While cliff to beaten cliff resounds with sullen roar.

The stock of Cadmus from old time, I know,   I 2
      Hath woe on woe,
Age following age, the living on the dead,
Fresh sorrow falling on each new-ris'n head,
None freed by God from ruthless overthrow.
      E'en now a smiling light
      Was spreading to our sight
O'er one last fibre of a blasted tree,—
When, lo ! the dust of cruel death,
      Tribute of Gods beneath,
And wildering thoughts, and fate-born ecstasy,
Quench the brief gleam in dark Nonentity.

What froward will of man, O Zeus ! can check thy
      might ?   II 1
Not all-enfeebling sleep, nor tireless months divine,
Can touch thee, who through ageless time
Rulest mightily Olympus' dazzling height.

This was in the beginning, and shall be
        Now and eternally,
Not here or there, but everywhere,
A law of misery that shall not spare.

For Hope, that wandereth wide, comforting many a
                head,   II 2
Entangleth many more with glamour of desire:
Unknowing they have trode the fire.
Wise was the famous word of one who said,
'Evil oft seemeth goodness to the mind
        An angry God doth blind.'
Few are the days that such as he
May live untroubled of calamity.

LEADER OF CHORUS.

Lo, Haemon, thy last offspring, now is come,
Lamenting haply for the maiden's doom.
Say, is he mourning o'er her young life lost,
Fiercely indignant for his bridal crossed?

Enter HAEMON.

CR. We shall know soon, better than seers could
        teach us.
Can it be so, my son, that thou art brought
By mad distemperature against thy sire,
On hearing of the irrevocable doom
Passed on thy promised bride? Or is thy love
Thy father's, be his actions what they may?
    HAEMON. I am thine, father, and will follow still
Thy good directions; nor would I prefer
The fairest bride to thy wise government.
    CR. That, O my son! should be thy constant mind,
In all to bend thee to thy father's will.
Therefore men pray to have around their hearths
Obedient offspring, to requite their foes
With harm, and honour whom their father loves;
But he whose issue proves unprofitable,
Begets what else but sorrow to himself
And store of laughter to his enemies?

Make not, my son, a shipwreck of thy wit
For a woman. Thine own heart may teach thee this :—
There's but cold comfort in a wicked wife
Yoked to the home inseparably. What wound
Can be more deadly than a harmful friend ?
Then spurn her like an enemy, and send her
To wed some shadow in the world below !
For since of all the city I have found
Her only recusant, caught in the act,
I will not break my word before the State.
I will take her life. At this let her invoke
The god of kindred blood ! For if at home
I foster rebels, how much more abroad ?
Whoso is just in ruling his own house,
Lives rightly in the commonwealth no less :
But he that wantonly defies the law,
Or thinks to dictate to authority,
Shall have no praise from me. What power soe'er
The city hath ordained, must be obeyed
In little things and great things, right or wrong.
The man who so obeys, I have good hope
Will govern and be governed as he ought,
And in the storm of battle at my side
Will stand a faithful and a trusty comrade.
But what more fatal than the lapse of rule ?
This ruins cities, this lays houses waste,
This joins with the assault of war to break
Full-numbered armies into hopeless rout ;
And in the unbroken host 'tis nought but rule
That keeps those many bodies from defeat.
I must be zealous to defend the law,
And not go down before a woman's will.
Else, if I fall, 'twere best a man should strike me ;
Lest one should say, ' a woman worsted him.'

    Ch. Unless our sense is weakened by long time,
Thou speakest not unwisely.

    Haem.   O my sire,
Sound wisdom is a God-implanted seed,
Of all possessions highest in regard.
I cannot, and I would not learn to say

That thou art wrong in this; though in another,
It may be such a word were not unmeet.
But as thy son, 'tis surely mine to scan
Men's deeds, and words, and muttered thoughts toward
                    thee.
Fear of thy frown restrains the citizen
In talk that would fall harshly on thine ear.
I under shadow may o'erhear, how all
Thy people mourn this maiden, and complain
That of all women least deservedly
She perishes for a most glorious deed.
' Who, when her own true brother on the earth
Lay weltering after combat in his gore,
Left him not graveless, for the carrion fowl
And raw-devouring field-dogs to consume—
Hath she not merited a golden praise ? '
Such the dark rumour spreading silently.
Now, in my valuing, with thy prosperous life,
My father, no possession can compare.
Where can be found a richer ornament
For children, than their father's high renown ?
Or where for fathers, than their children's fame ?
Nurse not one changeless humour in thy breast,
That nothing can be right but as thou sayest.
Whoe'er presumes that he alone hath sense,
Or peerless eloquence, or reach of soul,
Unwrap him, and you'll find but emptiness.
'Tis no disgrace even to the wise to learn
And lend an ear to reason. You may see
The plant that yields where torrent waters flow
Saves every little twig, when the stout tree
Is torn away and dies. The mariner
Who will not ever slack the sheet that sways
The vessel, but still tightens, oversets,
And so, keel-upward, ends his voyaging.
Relent, I pray thee, and give place to change.
If any judgement hath informed my youth,
I grant it noblest to be always wise,
But,—for omniscience is denied to man—
Tis good to hearken to admonishment.

CH. My lord, 'twere wise, if thou wouldst learn of him
In reason ; and thou, Haemon, from thy sire !
Truth lies between you.

CR.   Shall our age, forsooth,
Be taught discretion by a peevish boy ?

HAEM. Only in what is right. Respects of time
Must be outbalanced by the actual need.

CR. To cringe to rebels cannot be a need.

HAEM. I do not claim observance for the vile.

CR. Why, is not she so tainted ? Is 't not proved ?

HAEM. All Thebes denies it.

CR.   Am I ruled by Thebes ?

HAEM. If youth be folly, that is youngly said.

CR. Shall other men prescribe my government ?

HAEM. One only makes not up a city, father.

CR. Is not the city in the sovereign's hand ?

HAEM. Nobly you'd govern as the desert's king.

CR. This youngster is the woman's champion.

HAEM. You are the woman, then—for you I care.

CR. Villain, to bandy reasons with your sire !

HAEM. I plead against the unreason of your fault.

CR. What fault is there in reverencing my power ?

HAEM. There is no reverence when you spurn the
       Gods.

CR. Abominable spirit, woman-led !

HAEM. You will not find me following a base guide.

CR. Why, all your speech this day is spent for her.

HAEM. For you and me too, and the Gods below.

CR. She will not live to be your wife on earth.

HAEM. I know, then, whom she will ruin by her
       death.

CR. What, wilt thou threaten, too, thou audacious
       boy ?

HAEM. It is no threat to answer empty words.

CR. Witless admonisher, thou shalt pay for this !

HAEM. Thou art my sire, else would I call thee
       senseless.

CR. Thou woman's minion ! mince not terms with me.

HAEM. Wouldst thou have all the speaking on thy
       side ?

CR. Is 't possible ? By yon heaven ! thou 'lt not
    escape,
For adding contumely to words of blame.
Bring out the hated thing, that she may die
Immediately, before her lover's face !

HAEM. Nay, dream not she shall suffer in my sight.
Nor shalt thou ever see my face again.
Let those stay with you that can brook your rage !
                                        [*Exit*

CH. My lord, he is parted swiftly in deep wrath !
The youthful spirit offended makes wild work.

CR. Ay, let him do his worst. Let him give scope
To pride beyond the compass of a man !
He shall not free these maidens from their doom.

CH. Is death thy destination for them both ?

CR. Only for her who acted. Thou art right.

CH. And what hast thou determined for her death ?

CR. Where human footstep shuns the desert ground,
I'll hide her living in a cave-like vault,
With so much provender as may prevent
Pollution from o'ertaking the whole city.
And there, perchance, she may obtain of Death,
Her only deity, to spare her soul ;
Or else in that last moment she will learn
'Tis labour lost to worship powers unseen.   [*Exit* CREON

CHORUS

Love, never foiled in fight !   1
Warrior Love, that on Wealth workest havoc !
Love, who in ambush of young maid's soft cheek
All night keep'st watch !—Thou roamest over seas :
In lonely forest homes thou harbourest.
Who may avoid thee ? None !
Mortal, Immortal,
All are o'erthrown by thee, all feel thy frenzy.

Lightly thou draw'st awry   2
Righteous minds into wrong to their ruin.
Thou this unkindly quarrel hast inflamed
'Tween kindred men.—Triumphantly prevails

The heart-compelling eye of winsome bride,
Compeer of mighty Law
Thronèd, commanding.
Madly thou mockest men, dread Aphrodite.

LEADER OF CHORUS.

Ah! now myself am carried past the bound
Of law, nor can I check the rising tear,
When I behold Antigone even here
Touching the quiet bourne where all must rest.

Enter ANTIGONE *guarded.*

ANT. Ye see me on my way,   I 1
O burghers of my father's land!
With one last look on Helios' ray,
Led my last path toward the silent strand.
Alive to the wide house of rest I go;
 No dawn for me may shine,
No marriage-blessing e'er be mine,
No hymeneal with my praises flow!
The Lord of Acheron's unlovely shore
Shall be mine only husband evermore.
 CH. Yea, but with glory and fame,—
 Not by award of the sword,
 Not with blighting disease,
 But by a law of thine own,—
 Thou, of mortals alone,
 Goest alive to the deep
 Tranquil home of the dead.

ANT. Erewhile I heard men say,   I 2
How, in far Phrygia, Thebè's friend,
Tantalus' child, had dreariest end
On heights of Sipylus consumed away:
O'er whom the rock like clinging ivy grows,
 And while with moistening dew
Her cheek runs down, the eternal snows
Weigh o'er her, and the tearful stream renew
That from sad brows her stone-cold breast doth
  steep.
Like unto her the God lulls me to sleep.

CH. But she was a goddess born,
   We but of mortal line ;
   And sure to rival the fate
   Of a daughter of sires Divine
   Were no light glory in death.

ANT. O mockery of my woe !   II 1
I pray you by our fathers' holy Fear,
      Why must I hear
Your insults, while in life on earth I stand,
   O ye that flow
In wealth, rich burghers of my bounteous land ?
O fount of Dircè, and thou spacious grove,
Where Thebè's chariots move !
Ye are my witness, though none else be nigh,
By what enormity of lawless doom,
      Without one friendly sigh,
I go to the strong mound of yon strange tomb,—
All hapless, having neither part nor room
With those who live or those who die !
   CH. Thy boldness mounted high,
And thou, my child, 'gainst the great pedestal
Of Justice with unmeasured force didst fall.
Thy father's lot still presseth hard on thee.

ANT. That pains me more than all.   II 2
Ah ! thou hast touched my father's misery
      Still mourned anew,
With all the world-famed sorrows on us rolled
      Since Cadmus old.
O cursèd marriage that my mother knew !
O wretched fortune of my sire, who lay
      Where first he saw the day !
Such were the authors of my burdened life ;
      To whom, with curses dowered, never a wife,
      I go to dwell beneath.
O brother mine, thy princely marriage-tie
Hath been thy downfall, and in this thy death
Thou hast destroyed me ere I die.
   CH. 'Twas pious, we confess,
Thy fervent deed. But he, who power would show,

Must let no soul of all he rules transgress.
A self-willed passion was thine overthrow.

ANT. Friendless, uncomforted of bridal lay,   III
Unmourned, they lead me on my destined way.
Woe for my life forlorn ! I may not see
The sacred round of yon great light
Rising again to greet me from the night ;
No friend bemoans my fate, no tear hath fallen for me !

Enter CREON.

CR. If criminals were suffered to complain
In dirges before death, they ne'er would end.
Away with her at once, and closing her,
As I commanded, in the vaulty tomb,
Leave her all desolate, whether to die,
Or to live on in that sepulchral cell.
We are guiltless in the matter of this maid ;
Only she shall not share the light of day.

ANT. O grave ! my bridal chamber, prison-house
Eterne, deep-hollowed, whither I am led
To find mine own,—of whom Persephonè
Hath now a mighty number housed in death :—
I last of all, and far most miserably,
Am going, ere my days have reached their term !
Yet lives the hope that, when I go, most surely
Dear will my coming be, father, to thee,
And dear to thee, my mother, and to thee,
Brother ! since with these very hands I decked
And bathed you after death, and ministered
The last libations. And I reap this doom
For tending, Polynices, on thy corse.
Indeed I honoured thee, the wise will say.
For neither, had I children, nor if one
I had married were laid bleeding on the earth,
Would I have braved the city's will, or taken
This burden on me. Wherefore ? I will tell.
A husband lost might be replaced ; a son,
If son were lost to me, might yet be born ;
But, with both parents hidden in the tomb,
No brother may arise to comfort me.

Therefore above all else I honoured thee,
And therefore Creon thought me criminal,
And bold in wickedness, O brother mine!
And now by servile hands, for all to see,
He hastens me away, unhusbanded,
Before my nuptial, having never known
Or married joy or tender motherhood.
But desolate and friendless I go down
Alive, O horror! to the vaults of the dead.
For what transgression of Heaven's ordinance?
Alas! how can I look to Heaven? on whom
Call to befriend me? seeing that I have earned,
By piety, the meed of impious?—
Oh! if this act be what the Gods approve,
In death I may repent me of my deed;
But if they sin who judge me, be their doom
No heavier than they wrongly wreak on me!

    CH. With unchanged fury beats the storm of soul
That shakes this maiden.

    CR.   Then for that, be sure
Her warders shall lament their tardiness.

    ANT. Alas! I hear Death's footfall in that sound.

    CR. I may not reassure thee.—'Tis most true.

    ANT. O land of Thebè, city of my sires,
Ye too, ancestral Gods! I go—I go!
Even now they lead me to mine end.   Behold!
Founders of Thebes, the only scion left
Of Cadmus' issue, how unworthily,
By what mean instruments I am oppressed,
For reverencing the dues of piety.   [*Exit guarded*

CHORUS.

Even Danaë's beauty left the lightsome day.   I 1
Closed in her strong and brass-bound tower she lay
    In tomb-like deep confine.
Yet she was gendered, O my child!
       From sires of noblest line,
And treasured for the Highest the golden rain.
Fated misfortune hath a power so fell:
    Not wealth, nor warfare wild,

Nor dark spray-dashing coursers of the main
Against great Destiny may once rebel.

He too in darksome durance was compressed,   I 2
King of Edonians, Dryas' hasty son,
          In eyeless vault of stone
Immured by Dionysus' hest,
          All for a wrathful jest.
Fierce madness issueth in such fatal flower.
He found 'twas mad to taunt the Heavenly Power,
          Chilling the Maenad breast
Kindled with Bacchic fire, and with annoy
Angering the Muse that in the flute hath joy.

And near twin rocks that guard the Colchian sea,   II 1
Bosporian cliffs 'fore Salmydessus rise,
Where neighbouring Ares from his shrine beheld
Phineus' two sons by female fury quelled,
With cursèd wounding of their sight-reft eyes,
That cried to Heaven to 'venge the iniquity.
The shuttle's sharpness in a cruel hand
Dealt the dire blow, not struck with martial brand.

But chiefly for her piteous lot they pined,   II 2
Who was the source of their rejected birth.
She touched the lineage of Erechtheus old ;
Whence in far caves her life did erst unfold,
Cradled 'mid storms, daughter of Northern wind,
Steed-swift o'er all steep places of the earth.
Yet even on her, though reared of heavenly kind,
The long-enduring Fates at last took hold.

Enter TIRESIAS, *led by a boy.*

TIRESIAS.   We are come, my lords of Thebes, joint
                    wayfarers,
One having eyes for both.   The blind must still
Thus move in frail dependence on a guide.
    CR. And what hath brought thee, old Tirésias, now ?
    TI. I will instruct thee, if thou wilt hear my voice.
    CR. I have not heretofore rejected thee.
    TI. Therefore thy pilotage hath saved this city.

CR. Grateful experience owns the benefit.
TI.   Take heed.   Again thou art on an edge of
       peril.
CR. What is it? How I shudder at thy word!
TI.   The tokens of mine art shall make thee know.
As I was sitting on that ancient seat
Of divination, where I might command
Sure cognisance of every bird of the air,
I heard strange clamouring of fowl, that screeched
In furious dissonance; and, I could tell,
Talons were bloodily engaged—the whirr
Of wings told a clear tale. At once, in fear,
I tried burnt sacrifice at the high altar:
Where from the offering the fire-god refused
To gleam; but a dank humour from the bones
Dripped on the embers with a sputtering fume.
The gall was spirtled high in air; the thighs
Lay wasting, bared of their enclosing fat.
Such failing tokens of blurred augury
This youth reported, who is guide to me,
As I to others. And this evil state
Is come upon the city from thy will:
Because our altars—yea, our sacred hearths—
Are everywhere infected from the mouths
Of dogs or beak of vulture that hath fed
On Oedipus' unhappy slaughtered son.
And then at sacrifice the Gods refuse
Our prayers and savour of the thigh-bone fat—
And of ill presage is the thickening cry
Of bird that battens upon human gore.
Now, then, my son, take thought. A man may err;
But he is not insensate or foredoomed
To ruin, who, when he hath lapsed to evil,
Stands not inflexible, but heals the harm.
The obstinate man still earns the name of fool.
Urge not contention with the dead, nor stab
The fallen. What valour is 't to slay the slain?
I have thought well of this, and say it with care;
And careful counsel, that brings gain withal,
Is precious to the understanding soul.

CR. I am your mark, and ye with one consent
All shoot your shafts at me. Nought left untried,
Not even the craft of prophets, by whose crew
I am bought and merchandised long since. Go on!
Traffic, get gain, electrum from the mine
Of Lydia, and the gold of Ind! Yet know,
Grey-beard! ye ne'er shall hide him in a tomb.
No, not if heaven's own eagle chose to snatch
And bear him to the throne supreme for food,
Even that pollution should not daunt my heart
To yield permission for his funeral.
For well know I defilement ne'er can rise
From man to God. But, old Tirésias, hear!
Even wisest spirits have a shameful fall
That fairly speak base words for love of gain.
   TI. Ah! where is wisdom? who considereth?
   CR. Wherefore? what means this universal doubt?
   TI. How far the best of riches is good counsel!
   CR. As far as folly is the mightiest bane.
   TI. Yet thou art sick of that same pestilence.
   CR. I would not give the prophet blow for blow.
   TI. What blow is harder than to call me false?
   CR. Desire of money is the prophet's plague.
   TI. And ill-sought lucre is the curse of kings.
   CR. Know'st thou 'tis of thy sovereign thou speak'st
      this?
   TI. Yea, for my aid gives thee to sway this city.
   CR. Far-seeing art thou, but dishonest too.
   TI. Thou wilt provoke the utterance of my tongue
To that even thought refused to dwell upon.
   CR. Say on, so thou speak sooth, and not for gain.
   TI. You think me likely to seek gain from you?
   CR. You shall not make your merchandise on me!
   TI. Not many courses of the racing sun
Shalt thou fulfil, ere of thine own true blood
Thou shalt have given a corpse in recompense
For one on earth whom thou hast cast beneath,
Entombing shamefully a living soul,
And one whom thou hast kept above the ground
And disappointed of all obsequies,

Unsanctified and godlessly forlorn.
Such violence the powers beneath will bear
Not even from the Olympian gods. For thee
The avengers wait. Hidden but near at hand,
Lagging but sure, the Furies of the grave
Are watching for thee to thy ruinous harm,
With thine own evil to entangle thee.
Look well to it now whether I speak for gold!
A little while, and thine own palace-halls
Shall flash the truth upon thee with loud noise
Of men and women, shrieking o'er the dead.
And all the cities whose unburied sons,
Mangled and torn, have found a sepulchre
In dogs or jackals or some ravenous bird
That stains their incense with polluted breath,
Are forming leagues in troublous enmity.
Such shafts, since thou hast stung me to the quick,
I like an archer at thee in my wrath
Have loosed unerringly—carrying their pang,
Inevitable, to thy very heart.
Now, sirrah! lead me home, that his hot mood
Be spent on younger objects, till he learn
To keep a safer mind and calmer tongue.   [*Exit*

CH. Sire, there is terror in that prophecy.
He who is gone, since ever these my locks,
Once black, now white with age, waved o'er my brow,
Hath never spoken falsely to the state.

CR. I know it, and it shakes me to the core.
To yield is dreadful : but resistingly
To face the blow of fate, is full of dread.

CH. The time calls loud on wisdom, good my lord.

CR. What must I do ? Advise me. I will obey.

CH. Go and release the maiden from the vault,
And make a grave for the unburied dead.

CR. Is that your counsel ? Think you I will yield ?

CH. With all the speed thou mayest : swift harms
          from heaven
With instant doom o'erwhelm the froward man.

CR. Oh! it is hard. But I am forced to this
Against myself. I cannot fight with Destiny.

C. S.   D

CH. Go now to do it. Trust no second hand.

CR. Even as I am, I go. Come, come, my people,
Here or not here, with mattocks in your hands
Set forth immediately to yonder hill!
And, since I have ta'en this sudden turn, myself,
Who tied the knot, will hasten to unloose it.
For now the fear comes over me, 'tis best
To pass one's life in the accustomed round. [*Exeunt*

CHORUS.

O God of many a name!   I 1
Filling the heart of that Cadmeian bride
   With deep delicious pride,
Offspring of him who wields the withering flame!
    Thou for Italia's good
Dost care, and 'midst the all-gathering bosom wide
   Of Dèo dost preside ;
Thou, Bacchus, by Ismenus' winding waters
   'Mongst Thebè's frenzied daughters,
Keep'st haunt, commanding the fierce dragon's brood.

Thee o'er the forkèd hill   I 2
The pinewood flame beholds, where Bacchai rove,
   Nymphs of Corycian grove,
Hard by the flowing of Castalia's rill.
    To visit Theban ways,
By bloomy wine-cliffs flushing tender bright
   'Neath far Nyseian height
Thou movest o'er the ivy-mantled mound,
   While myriad voices sound
Loud strains of ' Evoe ! ' to thy deathless praise.

For Thebè thou dost still uphold,   II 1
First of cities manifold,
Thou and the nymph whom lightning made
Mother of thy radiant head.
Come then with healing for the violent woe
That o'er our peopled land doth largely flow,
Passing the high Parnassian steep
Or moaning narrows of the deep !

Come, leader of the starry quire   II 2
Quick-panting with their breath of fire!
Lord of high voices of the night,
Child born to him who dwells in light,
Appear with those who, joying in their madness,
Honour the sole dispenser of their gladness,
Thyiads of the Aegean main
Night-long trooping in thy train.

Enter Messenger.

MESS. Neighbours of Cadmus and Amphion's halls,
No life of mortal, howsoe'er it stand,
Shall once have praise or censure from my mouth;
Since human happiness and human woe
Come even as fickle Fortune smiles or lours;
And none can augur aught from what we see.
Creon erewhile to me was enviable,
Who saved our Thebè from her enemies;
Then, vested with supreme authority,
Ruled her aright; and flourish'd in his home
With noblest progeny. What hath he now?
Nothing. For when a man is lost to joy,
I count him not to live, but reckon him
A living corse. Riches belike are his,
Great riches and the appearance of a King;
But if no gladness come to him, all else
Is shadow of a vapour, weighed with joy.
CH. What new affliction heaped on sovereignty
Com'st thou to tell?
MESS.   They are dead; and they that live
Are guilty of the death.
CH.   The slayer, who?
And who the slain? Declare.
MESS.   Haemon is dead,
And by a desperate hand.
CH.   His own, or Creon's?
MESS. By his own hand, impell'd with violent wrath
At Creon for the murder of the maid.
CH. Ah, Seer! how surely didst thou aim thy word!
MESS. So stands the matter. Make of it what ye list.

CH. See, from the palace cometh close to us
Creon's unhappy wife, Eurydicè.
Is it by chance, or heard she of her son ?

Enter EURYDICE.

EURYDICE. Ye men of Thebes, the tidings met mine
          ear
As I was coming forth to visit Pallas
With prayerful salutation. I was loosening
The bar of the closed gate, when the sharp sound
Of mine own sorrow smote against my heart,
And I fell back astonied on my maids
And fainted. But the tale ? tell me once more ;
I am no novice in adversity.

MESS. Dear lady, I will tell thee what I saw,
And hide no grain of truth : why should I soothe
Thy spirit with soft tales, when the harsh fact
Must prove me a liar ? Truth is always best.
I duly led the footsteps of thy lord
To the highest point of the plain, where still was lying,
Forlorn and mangled by the dogs, the corse
Of Polynices. We besought Persephonè
And Pluto gently to restrain their wrath,
And wash'd him pure and clean, and then we burned
The poor remains with brushwood freshly pulled,
And heaped a lofty mound of his own earth
Above him. Then we turned us to the vault,
The maiden's stony bride-chamber of death.
And from afar, round the unhallowed cell,
One heard a voice of wailing loud and long,
And went and told his lord : who coming near
Was haunted by the dim and bitter cry,
And suddenly exclaiming on his fate
Said lamentably, 'My prophetic heart
Divined aright. I am going, of all ways
That e'er I went, the unhappiest to-day.
My son's voice smites me. Go, my men, approach
With speed, and, where the stones are torn away,
Press through the passage to that door of death,
Look hard, and tell me, if I hear aright

The voice of Haemon, or the gods deceive me.'
Thus urged by our despairing lord, we made
Th' espial. And in the farthest nook of the vault
We saw the maiden hanging by the neck
With noose of finest tissue firmly tied,
And clinging to her on his knees the boy,
Lamenting o'er his ruined nuptial-rite,
Consummated in death, his father's crime
And his lost love. And when the father saw him,
With loud and dreadful clamour bursting in
He went to him and called him piteously :
'What deed is this, unhappy youth ? What thought
O'ermaster'd thee ? Where did the force of woe
O'erturn thy reason ? O come forth, my son,
I beg thee !' But with savage eyes the youth
Glared scowling at him, and without a word
Plucked forth his two-edged blade. The father then
Fled and escaped : but the unhappy boy,
Wroth with himself, even where he stood, leant heavily
Upon his sword and plunged it in his side.—
And while the sense remained, his slackening arm
Enfolded still the maiden, and his breath,
Gaspingly drawn and panted forth with pain,
Cast ruddy drops upon her pallid face ;
Then lay in death upon the dead, at last
Joined to his bride in Hades' dismal hall :—
A monument unto mankind, that rashness
Is the worst evil of this mortal state.
                                    [*Exit* EURYDICE

   CH. What augur ye from this ? The queen is gone
Without word spoken either good or bad.
      MESS. I, too, am struck with dread. But hope con-
            soles me,
That having heard the affliction of her son,
Her pride forbids to publish her lament
Before the town, but to her maids within
She will prescribe to mourn the loss of the house.
She is too tried in judgement to do ill.
      CH. I cannot tell. The extreme of silence, too,
Is dangerous, no less than much vain noise

Mess. Well, we may learn, if there be aught unseen
Suppressed within her grief-distempered soul,
By going within the palace. Ye say well:
There is a danger, even in too much silence.

  Ch. Ah ! look where sadly comes our lord the King,
Bearing upon his arm a monument—
If we may speak it—of no foreign woe,
But of his own infirmity the fruit.

Enter Creon *with the body of* Haemon.

  Cr. O error of my insensate soul,   11
Stubborn, and deadly in the fateful end !
O ye who now behold
Slayer and slain of the same kindred blood !
O bitter consequence of seeming-wise decree !
Alas, my son !
Strange to the world wert thou, and strange the fate
That took thee off, that slew thee ; woe is me !
Not for thy rashness, but my folly. Ah me !
  Ch. Alas for him who sees the right too late !
  Cr. Alas !
I have learnt it now. But then upon my head
Some God had smitten with dire weight of doom ;
And plunged me in a furious course, woe is me !
Discomforting and trampling on my joy.
Woe ! for the bitterness of mortal pain !

Enter 2nd Messenger.

  2nd Mess. My lord and master. Thou art master
          here
Of nought but sorrows. One within thine arms
Thou bear'st with thee, and in thy palace hall
Thou hast possession of another grief,
Which soon thou shalt behold.
  Cr.   What more of woe,
Or what more woeful, sounds anew from thee ?
  2nd Mess. The honoured mother of that corse, thy
          queen,
Is dead, and bleeding with a new-given wound.

CR. O horrible ! O charnel gulf   I 2
Of death on death, not to be done away,
Why harrowest thou my soul ?
Ill-boding harbinger of woe, what word
Have thy lips uttered ? Oh, thou hast killed me
    again,
Before undone !
What say'st ? What were thy tidings ? Woe is me !
Saidst thou a slaughtered queen in yonder hall
Lay in her blood, crowning the pile of ruin ?
   CH. No longer hidden in the house. Behold !

         [*The Corpse of* EURYDICE *is disclosed*

   CR. Alas !
Again I see a new, a second woe.
What more calamitous stroke of Destiny
Awaits me still ? But now mine arms enfold
My child, and lo ! yon corse before my face !
Ah ! hapless, hapless mother, hapless son !
   2ND MESS. She with keen knife before the altar place
Closed her dark orbs ; but first lamented loud
The glorious bed of buried Megareus,
And then of Haemon ; lastly clamoured forth
The curse of murdered offspring upon thee.

   CR. Ay me ! Ay me !   II 1
I am rapt with terror. Is there none to strike me
With doubly-sharpened blade a mortal blow ?
Ah ! I am plunged in fathomless distress.
   2ND MESS. The guilt of this and of the former grief
By this dead lady was denounced on thee.
   CR. Tell us, how ended she her life in blood ?
   2ND MESS. Wounding herself to the heart, when she
    had heard
The loud lamented death of Haemon here.
   CR. O me ! This crime can come
On no man else, exempting me.
I slew thee—I, O misery !
I say the truth, 'twas I ! My followers,
Take me with speed—take me away, away !
Me, who am nothing now.

Ch. Thou sayest the best, if there be best in woe.
Briefest is happiest in calamity.

Cr. Ah! let it come,   Π 2
The day, most welcome of all days to me,
That brings the consummation of my doom.
Come! Come! I would not see another sun.
Ch. Time will determine that. We must attend
To present needs. Fate works her own dread work.
Cr. All my desire was gathered in my prayer.
Ch. But prayer is bootless. For to mortal men
There is no saviour from appointed woe.
Cr. Take me away, the vain-proud man that slew
Thee, O my son! unwittingly,—and thee!
Me miserable, which way shall I turn,
Which look upon? Since all that I can touch
Is falling,—falling,—round me, and o'erhead
Intolerable destiny descends.

LEADER OF CHORUS.

Wise conduct hath command of happiness
Before all else, and piety to Heaven
Must be preserved. High boastings of the proud
Bring sorrow to the height to punish pride:—
A lesson men shall learn when they are old.

AIAS

THE PERSONS

ATHENA.

ODYSSEUS.

AIAS, *the son of Telamon.*

CHORUS *of Salaminian Mariners.*

TECMESSA.

A Messenger.

TEUCER, *half brother of Aias.*

MENELAUS.

AGAMEMNON.

EURYSAKÈS, *the child of Aias and Tecmessa, appears,
but does not speak.*

SCENE.   Before the encampment of Aias on the shore
of the Troad.   Afterwards a lonely place beyond
Rhoeteum.

Time, towards the end of the Trojan War.

'A wounded spirit who can bear?'

AFTER the death of Achilles, the armour made for him by Hephaestus was to be given to the worthiest of the surviving Greeks. Although Aias was the most valiant, the judges made the award to Odysseus, because he was the wisest.

Aias in his rage attempts to kill the generals; but Athena sends madness upon him, and he makes a raid upon the flocks and herds of the army, imagining the bulls and rams to be the Argive chiefs. On awakening from his delusion, he finds that he has fallen irrecoverably from honour and from the favour of the Greeks. He also imagines that the anger of Athena is unappeasable. Under this impression he eludes the loving eyes of his captive-bride Tecmessa, and of his Salaminian comrades, and falls on his sword. ('The soul and body rive not more in parting Than greatness going off.')

But it is revealed through the prophet Calchas, that the wrath of Athena will last only for a day; and on the return of Teucer, Aias receives an honoured funeral, the tyrannical reclamations of the two sons of Atreus being overcome by the firm fidelity of Teucer and the magnanimity of Odysseus, who has been inspired for this purpose by Athena.

AIAS

ATHENA (*above*). ODYSSEUS.

ATHENA. Oft have I seen thee, Laërtiades,
Intent on some surprisal of thy foes;
As now I find thee by the seaward camp,
Where Aias holds the last place in your line,
Lingering in quest, and scanning the fresh print
Of his late footsteps, to be certified
If he keep house or no. Right well thy sense
Hath led thee forth, like some keen hound of Sparta!
The man is even but now come home, his head
And slaughterous hands reeking with ardent toil.
Thou, then, no longer strain thy gaze within
Yon gateway, but declare what eager chase
Thou followest, that a god may give thee light.
    ODYSSEUS. Athena, 'tis thy voice! Dearest in
                        heaven,
How well-discerned and welcome to my soul
From that dim distance doth thine utterance fly
In tones as of Tyrrhenian trumpet-clang!
Rightly hast thou divined mine errand here,
Beating this ground for Aias of the shield,
The lion-quarry whom I track to-day.
For he hath wrought on us to-night a deed
Past thought—if he be doer of this thing;
We drift in ignorant doubt, unsatisfied:—
And I unbidden have bound me to this toil.

Brief time hath flown since suddenly we knew
That all our gathered spoil was reaved and slaughtered,
Flocks, herds, and herdmen, by some human hand,
All tongues, then, lay this deed at Aias' door.
And one, a scout who had marked him, all alone,
With new-fleshed weapon bounding o'er the plain,

Gave me to know it, when immediately
I darted on the trail, and here in part
I find some trace to guide me, but in part
I halt, amazed, and know not where to look.
Thou com'st full timely. For my venturous course,
Past or to come, is governed by thy will.

ATH. I knew thy doubts, Odysseus, and came forth
Zealous to guard thy perilous hunting-path.

OD. Dear Queen! and am I labouring to an end?
ATH. Thou schem'st not idly. This is Aias' deed.
OD. What can have roused him to a work so wild?
ATH. His grievous anger for Achilles' arms.
OD. But wherefore on the flock this violent raid?
ATH. He thought to imbrue his hands with your
   heart's blood.
OD. What? Was this planned against the Argives,
   then?
ATH. Planned, and performed, had I kept careless
   guard.
OD. What daring spirit, what hardihood, was here!
ATH. Alone by night in craft he sought your tents.
OD. How? Came he near them? Won he to his goal?
ATH. He stood in darkness at the generals' gates.
OD. What then restrained his eager hand from murder?
ATH. I turned him backward from his baleful joy,
And overswayed him with blind phantasies,
To swerve against the flocks and well-watched herd
Not yet divided from the public booty.
There plunging in he hewed the horned throng,
And with him Havoc ranged: while now he thought
To kill the Atreidae with hot hand, now this
Now that commander, as the fancy grew.
I, joining with the tumult of his mind,
Flung the wild victim on the fatal net.
Anon, this toil being overpast, he draws
The living oxen and the panting sheep
With cords to his home, not as a hornèd prey,
But as in triumph marshalling his foes:
Whom now he tortures in their bonds within.

 Come, thou shalt see this madness in clear day,

And tell to the Argives all I show thee here.
Only stand firm and shrink not ; I will turn
His eyes askance, not to distinguish thee ;
Fear nought.—Ho ! thou that bindest to thy will
The limbs of those thy captives, come thou forth !
Aias ! advance before thy palace-gate !

OD. My Queen ! what dost thou ? Never call him
    forth.

ATH. Hush, hush ! Be not so timorous, but endure.

OD. Nay, nay ! Enough. He is there, and let him
    bide.

ATH. What fear you ? Dates his valour from to-day ?

OD. He was and is my valiant enemy.

ATH. Then is not laughter sweetest o'er a foe ?

OD. No more ! I care not he should pass abroad.

ATH. You flinch from seeing the madman in full view.

OD. When sane, I ne'er had flinched before his face.

ATH. Well, but even now he shall not know thee near.

OD. How, if his eyes be not transformed or lost ?

ATH. I will confound his sense although he see.

OD. Well, nothing is too hard for Deity.

ATH. Stand still and keep thy place without a word.

OD. I must. Would I were far away from here !

ATH. Aias ! Again I summon thee. Why pay
So scanty heed to her who fights for thee ?

Enter AIAS *with a bloody scourge.*

AIAS. Hail, offspring of the Highest ! Pallas, hail !
Well hast thou stood by me. Triumphal gold
Shall crown thy temple for this lordly prey.

ATH. A fair intention ! But resolve me this :
Hast dyed thy falchion deep in Argive blood ?

AI. There is my boast ; that charge I'll ne'er deny.

ATH. Have Atreus' sons felt thy victorious might ?

AI. They have. No more they'll make a scorn of
    me !

ATH. I take it, then, they are dead.

AI.   Ay, now they are dead,
Let them arise and rob me of mine arms !

ATH. Good. Next inform us of Laërtes' son;
How stands his fortune ? Hast thou let him go ?
　　AI. The accursed fox ! Dost thou inquire of him ?
　　ATH. Ay, of Odysseus, thy late adversary.
　　AI. He sits within, dear lady, to my joy,
Bound ; for I mean him not just yet to die.
　　ATH. What fine advantage wouldst thou first
　　　　achieve ?
　　AI. First, tie him to a pillar of my hall—
　　ATH. Poor wretch ! What torment wilt thou wreak
　　　　on him ?
　　AI. Then stain his back with scourging till he die.
　　ATH. Nay, 'tis too much. Poor caitiff ! Not the
　　　　scourge !
　　AI. Pallas, in all things else have thou thy will,
But none shall wrest Odysseus from this doom.
　　ATH. Well, since thou art determined on the deed,
Spare nought of thine intent : indulge thy hand !
　　AI. (waving the bloody scourge). I go ! But thou, I
　　　　charge thee, let thine aid
Be evermore like valiant as to-day.   [Exit
　　ATH. The gods are strong, Odysseus. Dost thou see?
What man than Aias was more provident,
Or who for timeliest action more approved ?
　　OD. I know of none. But, though he hates me sore,
I pity him, poor mortal, thus chained fast
To a wild and cruel fate,—weighing not so much
His fortune as mine own. For now I feel
All we who live are but an empty show
And idle pageant of a shadowy dream.
　　ATH. Then, warned by what thou seest, be thou not
　　　　rash
To vaunt high words toward Heaven, nor swell thy
　　　　port
Too proudly, if in puissance of thy hand
Thou passest others, or in mines of wealth.
Since Time abases and uplifts again
All that is human, and the modest heart
Is loved by Heaven, who hates the intemperate will.
                                              [Exeunt

CHORUS (*entering*).

Telamonian child, whose hand
Guards our wave-encircled land,
Salamis that breasts the sea,
Good of thine is joy to me;
But if One who reigns above
Smite thee, or if murmurs move
From fierce Danaäns in their hate
Full of threatening to thy state,
All my heart for fear doth sigh,
Shrinking like a dove's soft eye.

Half-Chorus I.

Hardly had the darkness waned,
When our ears were filled and pained
With huge scandal on thy fame.
Telling, thine the arm that came
To the cattle-browsèd mead,
Wild with prancing of the steed,
And that ravaged there and slew
With a sword of fiery hue
All the spoils that yet remain,
By the sweat of spearmen ta'en.

Such report against thy life,   *Half-Chorus II.*
Whispered words with falsehood rife,
Wise Odysseus bringing near
Shrewdly gaineth many an ear:
Since invention against thee
Findeth hearing speedily,
Tallying with the moment's birth;
And with loudly waxing mirth
Heaping insult on thy grief,
Each who hears it glories more
Than the tongue that told before.
Every slander wins belief
Aimed at souls whose worth is chief:
Shot at me, or one so small,
Such a bolt might harmless fall.

Ever toward the great and high
Creepeth climbing jealousy.
Yet the low without the tall
Make at need a tottering wall.
Let the strong the feeble save
And the mean support the brave.

CHORUS.

Ah ! 'twere vain to tune such song
'Mid the nought-discerning throng
Who are clamouring now 'gainst thee
Long and loud ; and strengthless we,
Mighty chieftain, thou away,
To withstand the gathering fray.
Flocking fowl with carping cry
Seem they, lurking from thine eye ;
Till the royal eagle's poise
Overawe the paltry noise :
Till before thy presence hushed
Sudden sink they, mute and crushed.

Did bull-slaying Artemis, Zeus' cruel daughter   I 1
  (Ah, fearful rumour, fountain of my shame !)
Prompt thy fond heart to this disastrous slaughter
  Of the full herd stored in our army's name ?
Say, had her blood-stained temple missed the kindness
  Of some vow-promised fruit of victory,
Foiled of some glorious armour through thy blindness,
  Or fell some stag ungraced by gift from thee ?
Or did stern Ares venge his thankless spear
Through this night-foray that hath cost thee dear ?

For never, if thy heart were not distracted   I 2
  By stings from Heaven, O child of Telamon,
Wouldst thou have bounded leftward, to have acted
  Thus wildly, spoiling all our host hath won !
Madness might fall : some heavenly power forfend it !
  But if Odysseus and the tyrant lords
Suggest a forgèd tale, O rise to end it,
  Nor fan the fierce flame of their withering words !

Forth from thy tent, and let thine eye confound
The brood of Sisyphus that would thee wound!

Too long hast thou been fixed in grim repose, III
  Heightening the haughty malice of thy foes,
That, while thou porest by the sullen sea,
  Through breezy glades advanceth fearlessly,
A mounting blaze with crackling laughter fed
From myriad throats; whence pain and sorrow bred
Within my bosom are establishèd.

Enter TECMESSA.

TECMESSA. Helpers of Aias' vessel's speed,
Erechtheus' earth-derivèd seed,
Sorrows are ours who truly care
For the house of Telamon afar.
The dread, the grand, the rugged form
    Of him we know,
Is stricken with a troublous storm;
  Our Aias' glory droopeth low.
CHORUS. What burden through the darkness fell
Where still at eventide 'twas well?
Phrygian Teleutas' daughter, say;
Since Aias, foremost in the fray,
Disdaining not the spear-won bride,
Still holds thee nearest at his side,
And thou may'st solve our doubts aright.
TEC. How shall I speak the dreadful word?
How shall ye live when ye have heard?
Madness hath seized our lord by night
And blasted him with hopeless blight.
Such horrid victims mightst thou see
Huddled beneath yon canopy,
Torn by red hands and dyed in blood,
Dread offerings to his direful mood.

CH. What news of our fierce lord thy story showeth, I
  Sharp to endure, impossible to fly!
News that on tongues of Danaäns hourly groweth,
  Which Rumour's myriad voices multiply!

Alas! the approaching doom awakes my terror.
 The man will die, disgraced in open day,
Whose dark-dyed steel hath dared through mad-
        brained error
 The mounted herdmen with their herds to slay.

Tec. O horror! Then 'twas there he found
  The flock he brought as captives tied;
And some he slew upon the ground,
  And some, side-smiting, sundered wide.
Two white-foot rams he backward drew,
And bound. Of one he shore and threw
The tipmost tongue and head away;
The other to an upright stay
He tied, and with a harness thong
  Doubled in hand, gave whizzing blows,
Echoing his lashes with a song
  More dire than mortal fury knows.

Ch. Ah! then 'tis time, our heads in mantles hiding, 2
  Our feet on some stol'n pathway now to ply,
Or with swift oarage o'er the billows gliding,
  With ordered stroke to make the good ship fly.
Such threats the Atridae, armed with two-fold power,
  Launch to assail us. Oh, I sadly fear
Stones from fierce hands on us and him will shower,
  Whose heavy plight no comfort may come near.

Tec. 'Tis changed; his rage, like sudden blast,
Without the lightning-gleam is past.
And now that Reason's light returns,
New sorrow in his spirit burns.
For when we look on self-made woe,
  In which no hand but ours had part,
Thought of such griefs and whence they flow
  Brings aching misery to the heart.

Ch. If he hath ceased to rave, he should do well.
The account of evil lessens when 'tis past.
  Tec. If choice were given you, would you rather
        choose
Hurting your friends, yourself to feel delight,

Or share with them in one commingled pain ?
  CH. The two-fold trouble is more terrible.
  TEC. Then comes our torment now the fit is o'er.
  CH. How mean'st thou by that word ? I fail to see.
  TEC. He in his rage had rapture of delight
And knew not how he grieved us who stood near
And saw the madding tempest ruining him.
But now 'tis over and he breathes anew,
The counterblast of sorrow shakes his soul,
Whilst our affliction vexeth as before,
Have we not double for our single woe ?
  CH. I feel thy reasoning move me, and I fear
Some heavenly stroke hath fallen.   How else, when the
      end
Of stormy sickness brings no cheering ray ?
  TEC. Our state is certain.   Dream not but 'tis so.
  CH. How first began the assault of misery ?
Tell us the trouble, for we share the pain.
  TEC. It toucheth you indeed, and ye shall hear
All from the first.   'Twas midnight, and the lamp
Of eve had died, when, seizing his sharp blade,
He sought on some vain errand to creep forth.
I broke in with my word : ' Aias, what now ?
Why thus uncalled for salliest thou ? No voice
Of herald summoned thee. No trumpet blew.
What wouldst thou when the camp is hushed in
    sleep ? '
He with few words well known to women's ears
Checked me : ' The silent partner is the best.'
I saw how 'twas and ceased.   Forth then he fared
Alone.—What horror passed upon the plain
This night, I know not.   But he drags within,
Tied in a throng, bulls, shepherd-dogs, and spoil
Of cattle and sheep.   Anon he butchers them,
Felling or piercing, hacking or tearing wide,
Ribs from breast, limb from limb.   Others in rage
He seized and bound and tortured, brutes for men.
Last, out he rushed before the doors, and there
Whirled forth wild language to some shadowy form,
Flouting the generals and Laërtes' son

With torrent laughter and loud triumphing
What in his raid he had wreaked to their despite.
Then diving back within—the fitful storm
Slowly assuaging left his spirit clear.
And when his eye had lightened through the room
Cumbered with ruin, smiting on his brow
He roared ; and, tumbling down amid the wreck
Of woolly carnage he himself had made,
Sate with clenched hand tight twisted in his hair.
Long stayed he so in silence. Then flashed forth
Those frightful words of threatening vehemence,
That bade me show him all the night's mishap,
And whither he was fallen. I, dear my friends,
Prevailed on through my fear, told all I knew.
And all at once he raised a bitter cry,
Which heretofore I ne'er had heard ; for still
He made us think such doleful utterance
Betokened the dull craven spirit, and still
Dumb to shrill wailings, he would inly moan
With half-heard muttering, like an angry bull.
But now, by such dark fortune overpowered,
Foodless and dry, amid the quivering heap
His steel hath quelled, all quietly he broods ;
And out of doubt his mind intends some harm :
Such words, such groans, burst from him. O my
            friends,—
Therefore I hastened,—enter and give aid
If aught ye can ! Men thus forgone will oft
Grow milder through the counsel of a friend.

  CH. Teleutas' child ! we shudder at thy tale
That fatal frenzy wastes our hero's soul.

  AIAS (*within*). Woe 's me, me, me !

  TEC. More cause anon ! Hear ye not Aias there,
How sharp the cry that shrills from him ?
  AI.   Woe ! Woe !
  CH. Madly it sounds.—Or springs it of deep grief
For proofs of madness harrowing to his eye ?
  AI. Boy, boy !
  TEC.   What means he ? Oh, Eurysakès !
He cries on thee. Where art thou ? O my heart !

Aɪ. Teucer I call! Where's Teucer? Will he ne'er
Come from the chase, but leave me to my doom?

Cʜ. Not madness now.   Disclose him.   Let us look.
Haply the sight of us may calm his soul.

Tᴇᴄ. There, then; I open to your view the form
Of Aias, and his fortunes as they are.

[Aɪᴀs *is discovered*

Aɪ. Dear comrades of the deep, whose truth and
        love   I 1
    Stand forth alone unbroken in my woe,
            Behold what gory sea
            Of storm-lashed agony
    Doth round and round me flow!

Cʜ. (*to* Tᴇᴄ.) Too true thy witness: for the fact
        cries out
Wild thoughts were here and Reason's lamp extinct.

Aɪ. Strong helpers of sea-speed, whose nimble
        hand   I 2
    Plied hither the salt oar with circling stroke,
            No shepherd there was found
            To give the avenging wound.
    Come, lay me with the flock!

Cʜ. Speak no rash word! nor curing ill with ill
Augment the plague of this calamity.

Aɪ.   Mark ye the brave and bold,   II 1
        Whom none could turn of old,
    When once he set his face to the fierce fight?
            Now beasts that thought no harm
            Have felt this puissant arm.
    O laughter of my foes! O mockery of my might!

Tᴇᴄ. Aias, my lord! I entreat thee, speak not so!

Aɪ. Thou here! Away! begone, and trouble me not!
O! O!

Cʜ.   Be softened! bear a steadier mind!

Aɪ. O heaven-accursèd hand
        That let the ruffians go,
    But falling 'midst the horn'd and bleating band,
        Made darkling blood-streams flow!

CH. Why vex thy heart with what is over and done ?
Do what we may, this ne'er will alter now.

AI.   Child of Laërtes old,   II 2
          Thou that dost still behold
    And still contrive all shapes of monstrous ill,
          Winding in foulest ways
          Through the army's sinful maze,—
    Now even for pleasure thou may'st laugh thy fill.

CH. Laughter and tears are in the gift of God.
AI. Ay, might I see him, though thus broken,—ay
me !
Even yet—
CH. Nay, vaunt not. Look where thou art fallen.

AI.   Source where my life-blood springs,
          O Zeus, might I but slay
    That crafty plague, with those twin-sceptred
          kings,
          Then breathe my life away !

TEC. Pray thus, and pray that I too be no more !
If thou wert gone, what were my life to me ?

AI. Darkness ! my only light !   III 1
    O nether gloom, to me
    Brighter than morning to the wakeful eye !
    Take me to dwell with thee.
    Take me ! What help? Zeus' daughter with fell
          might
    Torments me sore. I may not look on high,
    Nor to the tribe of momentary men.—
    Oh, whither, then,
    Should it avail to fly ?
    Ah ! whither should I go and stay ?
    All here is ruin. This mad prey
    Shames me for evermore :
    Vengeance is at the door ;
    Yea, all the Achaean host, with armèd hand,
    Is ready at command
    To slay me o'er and o'er.

TAC. Woe 's me ! to hear from one so good and true
Words he had scorned to utter in past days.

AI. Grey firths of foaming brine,   III 2
And ye, deep groves, that crown
The sea-caves and long cliffs upon the shore,
Too long did ye confine
My life about the walls of Troia's town :
But no more now ! a breathing man, no more !
The wise in heart may duly learn that lore.
Let Xanthus know,
Whose waters neighbouring flow,
And minister to Argive men :
One man he ne'er shall see again ;
One, I will vaunt it forth !
Highest in warlike worth
Of all Greek forms that Troia's towers have eyed :
Now, shorn of all that pride,
I lie thus low.

CH. I know not how to let thee speak, nor how
To silence thee. Such evils close thee round.
AI. Ay me !
               Could human thought have prophesied
My name would thus give echo to mine ill ?
'Ai' now for Aias, doubly, trebly said,
Sorts all too well to mark my misery ;
Whose father from this land of Troy, as noblest
Of all the host, carrying the fairest prize,
Came girt about with glory to his home.
But I his son, not less of might than he,
Nor poorer in the achievements of my hand,
To this same region following in my prime,
Am scouted by the Achaeans and destroyed.
Yet know I one thing well. Had Peleus' child,
Living, adjudged his armour as a meed
Of well-tried bravery, no grasp save mine
Had clutched it. But the Atridae with mean craft
Conveyed his heirloom to a wit-proud knave,
Whilst Aias' peerless prowess was despised.
And had not this mine eye and mind distraught

Glanced from my purpose, ne'er again had they
Perverted judgement. But the invincible
Stern daughter of the Highest, with baneful eye,
Even as mine arm descended, baffled me,
And hurled upon my soul a frenzied plague,
To stain my hand with these dumb victims' blood.
And those mine enemies exult in safety,—
Not with my will; but where a God misguides,
Strong arms are thwarted and the weakling lives.

Now, what remains ? Heaven hates me, 'tis too clear :
The Grecian host abhor me : Troy, with all
This country round our camp, is my sworn foe.
Shall I, across the Aegean sailing home,
Leave these Atridae and their fleet forlorn ?
How shall I dare to front my father's eye ?
How will he once endure to look on me,
Denuded of the prize of high renown,
Whose coronal stood sparkling on his brow ?
No ! 'twere too dreadful. Then shall I advance
Before the Trojan battlements, and there
In single conflict doing valiantly
Last die upon their spears ? Nay, for by this
I might perchance make Atreus' offspring glad.
That may not be imagined. I must find
Some act to let my grey-haired father feel
No heartless recreant once called him sire.
Shame on the wight who when beset with ill
Cares to live on in misery unrelieved.
Can hour outlasting hour make less or more
Of death ? Whereby then can it furnish joy ?
That mortal weighs for nothing-worth with me,
Whom Hope can comfort with her fruitless fire.
Honour in life or honour in the grave
Befits the noble heart. You hear my will.

CN. From thine own spirit, Aias, all may tell,
That utterance came, and none have prompted thee.
Yet stay thy hurrying thought, and by thy friends
Be ruled to loose this burden from thy mind.

TEC. O my great master ! heaviest of all woe
Is theirs whose life is crushed beyond recall.

I, born of one the mightiest of the free
And wealthiest in the Phrygian land, am now
A captive. So Heaven willed, and thy strong arm
Determined. Therefore, since the hour that made
My being one with thine, I breathe for thee;
And I beseech thee by the sacred fire
Of home, and by the sweetness of the night
When from thy captive I became thy bride,
Leave me not guardless to the unworthy touch
And cruel taunting of thine enemies!
For, shouldst thou die and leave us, then shall I
Borne off by Argive violence with thy boy
Eat from that day the bread of slavery.
And some one of our lords shall smite me there
With galling speech: Behold the concubine
Of Aias, first of all the Greeks for might,
How envied once, worn with what service now!
So will they speak; and while my quailing heart
Shall sink beneath its burden, clouds of shame
Will dim thy glory and degrade thy race.
Oh! think but of thy father, left to pine
In doleful age, and let thy mother's grief—
Who, long bowed down with many a careful year,
Prays oftentimes thou may'st return alive—
O'er-awe thee. Yea, and pity thine own son,
Unsheltered in his boyhood, lorn of thee,
With bitter foes to tend his orphanhood,
Think, O my lord, what sorrow in thy death
Thou send'st on him and me. For I have nought
To lean to but thy life. My fatherland
Thy spear hath ruined. Fate—not thou—hath sent
My sire and mother to the home of death.
What wealth have I to comfort me for thee?
What land of refuge? Thou art all my stay.
Oh, of me too take thought! Shall men have joy,
And not remember? Or shall kindness fade?
Say, can the mind be noble, where the stream
Of gratitude is withered from the spring?

    Ch. Aias, I would thy heart were touched like mine
With pity; then her words would win thy praise.

Aɪ. My praise she shall not miss, if she perform
My bidding with firm heart, and fail not here.
 Tᴇᴄ. Dear Aias, I will fail in nought thou bidst me.
 Aɪ. Bring me my boy, that I may see his face.
 Tᴇᴄ. Oh, in my terror I conveyed him hence!
 Aɪ. Clear of this mischief, mean'st thou? or for what?
 Tᴇᴄ. Lest he might run to thee, poor child, and die.
 Aɪ. That issue had been worthy of my fate!
 Tᴇᴄ. But I kept watch to fence his life from harm.
 Aɪ. 'Twas wisely done. I praise thy foresight there.
 Tᴇᴄ. Well, since 'tis so, how can I help thee now?
 Aɪ. Give me to speak to him and see him near.
 Tᴇᴄ. He stands close by with servants tending him.
 Aɪ. Then why doth he not come, but still delay?
 Tᴇᴄ. Thy father calls thee, child. Come, lead him
    hither,
Whichever of you holds him by the hand.
 Aɪ. Moves he? or do thine accents idly fall?
 Tᴇᴄ. See, where thy people bring him to thine eye.
 Aɪ. Lift him to me: lift him! He will not fear
At sight of this fresh havoc of the sword,
If rightly he be fathered of my blood.
Like some young colt he must be trained and taught
To run fierce courses with his warrior sire.
Be luckier than thy father, boy! but else
Be like him, and thy life will not be low.
One thing even now I envy thee, that none
Of all this misery pierces to thy mind.
For life is sweetest in the void of sense,
Ere thou know joy or sorrow. But when this
Hath found thee, make thy father's enemies
Feel the great parent in the valiant child.
Meantime grow on in tender youthfulness,
Nursed by light breezes, gladdening this thy mother.
No Greek shall trample thee with brutal harm,
That I know well, though I shall not be near—
So stout a warder to protect thy life
I leave in Teucer. He'll not fail, though now
He follow far the chase upon his foes.
My trusty warriors, people of the sea,

Be this your charge, no less,—and bear to him
My clear commandment, that he take this boy
Home to my fatherland, and make him known
To Telamon, and Eriboea too,
My mother. Let him tend them in their age.
And, for mine armour, let not that be made
The award of Grecian umpires or of him
Who ruined me. But thou, named of the shield,
Eurysakès, hold mine, the unpierceable
Seven-hided buckler, and by the well-stitched thong
Grasp firm and wield it mightily.—The rest
Shall lie where I am buried.—Take him now,
Quickly, and close the door. No tears ! What ! weep
Before the tent ? How women crave for pity !
Make fast, I say. No wise physician dreams
With droning charms to salve a desperate sore.
  Ch. There sounds a vehement ardour in thy words
That likes me not. I fear thy sharpened tongue.
  Tec. Aias, my lord, what act is in thy mind ?
  Ai. Inquire not, question not ; be wise, thou'rt best.
  Tec. How my heart sinks ! Oh, by thy child, by
            Heaven,
I pray thee on my knees, forsake us not !
  Ai. Thou troublest me. What ! know'st thou not
            that Heaven
Hath ceased to be my debtor from to-day ?
  Tec. Hush ! Speak not so.
  Ai.   Speak thou to those that hear.
  Tec. Will you not hear me ?
  Ai.   Canst thou not be still ?
  Tec. My fears, my fears !
  Ai. (to the Attendants). Come, shut me in, I say.
  Tec. Oh, yet be softened !
  Ai.   'Tis a foolish hope,
If thou deem'st now to mould me to thy will.
                [Aias is withdrawn. Exit Tecmessa

CHORUS.

Island of glory ! whom the glowing eyes   I 1
Of all the wondering world immortalize,

Thou, Salamis, art planted evermore,
Happy amid the wandering billows' roar;
While I—ah, woe the while!—this weary time,
  By the green wold where flocks from Ida stray,
Lie worn with fruitless hours of wasted prime,
  Hoping—ah, cheerless hope!—to win my way
Where Hades' horrid gloom shall hide me from the day.

Aias is with me, yea, but crouching low,   I 2
Where Heaven-sent madness haunts his overthrow,
Beyond my cure or tendance: woful plight!
Whom thou, erewhile, to head the impetuous fight,
Sent'st forth, thy conquering champion. Now he feeds
  His spirit on lone paths, and on us brings
Deep sorrow; and all his former peerless deeds
Of prowess fall like unremembered things
From Atreus' loveless brood, this caitiff brace of kings.

Ah! when his mother, full of days and bowed II 1
With hoary eld, shall hear his ruined mind,
     How will she mourn aloud!
    Not like the warbler of the dale,
     The bird of piteous wail,
But in shrill strains far borne upon the wind,
While on the withered breast and thin white hair
Falls the resounding blow, the rending of despair.

Best hid in death were he whom madness drives II 2
Remediless; if, through his father's race
    Born to the noblest place
Among the war-worn Greeks, he lives
     By his own light no more,
Self-aliened from the self he knew before.
Oh, hapless sire, what woe thine ear shall wound!
One that of all thy line no life save this hath found.

Enter AIAS *with a bright sword, and* TECMESSA, *severally.*

  AI. What change will never-terminable Time
Not heave to light, what hide not from the day?
What chance shall win men's marvel? Mightiest
  oaths

Fall frustrate, and the steely-tempered will.
Ay, and even mine, that stood so diamond-keen
Like iron lately dipped, droops now dis-edged
And weakened by this woman, whom to leave
A widow with her orphan to my foes,
Dulls me with pity. I will go to the baths
And meadows near the cliff, and purging there
My dark pollution, I will screen my soul
From reach of Pallas' grievous wrath. I will find
Some place untrodden, and digging of the soil
Where none shall see, will bury this my sword,
Weapon of hate! for Death and Night to hold
Evermore underground. For, since my hand
Had this from Hector mine arch-enemy,
No kindness have I known from Argive men.
So true that saying of the bygone world,
'A foe's gift is no gift, and brings no good.'
    Well, we will learn of Time. Henceforth I'll bow
To heavenly ordinance and give homage due
To Atreus' sons. Who rules, must be obeyed.
Since nought so fierce and terrible but yields
Place to Authority. Wild Winter's snows
Make way for bounteous Summer's flowery tread,
And Night's sad orb retires for lightsome Day
With his white steeds to illumine the glad sky.
The furious storm-blast leaves the groaning sea
Gently to rest. Yea, the all-subduer Sleep
Frees whom he binds, nor holds enchained for aye.
And shall not men be taught the temperate will?
Yea, for I now know surely that my foe
Must be so hated, as being like enough
To prove a friend hereafter, and my friend
So far shall have mine aid, as one whose love
Will not continue ever. Men have found
But treacherous harbour in companionship.
    Our ending, then, is peaceful. Thou, my girl,
Go in and pray the Gods my heart's desire
Be all fulfilled. My comrades, join her here,
Honouring my wishes; and if Teucer come,
Bid him toward us be mindful, kind toward you.

I must go—whither I must go. Do ye
But keep my word, and ye may learn, though now
Be my dark hour, that all with me is well.

[Exit towards the country. TECMESSA *retires*

CHORUS.

A shudder of love thrills through me. Joy! I soar. 1
      O Pan, wild Pan!   *[They dance*
      Come from Cyllenè hoar—
Come from the snowdrift, the rock-ridge, the glen!
      Leaving the mountain bare
      Fleet through the salt sea-air,
Mover of dances to Gods and to men.
Whirl me in Cnossian ways—thrid me the Nysian
    maze!
Come, while the joy of the dance is my care!
      Thou too, Apollo, come
      Bright from thy Delian home,
        Bringer of day,
      Fly o'er the southward main
      Here in our hearts to reign,
Loved to repose there and kindly to stay.

Horror is past. Our eyes have rest from pain.   2
      O Lord of Heaven!   *[They dance*
      Now blithesome day again
Purely may smile on our swift-sailing fleet,
      Since, all his woe forgot,
      Aias now faileth not
Aught that of prayer and Heaven-worship is meet.
Time bringeth mighty aid—nought but in time doth
    fade:
Nothing shall move me as strange to my thought.
      Aias our lord hath now
      Cleared his wrath-burdened brow
        Long our despair,
      Ceased from his angry feud
      And with mild heart renewed
Peace and goodwill to the high-sceptred pair.

Enter Messenger.

MESSENGER. Friends, my first news is Teucer's
                presence here,
Fresh from the Mysian heights; who, as he came
Right toward the generals' quarter, was assailed
With outcry from the Argives in a throng:
For when they knew his motion from afar
They swarmed around him, and with shouts of blame
From each side one and all assaulted him
As brother to the man who had gone mad
And plotted 'gainst the host,—threatening aloud,
Spite of his strength, he should be stoned, and die.
—So far strife ran, that swords unscabbarded
Crossed blades, till as it mounted to the height
Age interposed with counsel, and it fell.
  But where is Aias to receive my word?
Tidings are best told to the rightful ear.

  CH. Not in the hut, but just gone forth, preparing
New plans to suit his newly altered mind.

  MESS. Alas!
Too tardy then was he who sped me hither;
Or I have proved too slow a messenger.

  CH. What point is lacking for thine errand's speed?

  MESS. Teucer was resolute the man should bide
Close held within-doors till himself should come.

  CH. Why, sure his going took the happiest turn
And wisest, to propitiate Heaven's high wrath.

  MESS. The height of folly lives in such discourse,
If Calchas have the wisdom of a seer.

  CH. What knowest thou of our state? What saith
                he? Tell.

  MESS. I can tell only what I heard and saw.
Whilst all the chieftains and the Atridae twain
Were seated in a ring, Calchas alone
Rose up and left them, and in Teucer's palm
Laid his right hand full friendly; then out-spake
With strict injunction by all means i' the world
To keep beneath yon covert this one day
Your hero, and not suffer him to rove,

If he would see him any more alive.
For through this present light—and ne'er again—
Holy Athena, so he said, will drive him
Before her anger. Such calamitous woe
Strikes down the unprofitable growth that mounts
Beyond his measure and provokes the sky.
'Thus ever,' said the prophet, 'must he fall
Who in man's mould hath thoughts beyond a man.
And Aias, ere he left his father's door,
Made foolish answer to his prudent sire.

'My son,' said Telamon, 'choose victory
Always, but victory with an aid from Heaven.'
How loftily, how madly, he replied !
'Father, with heavenly help men nothing worth
May win success. But I am confident
Without the Gods to pluck this glory down.'
So huge the boast he vaunted ! And again
When holy Pallas urged him with her voice
To hurl his deadly spear against the foe,
He turned on her with speech of awful sound :
'Goddess, by other Greeks take thou thy stand ;
Where I keep rank, the battle ne'er shall break.'
Such words of pride beyond the mortal scope
Have won him Pallas' wrath, unlovely meed.
But yet, perchance, so be it he live to-day,
We, with Heaven's succour, may restore his peace.'—
Thus far the prophet, when immediately
Teucer dispatched me, ere the assembly rose,
Bearing to thee this missive to be kept
With all thy care. But if my speed be lost,
And Calchas' word have power, the man is dead.

CH. O trouble-tost Tecmessa, born to woe,
Come forth and see what messenger is here !
This news bites near the bone, a death to joy.

Enter TECMESSA.

TEC. Wherefore again, when sorrow's cruel storm
Was just abating, break ye my repose ?
CH. (*pointing to the* Messenger). Hear what he saith,
                              and how he comes to bring

News of our Aias that hath torn my heart.

TEC. Oh me! what is it, man? Am I undone?

MESS. Thy case I know not; but of Aias this,
That if he roam abroad, 'tis dangerous.

TEC. He is, indeed, abroad. Oh! tell me quickly!

MESS. 'Tis Teucer's strong command to keep him close
Beneath this roof, nor let him range alone.

TEC. But where is Teucer? and what means his word?

MESS. Even now at hand, and eager to make known
That Aias, if he thus go forth, must fall.

TEC. Alas! my misery! Whence learned he this?

MESS. From Thestor's prophet-offspring, who to-day
Holds forth to Aias choice of life or death.

TEC. Woe's me! O friends, this desolating blow
Is falling! Oh, stand forward to prevent!
And some bring Teucer with more haste, while some
Explore the western bays and others search
Eastward to find your hero's fatal path!
For well I see I am cheated and cast forth
From the old favour. Child, what shall I do?

                                    [Looking at EURYSAKES
We must not stay. I too will fare along,
So far as I have power. Come, let us go.
Bestir ye! 'Tis no moment to sit still.
If we would save him who now speeds to die.

CH. I am ready. Come! Fidelity of foot,
And swift performance, shall approve me true.

                                    [Exeunt omnes

The scene changes to a lonely wooded spot.

AIAS (discovered alone).

The sacrificer stands prepared,—and when
More keen? Let me take time for thinking, too!
This gift of Hector, whom of stranger men
I hated most with heart and eyes, is set
In hostile Trojan soil, with grinding hone
Fresh-pointed, and here planted by my care

C. S.   F

Thus firm, to give me swift and friendly death.
Fine instrument, so much for thee! Then, first,
Thou, for 'tis meet, great Father, lend thine aid.
For no great gift I sue thee. Let some voice
Bear Teucer the ill news, that none but he
May lift my body, newly fallen in death
About my bleeding sword, ere I be spied
By some of those who hate me, and be flung
To dogs and vultures for an outcast prey.
So far I entreat thee, Lord of Heaven. And thou,
Hermes, conductor of the shadowy dead,
Speed me to rest, and when with this sharp steel
I have cleft a sudden passage to my heart,
At one swift bound waft me to painless slumber!
But most be ye my helpers, awful Powers,
Who know no blandishments, but still perceive
All wicked deeds i' the world—strong, swift, and sure,
Avenging Furies, understand my wrong,
See how my life is ruined, and by whom.
Come, ravin on Achaean flesh—spare none;
Rage through the camp!—Last, thou that driv'st thy
                                                        course
Up yon steep Heaven, thou Sun, when thou behold'st
My fatherland, checking thy golden rein,
Report my fall, and this my fatal end,
To my old sire, and the poor soul who tends him.
Ah, hapless one! when she shall hear this word,
How she will make the city ring with woe!
   'Twere from the business idly to condole.
To work, then, and dispatch. O Death! O Death!
Now come, and welcome! Yet with thee, hereafter,
I shall find close communion where I go.
But unto thee, fresh beam of shining Day,
And thee, thou travelling Sun-god, I may speak
Now, and no more for ever. O fair light!
O sacred fields of Salamis my home!
Thou, firm-set natal hearth: Athens renowned,
And ye her people whom I love; O rivers,
Brooks, fountains here—yea, even the Trojan plain
I now invoke!—kind fosterers, farewell!

This one last word from Aias peals to you:
Henceforth my speech will be with souls unseen.

[*Falls on his sword*

CHORUS (*re-entering severally*).

CH. A.   Toil upon toil brings toil,
   And what save trouble have I ?
   Which path have I not tried ?
   And never a place arrests me with its tale.
   Hark ! lo, again a sound !
CH. B.   'Tis we, the comrades of your good ship's crew.
CH. A.   Well, sirs ?
CH. B.   We have trodden all the westward arm o' the
   bay.
CH. A.   Well, have ye found ?
CH. B.   Troubles enow, but nought to inform our sight.
CH. A.   Nor yet along the road that fronts the dawn
   Is any sign of Aias to be seen.

CH.   Who then will tell me, who ? What hard sea-
   liver,   1
 What toiling fisher in his sleepless quest,
What Mysian nymph, what oozy Thracian river,
 Hath seen our wanderer of the tameless breast?
   Where ? tell me where !
'Tis hard that I, far-toiling voyager,
   Crossed by some evil wind,
   Cannot the haven find,
 Nor catch his form that flies me, where? ah! where?
TEC. (*behind*). Oh, woe is me ! woe, woe !
CH. A.   Who cries there from the covert of the grove ?
TEC.   O boundless misery !
CH. B.   Steeped in this audible sorrow I behold
Tecmessa, poor fate-burdened bride of war.
TEC.   Friends, I am spoiled, lost, ruined, overthrown !
CH. A.   What ails thee now ?
TEC.   See where our Aias lies, but newly slain,
Fallen on his sword concealed within the ground.
 CH.   Woe for my hopes of home !
   Aias, my lord, thou hast slain

Thy ship-companion on the salt sea foam.
    Alas for us, and thee,
      Child of calamity!

Tec. So lies our fortune. Well may'st thou complain.
Ch. a. Whose hand employed he for the deed of
    blood?
Tec. His own, 'tis manifest. This planted steel,
Fixed by his hand, gives verdict from his breast.

Ch. Woe for my fault, my loss!
    Thou hast fallen in blood alone,
    And not a friend to cross
      Or guard thee. I, deaf, senseless as a stone,
Left all undone. Oh, where, then, lies the stern
Aias, of saddest name, whose purpose none might turn?

Tec. No eye shall see him. I will veil him round
With this all-covering mantle; since no heart
That loved him could endure to view him there,
With ghastly expiration spouting forth
From mouth and nostrils, and the deadly wound,
The gore of his self-slaughter. Ah, my lord!
What shall I do? What friend will carry thee?
Oh, where is Teucer! Timely were his hand,
Might he come now to smooth his brother's corse.
O thou most noble, here ignobly laid,
Even enemies methinks must mourn thy fate!

Ch. Ah! 'twas too clear thy firm-knit thoughts
      would fashion,   2
    Early or late, an end of boundless woe!
  Such heaving groans, such bursts of heart-
      bruised passion,
    Midnight and morn, bewrayed the fire below.
      'The Atridae might beware!'
A plenteous fount of pain was opened there,
    What time the strife was set,
    Wherein the noblest met,
  Grappling the golden prize that kindled thy despair!
Tec. Woe, woe is me!
Ch. Deep sorrow wrings thy soul, I know it well.

Tec. O woe, woe, woe!

Ch. Thou may'st prolong thy moan, and be believed,
Thou that hast lately lost so true a friend.

Tec. Thou may'st imagine; 'tis for me to know.

Ch. Ay, ay, 'tis true.

Tec. Alas, my child! what slavish tasks and hard
We are drifting to! What eyes control our will!

Ch.   Ay me! Through thy complaint
        I hear the wordless blow
    Of two high-throned, who rule without restraint
        Of Pity.   Heaven forfend
        What evil they intend!

Tec. The work of Heaven hath brought our life thus
        low.

Ch. 'Tis a sore burden to be laid on men.

Tec. Yet such the mischief Zeus' resistless maid,
Pallas, hath planned to make Odysseus glad.

Ch.   O'er that dark-featured soul
        What waves of pride shall roll,
        What floods of laughter flow,
    Rudely to greet this madness-prompted woe,
Alas! from him who all things dares endure,
And from that lordly pair, who hear, and seat them
        sure!

Tec. Ay, let them laugh and revel o'er his fall!
Perchance, albeit in life they missed him not,
Dead, they will cry for him in straits of war.
For dullards know not goodness in their hand,
Nor prize the jewel till 'tis cast away.
To me more bitter than to them 'twas sweet,
His death to him was gladsome, for he found
The lot he longed for, his self-chosen doom.
What cause have they to laugh? Heaven, not their crew,
Hath glory by his death.   Then let Odysseus
Insult with empty pride.   To him and his
Aias is nothing; but to me, to me,
He leaves distress and sorrow in his room!

Teucer (within). Alas, undone!

LEADER OF CH. Hush ! .that was Teucer's cry. Me-
        thought I heard
His voice salute this object of dire woe.

Enter TEUCER.

TEU. Aias, dear brother, comfort of mine eye,
Hast thou then done even as the rumour holds ?
    CH. Be sure of that, Teucer. He lives no more.
    TEU. Oh, then how heavy is the lot I bear !
    CH. Yes, thou hast cause—
    TEU.   O rash assault of woe !—
    CH. To mourn full loud.
    TEU.   Ay me ! and where, oh where
On Trojan earth, tell me, is this man's child ?
    CH. Beside the huts, untended.
    TEU. (*to* TEC).   Oh, with haste
Go bring him hither, lest some enemy's hand
Snatch him, as from the lion's widowed mate
The lion-whelp is taken. Spare not speed.
All soon combine in mockery o'er the dead.
                    [*Exit* TECMESSA
    CH. Even such commands he left thee ere he died.
As thou fulfillest by this timely care.
    TEU. O sorest spectacle mine eyes e'er saw !
Woe for my journey hither, of all ways
Most grievous to my heart, since I was ware,
Dear Aias, of thy doom, and sadly tracked
Thy footsteps. For there darted through the host,
As from some God, a swift report of thee
That thou wert lost in death. I, hapless, heard,
And mourned even then for that whose presence kills me.
Ay me ! But come,
Unveil. Let me behold my misery.
             [*The corpse of* AIAS *is uncovered*
O sight unbearable ! Cruelly brave !
Dying, what store of griefs thou sow'st for me !
Where, amongst whom of mortals, can I go,
That stood not near thee in thy troublous hour ?
Will Telamon, my sire and thine, receive me
With radiant countenance and favouring brow

Returning without thee ? Most like ! being one
Who smiles no more, yield Fortune what she may.
Will he hide aught or soften any word,
Rating the bastard of his spear-won thrall,
Whose cowardice and dastardly betrayed
Thy life, dear Aias,—or my murderous guile,
To rob thee of thy lordship and thy home ?
Such greeting waits me from the man of wrath,
Whose testy age even without cause would storm.
Last, I shall leave my land a castaway,
Thrust forth an exile, and proclaimed a slave ;
So should I fare at home. And here in Troy
My foes are many and my comforts few.
All these things are my portion through thy death.
Woe 's me, my heart ! how shall I bear to draw thee,
O thou ill-starr'd ! from this discoloured blade,
Thy self-shown slayer ? Didst thou then perceive
Dead Hector was at length to be thine end ?—
I pray you all, consider these two men.
Hector, whose gift from Aias was a girdle,
Tight-braced therewith to the car's rim, was dragged
And scarified till he breathed forth his life.
And Aias with this present from his foe
Finds through such means his death-fall and his
    doom.
Say then what cruel workman forged the gifts,
But Fury this sharp sword, Hell that bright band ?
In this, and all things human, I maintain,
Gods are the artificers. My thought is said.
And if there be who cares not for my thought,
Let him hold fast his faith and leave me mine.

   Ch. Spare longer speech, and think how to secure
Thy brother's burial, and what plea will serve ;
Since one comes here hath no good will to us
And like a villain haply comes in scorn.

    Teu. What man of all the host hath caught thine
    eye?

    Ch. The cause for whom we sailed, the Spartan
    King.

    Teu. Yes ; I discern him, now he moves more near.

Enter MENELAUS.

MENELAUS. Fellow, give o'er. Cease tending yon
        dead man!
Obey my voice, and leave him where he lies.
    TEU. Thy potent cause for spending so much breath?
    MEN. My will, and his whose word is sovereign here.
    TEU. May we not know the reasons of your will?
    MEN. Because he, whom we trusted to have brought
To lend us loyal help with heart and hand,
Proved in the trial a worse than Phrygian foe;
Who lay in wait for all the host by night,
And sallied forth in arms to shed our blood;
That, had not one in Heaven foiled this attempt,
Our lot had been to lie as he doth here
Dead and undone for ever, while he lived
And flourished. Heaven hath turned this turbulence
To fall instead upon the harmless flock.
Wherefore no strength of man shall once avail
To encase his body with a seemly tomb,
But outcast on the wide and watery sand,
He'll feed the birds that batten on the shore.
Nor let thy towering spirit therefore rise
In threatening wrath. Wilt thou or not, our hand
Shall rule him dead, howe'er he braved us living,
And that by force; for never would he yield,
Even while he lived, to words from me. And yet
It shows base metal when the subject-wight
Deigns not to hearken to the chief in power.
Since without settled awe, neither in states
Can laws have rightful sway, nor can a host
Be governed with due wisdom, if no fear
Or wholesome shame be there to shield its safety.
And though a man wax great in thews and bulk,
Let him be warned: a trifling harm may ruin him.
Whoever knows respect and honour both
Stands free from risk of dark vicissitude.
But whereso pride and licence have their fling,
Be sure that state will one day lose her course
And founder in the abysm. Let fear have place

Still where it ought, say I, nor let men think
To do their pleasure and not bide the pain.
That wheel comes surely round. Once Aias flamed
With insolent fierceness. Now I mount in pride,
And loudly bid thee bury him not, lest burying
Thy brother thou be burrowing thine own grave.

  Ch. Menelaüs, make not thy philosophy
A platform whence to insult the valiant dead.

  Teu. I nevermore will marvel, sirs, when one
Of humblest parentage is prone to sin,
Since those reputed men of noble strain
Stoop to such phrase of prating frowardness.
Come, tell it o'er again,—said you ye brought
My brother bound to aid you with his power ?
Sailed he not forth of his own sovereign will ?
Where is thy voucher of command o'er him ?
Where of thy right o'er those that followed him ?
Sparta, not we, shall buckle to thy sway.
'Twas written nowhere in the bond of rule
That thou shouldst check him rather than he thee.
Thou sailedst under orders, not in charge
Of all, much less of Aias. Then pursue
Thy limited direction, and chastise,
In haughty phrase, the men who fear thy nod.
But I will bury Aias, whether thou
Or the other general give consent or no.
'Tis not for me to tremble at your word.
Not to reclaim thy wife, like those poor souls
Thou fill'st with labour, issued this man forth,
But caring for his oath, and not for thee,
Or any other nobody. Then come
With heralds all arow, and bring the man
Called king of men with thee ! For thy sole noise
I budge not, wert thou twenty times thy name.

  Ch. The sufferer should not bear a bitter tongue.
Hard words, how just soe'er, will leave their sting.

  Men. Our bowman carries no small pride, I see.

  Teu. No mere mechanic's menial craft is mine.

  Men. How wouldst thou vaunt it hadst thou but a
      shield !

TEU. Unarmed I fear not thee in panoply.

MEN. Redoubted is the wrath lives on thy tongue.

TEU. Whose cause is just hath licence to be proud.

MEN. Just, that my murderer have a peaceful end ?

TEU. Thy murderer ? Strange, to have been slain and
    live !

MEN. Yea, through Heaven's mercy. By his will,
    I am dead.

TEU. If Heaven have saved thee, give the Gods their
    due.

MEN. Am I the man to spurn at Heaven's command ?

TEU. Thou dost, to come and frustrate burial.

MEN. Honour forbids to yield my foe a tomb.

TEU. And Aias was thy foeman ? Where and when ?

MEN. Hate lived between us ; that thou know'st
    full well.

TEU. For thy proved knavery, coining votes i' the
    court.

MEN. The judges voted. He ne'er lost through me.

TEU. Guilt-hiding guile wears often fairest front.

MEN. I know whom pain shall harass for that word.

TEU. Not without giving equal pain, 'tis clear.

MEN. No more, but this. No burial for this man !

TEU. Yea, this much more. He shall have instant
    burial.

MEN. I have seen ere now a man of doughty tongue
Urge sailors in foul weather to unmoor,
Who, caught in the sea-misery by-and-by,
Lay voiceless, muffled in his cloak, and suffered
Who would of the sailors over-trample him.
Even so methinks thy truculent mouth ere long
Shall quench its outcry, when this little cloud
Breaks forth on thee with the full tempest's might.

TEU. I too have seen a man whose windy pride
Poured forth loud insults o'er a neighbour's fall,
Till one whose cause and temper showed like mine
Spake to him in my hearing this plain word :
'Man, do the dead no wrong ; but, if thou dost,
Be sure thou shalt have sorrow.' Thus he warned
The infatuate one : ay, one whom I behold ;

For all may read my riddle—thou art he.

MEN. I will be gone.   'Twere shame to me, if known,
To chide when I have power to crush by force.

TEU. Off with you, then !   'Twere triple shame in me
To list the vain talk of a blustering fool.

[*Exit* MENELAUS

LEADER OF CHORUS.

High the quarrel rears his head !
    Haste thee, Teucer, trebly haste,
Grave-room for the valiant dead
    Furnish with what speed thou mayst,
Hollowed deep within the ground,
Where beneath his mouldering mound
Aias aye shall be renowned.

Re-enter TECMESSA *with* EURYSAKES.

TEU. Lo ! where the hero's housemate and his child,
Hitting the moment's need, appear at hand,
To tend the burial of the ill-fated dead.
Come, child, take thou thy station close beside :
Kneel and embrace the author of thy life,
In solemn suppliant fashion holding forth
This lock of thine own hair, and hers, and mine
With threefold consecration, that if one
Of the army force thee from thy father's corse,
My curse may banish him from holy ground,
Far from his home, unburied, and cut off
From all his race, even as I cut this curl.
There, hold him, child, and guard him ; let no hand
Stir thee, but lean to the calm breast and cling.
(*To* CHORUS) And ye, be not like women in this scene,
Nor let your manhoods falter ; stand true men
To this defence, till I return prepared,
Though all cry No, to give him burial.   [*Exit*

CHORUS.

When shall the tale of wandering years be done ? I 1
When shall arise our exile's latest sun ?

Oh, where shall end the incessant woe
Of troublous spear-encounter with the foe,
   Through this vast Trojan plain,
Of Grecian arms the lamentable stain ?

Would he had gone to inhabit the wide sky,   I 2
Or that dark home of death where millions lie,
Who taught our Grecian world the way
To use vile swords and knit the dense array !
   His toil gave birth to toil
In endless line. He made mankind his spoil.

His tyrant will hath forced me to forgo   II 1
The garland, and the goblet's bounteous flow:
   Yea, and the flute's dear noise,
   And night's more tranquil joys;
   Ay me ! nor only these,
   The fruits of golden ease,
But Love, but Love—O crowning sorrow !—
Hath ceased for me. I may not borrow
   Sweet thoughts from him to smooth my dreary bed,
Where dank night-dews fall ever on my head,
Lest once I might forget the sadness of the morrow.

Even here in Troy, Aias was erst my rock,   II 2
From darkling fears and 'mid the battle-shock
   To screen me with huge might :
   Now he is lost in night
   And horror. Where again
   Shall gladness heal my pain ?
O were I where the waters hoary,
Round Sunium's pine-clad promontory,
   Plash underneath the flowery upland height.
   Then holiest Athens soon would come in sight,
And to Athena's self I might declare my story.

Enter TEUCER.

TEU. My steps were hastened, brethren, when I saw
Great Agamemnon hitherward afoot.
He means to talk perversely, I can tell.

Enter AGAMEMNON.

AG. And so I hear thou'lt stretch thy mouth agape
With big bold words against us undismayed—
Thou, the she-captive's offspring ! High would scale
Thy voice, and pert would be thy strutting gait,
Were but thy mother noble ; since, being naught,
So stiff thou stand'st for him who is nothing now,
And swear'st we came not as commanders here
Of all the Achaean navy, nor of thee ;
But Aias sailed, thou say'st, with absolute right.
Must we endure detraction from a slave ?
What was the man thou noisest here so proudly ?
Have I not set my foot as firm and far ?
Or stood his valour unaccompanied
In all this host ? High cause have we to ruc
That prize-encounter for Pelides' arms,
Seeing Teucer's sentence stamps our knavery
For all to know it ; and nought will serve but ye,
Being vanquished, kick at the award that passed
By voice of the majority in the court,
And either pelt us with rude calumnies,
Or stab at us, ye laggards ! with base guile.
Howbeit, these ways will never help to build
The wholesome order of established law,
If men shall hustle victors from their right,
And mix the hindmost rabble with the van.
That craves repression. Not by bulky size,
Or shoulders' breadth, the perfect man is known ;
But wisdom gives chief power in all the world.
The ox hath a huge broadside, yet is held
Right in the furrow by a slender goad ;
Which remedy, I perceive, will pass ere long
To visit thee, unless thy wisdom grow ;
Who hast uttered forth such daring insolence
For the pale shadow of a vanished man.
Learn modestly to know thy place and birth,
And bring with thee some freeborn advocate
To plead thy cause before us in thy room.

I understand not in the barbarous tongue,
And all thy talk sounds nonsense to mine ear.

CH. Would ye might both have sense to curb your ire!
No better hope for either can I frame.

TEU. Fie! How doth gratitude when men are dead
Prove renegade and swiftly pass away!
This Agamemnon hath no slightest word
Of kind remembrance any more for thee,
Aias, who oftentimes for his behoof
Hast jeoparded thy life in labour of war.
Now all is clean forgotten and out of mind.
Thou who hast multiplied words void of sense,
Hast thou no faintest memory of the time
When who but Aias came and rescued you
Already locked within the toils,—all lost,
The rout began: when close abaft the ships
The torches flared, and o'er the bootless trench
Hector was bounding high to board our fleet?
Who stayed that onset? Was not Aias he?
Whom thou deny'st to have once set foot by thine.
Find ye no merit there? And once again
When he met Hector singly, man to man,
Not by your bidding, but the lottery's choice,
His lot, that skulked not low adown i' the heap,
A moist earth-clod, but sure to spring in air,
And first to clear the plumy helmet's brim.
Yes, Aias was the man, and I too there
Kept rank, the 'barbarous mother's servile son.'
I pity thee the blindness of that word.
Who was thy father's father? A barbarian,
Pelops, the Phrygian, if you trace him far!
And what was Atreus, thine own father? One
Who served his brother with the abominable
Dire feast of his own flesh. And thou thyself
Cam'st from a Cretan mother, whom her sire
Caught with a man who had no right in her
And gave dumb fishes the polluted prey.
Such was thy race. What is the race thou spurnest?
My father, Telamon, of all the host
Being foremost proved in valour, took as prize

My mother for his mate : a princess she,
Born of Laomedon ; Alcmena's son
Gave her to grace him—a triumphant meed.
Thus royally descended and thus brave,
Shall I renounce the brother of my blood,
Or suffer thee to thrust him in his woes
Far from all burial, shameless that thou art ?
Be sure that, if ye cast him forth, ye'll cast
Three bodies more beside him in one spot ;
For nobler should I find it here to die
In open quarrel for my kinsman's weal,
Than for thy wife—or Menelaüs', was 't ?
Consider then, not my case, but your own.
For if you harm me you will wish some day
To have been a coward rather than dare me.

CH. Hail, Lord Odysseus ! thou art come in time
Not to begin, but help to end, a fray.

Enter ODYSSEUS.

OD. What quarrel, sirs ? I well perceived from far
The kings high-voicing o'er the valiant dead.

AG. Yea, Lord Odysseus, for our ears are full
Of this man's violent heart-offending talk.

OD. What words have passed ? I cannot blame the
        man
Who meets foul speech with bitterness of tongue.

AG. My speech was bitter, for his deeds were foul.

OD. What deed of his could harm thy sovereign head ?

AG. He boldly says this corse shall not be left
Unburied, but he'll bury it in our spite.

OD. May I then speak true counsel to my friend,
And pull with thee in policy as of yore ?

AG. Speak. I were else a madman ; for no friend
Of all the Argeians do I count thy peer.

OD. Then hear me in Heaven's name ! Be not so hard
Thus without ruth tombless to cast him forth ;
Nor be so vanquished by a vehement will,
That to thy hate even Justice' self must bow.
I, too, had him for my worst enemy,
Since I gained mastery o'er Pelides' arms.

But though he used me so, I ne'er will grudge
For his proud scorn to yield him thus much honour,
That, save Achilles' self, I have not seen
So noble an Argive on the fields of Troy.
Then 'twere not just in thee to slight him now ;
Nor would thy treatment wound him, but confound
The laws of Heaven. No hatred should have scope
To offend the noble spirits of the dead.

AG. Wilt thou thus fight against me on his side ?

OD. Yea, though I hated him, while hate was comely.

AG. Why, thou shouldst trample him the more, being
       dead.

OD. Rejoice not, King, in feats that soil thy fame !

AG. 'Tis hard for power to observe each pious rule.

OD. Not hard to grace the good words of a friend.

AG. The 'noble spirit' should hearken to command.

OD. No more ! 'Tis conquest to be ruled by love.

AG. Remember what he was thou gracest so.

OD. A noisome enemy ; but his life was great.

AG. And wilt thou honour such a pestilent corse ?

OD. Hatred gives way to magnanimity.

AG. With addle-pated fools.

OD.   Full many are found
Friends for an hour, yet bitter in the end.

AG. And wouldst thou have us gentle to such friends ?

OD. I would not praise ungentleness in aught.

AG. We shall be known for weaklings through thy
       counsel.

OD. Not so, but righteous in all Grecian eyes.

AG. Thou bidst me then let bury this dead man ?

OD. I urge thee to the course myself shall follow.

AG. Ay, every man for his own line ! That holds.

OD. Why not for my own line ? What else were
       natural ?

AG. 'Twill be thy doing then, ne'er owned by me.

OD. Own it or not, the kindness is the same.

AG. Well, for thy sake I'd grant a greater boon ;
Then why not this ? However, rest assured
That in the grave or out of it, Aias still
Shall have my hatred. Do thou what thou wilt. [*Exit*

Сн. Whoso would sneer at thy philosophy,
While such thy ways, Odysseus, were a fool.

Od. And now let Teucer know that from this hour
I am more his friend than I was once his foe,
And fain would help him in this burial-rite
And service to his brother, nor would fail
In aught that mortals owe their noblest dead.

Teu. Odysseus, best of men, thine every word
Hath my heart's praise, and my worst thought of thee
Is foiled by thy staunch kindness to the man
Who was thy rancorous foe. Thou wast not keen
To insult in present of his corse, like these,
The insensate general and his brother-king,
Who came with proud intent to cast him forth
Foully debarred from lawful obsequy.
Wherefore may he who rules in yon wide heaven,
And the unforgetting Fury-spirit, and she,
Justice, who crowns the right, so ruin them
With cruellest destruction, even as they
Thought ruthlessly to rob him of his tomb!
For thee, revered Laërtes' lineal seed,
I fear to admit thy hand unto this rite,
Lest we offend the spirit that is gone.
But for the rest, I hail thy proffered aid;
And bring whom else thou wilt, I'll ne'er resent it.
This work shall be my single care; but thou,
Be sure I love thee for thy generous heart.

Od. I had gladly done it; but, since thou declinest,
I bow to thy decision, and depart.   [*Exit*

Teu. Speed we, for the hour grows late:
        Some to scoop his earthy cell,
    Others by the cauldron wait,
        Plenished from the purest well.
    Hoist it, comrades, here at hand,
    High upon the three-foot stand!
    Let the cleansing waters flow;
    Brightly flame the fire below!
    Others in a stalwart throng
    From his chamber bear along

All the arms he wont to wield
Save alone the mantling shield.
Thou with me thy strength employ,
Lifting this thy father, boy;
Hold his frame with tender heed—
Still the gashed veins darkly bleed.
Who professes here to love him?
Ply your busy cares above him.
Come and labour for the man,
Nobler none since time began,
Aias, while his life-blood ran.

LEADER OF CH. Oft we know not till we see.
Weak is human prophecy.
Judge not, till the hour have taught thee
What the destinies have brought thee.

KING OEDIPUS

THE PERSONS

OEDIPUS, *King of Thebes.*
Priest of Zeus.
CREON, *brother of Jocasta.*
CHORUS *of Theban Elders.*
TIRESIAS, *the Blind Prophet.*
JOCASTA, *the Queen, sister to Creon.*
A Corinthian Shepherd.
A Theban Shepherd.
Messenger.

The following also appear, but do not speak:
A Train of Suppliants.
The children ANTIGONE *and* ISMENE.

SCENE. Before the Royal Palace in the Cadmean
citadel of Thebes.

LAIUS, the descendant of Cadmus, and king of Thebes (or Thebè), had been told by an oracle that if a son were born to him by his wife Jocasta the boy would be his father's death.

Under such auspices Oedipus was born, and to elude the prophecy was exposed by his parents on Mount Cithaeron. But he was saved by a compassionate shepherd, and became the adopted son of Polybus, king of Corinth. When he grew up he was troubled by a rumour that he was not his father's son. He went to consult the oracle of Apollo at Delphi, and was told—not of his origin but of his destiny —that he should be guilty of parricide and incest.

He was too horror-stricken to return to Corinth, and as he travelled the other way, he met Laius going from Thebes to Delphi. The travellers quarrelled and the son killed his father, but knew not whom he had slain. He went onward till he came near Thebes, where the Sphinx was making havoc of the noblest citizens, devouring all who failed to solve her riddle. But Oedipus succeeded and overcame her, and, as Laius did not return, was rewarded with the regal sceptre,—and with the hand of the queen.

He reigned nobly and prosperously, and lived happily with Jocasta, by whom he had four children.

But after some years a plague descended on the people, and Apollo, on being inquired of, answered that it was for Laius' death. The act of regicide must be avenged. Oedipus undertakes the task of discovering the murderer,— and in the same act discovers his own birth, and the fulfilment of both the former prophecies.

Jocasta hangs herself, and Oedipus in his despair puts out his eyes.

KING OEDIPUS

OEDIPUS—Priest of Zeus
(*with the* Train of Suppliants *grouped before an altar*).

OEDIPUS. Nurslings of Cadmus, children of my care,
Why press ye now to kneel before my gate
With sacred branches in those suppliant hands,
While o'er your city clouds of incense rise
And sounds of praise, mingling with sounds of woe?
I would not learn of your estate, my sons,
Through others; wherefore I myself am come,
Your Oedipus,—a name well known to men.
Speak, aged friend, whose look proclaims thee meet
To be their spokesman:—What desire, what fear
Hath brought you? Doubt not of my earnest will
To lend all succour. Hard would be the heart
That looked unmoved on such a kneeling throng.
 PRIEST. Great ruler of my country, thou beholdest
The different ages of our flock who here
Are gathered round thine altar;—some, whose wing
Hath not yet ventured far from home; and some
Burdened with many years, priests of the Gods,
Myself the arch-priest of Zeus; and these fresh youths,
A chosen few. Others there are who crowd
The holy agora and the temples twain
Of Pallas, and Ismenus' hallowed fires,
A suppliant host. For, as thyself perceivest,
Our city is tempest-tost, and all too weak
To lift above the waves her weary prow
That plunges in a rude and ravenous sea.
Earth's buds are nipped, withering the germs within;
Our cattle lose their increase, and our wives
Have fruitless travail; and that scourge from Heaven,
The fiery Pestilence abhorred of men,
Descending on our people with dire stroke

Lays waste the Home of Cadmus, while dark Death
Wins ample tribute of laments and groans.

  We kneel, then, at thy hearth; not likening thee
Unto the gods, I nor these children here,
But of men counting thee the first in might
Whether to cope with earthly casualty
Or visiting of more than earthly Power.
Thou, in thy coming to this Theban land,
Didst take away the hateful tax we paid
To that stern songstress,—aided not by us
With hint nor counsel, but, as all believe,
Gifted from heaven with life-restoring thought.
Now too, great Oedipus of matchless fame,
We all uplift our suppliant looks to thee,
To find some help for us, whether from man,
Or through the prompting of a voice Divine.
Experienced counsel, we have seen and know,
Hath ever prosperous issue. Thou, then, come,
Noblest of mortals, give our city rest
From sorrow! come, take heed! seeing this our land
Now calls thee Saviour for thy former zeal;
And 'twere not well to leave this memory
Of thy great reign among Cadmean men,
'He raised us up, only again to fall.'
Let the salvation thou hast wrought for us
Be flawless and assured! As once erewhile
Thy lucky star gave us prosperity,
Be the same man to-day. Wouldst thou be king
In power, as in command, 'tis greater far
To rule a people than a wilderness.
Since nought avails or city or buttressed wall
Or gallant vessel, if unmanned and void.

  OED. Ye touch me to the core. Full well I know
Your trouble and your desire. Think not, my sons,
I have no feeling of your misery!
Yet none of you hath heaviness like mine.
Your grief is held within the single breast
Of each man severally. My burdened heart
Mourns for myself, for Thebè, and for you.
Your coming hath not roused me from repose:

I have watched, and bitterly have wept; my mind
Hath travelled many a labyrinth of thought.
And now I have tried in act the only plan
Long meditation showed me. I have sent
The brother of my queen, Menoeceus' son,
Creon, to learn, in Phoebus' Delphian Hall,
What word or deed of mine may save this city.
And when I count the time, I am full of pain
To guess his speed; for he is absent long,
Beyond the limit of expectancy.
But when he shall appear, base then were I
In aught to disobey the voice of Heaven.

  PR. Lo, in good time, crowning thy gracious word,
'Tis told me by these youths, Creon draws near.

  OED. Apollo! may his coming be as blest
With saving fortune, as his looks are bright.

  PR. Sure he brings joyful news; else had he ne'er
Worn that full wreath of thickly-berried bay.

  OED. We have not long to doubt. He can hear now.

Enter CREON.

Son of Menoeceus, brother of my queen,
What answer from Apollo dost thou bring?

  CREON. Good; for my message is that even our woes,
When brought to their right issue, shall be well.

  OED. What saith the oracle? Thy words so far
Neither embolden nor dishearten me.

  CR. Say, must I tell it with these standing by,
Or go within? I am ready either way.

  OED. Speak forth to all. The burden of their grief
Weighs more on me than my particular fear.

  CR. My lips shall utter what the God hath said.
Sovereign Apollo clearly bids us drive
Forth from this region an accursed thing
(For such is fostered in the land and stains
Our sacred clime), nor cherish it past cure.

  OED. What is the fault, and how to be redressed?

  CR. By exile, or by purging blood with blood.
Since blood it is that shakes us with this storm.

  OED. Whose murder doth Apollo thus reveal?

CR. My gracious lord, before thy prosperous reign,
King Laius was the leader of our land.

OED. Though I ne'er saw him, I have heard, and
    know.

CR. Phoebus commands us now to punish home,
Whoe'er they are, the authors of his death.

OED. But they, where are they ? Where shall now be
    read
The fading record of this ancient guilt ?

CR. He saith, 'tis in this land. And what is sought
Is found, while things uncared for glide away.

OED. But where did Laius meet this violent end ?
At home, afield, or on some foreign soil ?

CR. He had left us, as he said, to visit Delphi ;
But nevermore returned since he set forth.

OED. And was there none, no fellow-traveller,
To see, and tell the tale, and help our search ?

CR. No, they were slain ; save one, who, flying in
    fear,
Had nought to tell us but one only thing.

OED. What was that thing ? A little door of hope,
Once opened, may discover much to view.

CR. A random troop of robbers, meeting him,
Outnumbered and o'erpowered him. So 'twas told.

OED. What robber would have ventured such a deed,
If unsolicited with bribes from hence ?

CR. We thought of that. But Laius being dead,
We found no helper in our miseries.

OED. When majesty was fallen, what misery
Could hinder you from searching out the truth ?

CR. A present trouble had engrossed our care.
The riddling Sphinx compelled us to observe
The moment's grief, neglecting things unknown.

OED. But I will track this evil to the spring
And clear it to the day. Most worthily
Doth great Apollo, worthily dost thou
Prompt this new care for the unthought-of dead.
And me too ye shall find a just ally,
Succouring the cause of Phoebus and the land.
Since, in dispelling this dark cloud, I serve

No indirect or distant claim on me,
But mine own life ; for he that slew the king
May one day turn his guilty hand 'gainst me
With equal rage. In righting Laius, then,
I forward mine own cause.—Now, children, rise
From the altar-steps, and lift your suppliant boughs,
And let some other summon to this place
All Cadmus' people, and assure them, I
Will answer every need. This day shall see us
Blest with glad fortune through God's help, or fallen.
    PR. Rise then, my children. Even for this we
        came
Which our good lord hath promised of himself.
Only may Phoebus, who hath sent this word,
With healing power descend, and stay the plague.
                                [*Exeunt severally*

CHORUS (*entering*).

Kind voice of Heaven, soft-breathing from the
        height   I 1
Of Pytho's opulent home to Thebè bright,
        What wilt thou bring to-day ?
        Ah, Delian Healer, say !
My heart hangs on thy word with trembling awe :
        What new-giv'n law,
Or what returning in Time's circling round
Wilt thou unfold ? Tell us, immortal sound,
Daughter of golden Hope, tell us, we pray, we pray !

First, child of Zeus, Pallas, to thee appealing,   I 2
Then to sweet Artemis, thy sister, kneeling,
        Who with benignant hand
        Still guards our sacred land,
Throned o'er the circling mart that hears her praise,
        And thou, whose rays
Pierce evil from afar, ho ! come and save,
Ye mighty three ! if e'er before ye drave
The threatening fire of woe from Thebè, come to-day !

    For ah ! the griefs that on me weigh   II 1
    Are numberless ; weak are my helpers all,

And thought finds not a sword to fray
This hated pestilence from hearth or hall.
    Earth's blossoms blasted fall:
    Nor can our women rise
    From childbed after pangs and cries;
    But flocking more and more
    Toward the western shore,
Soul after soul is known to wing her flight,
Swifter than quenchless flame, to the far realm of Night.

    So deaths innumerable abound.   II 2
My city's sons unpitied lie around
Over the plague-encumbered ground
And wives and matrons old on every hand
    Along the altar-strand
    Groaning in saddest grief
    Pour supplication for relief.
    Loud hymns are sounding clear
    With wailing voices near.
Then, golden daughter of the heavenly sire,
Send bright-eyed Succour forth to drive away this fire.

    And swiftly speed afar,   III 1
    Windborne on backward car,
The viewless fiend who scares me with wild cries,
    To oarless Thracian tide,
    Or ocean-chambers wide,
About the bed where Amphitritè lies.
Day blights what night hath spared. O thou whose
        hand
Wields lightning, blast him with thy thundrous brand.

    Shower from the golden string   III 2
    Thine arrows Lycian King!
O Phoebè, let thy fiery lances fly
    Resistless, as they rove
    Through Xanthus' mountain-grove!
O Theban Bacchus of the lustrous eye,
With torch and trooping Maenads and bright crown
Blaze on the god whom all in Heaven disown.
       [OEDIPUS *has entered during the Choral song*

OED. Your prayers are answered. Succour and
    relief
Are yours, if ye will heed my voice and yield
What help the plague requires. Hear it from me,
Who am hitherto a stranger to the tale.
As to the crime. Being nought concerned therewith,
I could not of myself divine the truth.
But now, as one adopted to your state,
To all of you Cadmeans I speak this:
Whoe'er among you knoweth the murderer
Of Laius, son of royal Labdacus,
Let him declare the deed in full to me.
First, if the man himself be touched with fear,
Let him depart, carrying the guilt away;
No harm shall follow him:—he shall go free.
Or if there be who knows another here,
Come from some other country, to have wrought
This murder, let him speak. Reward from me
And store of kind remembrance shall be his.
But if ye are silent, and one present here
Who might have uttered this, shall hold his peace,
As fearing for himself, or for his friend,
What then shall be performed, hear me proclaim.
I here prohibit all within this realm
Whereof I wield the sceptre and sole sway,
To admit the murderer, whosoe'er he be,
Within their houses, or to speak with him,
Or share with him in vow or sacrifice
Or lustral rite. All men shall thrust him forth,
Our dark pollution, so to me revealed
By this day's oracle from Pytho's cell.
    So firm is mine allegiance to the God
And your dead sovereign in this holy war.
Now on the man of blood, whether he lurk
In lonely guilt, or with a numerous band,
I here pronounce this curse:—Let his crushed life
Wither forlorn in hopeless misery.
Next, I pray Heaven, should he or they be housed
With mine own knowledge in my home, that I
May suffer all I imprecate on them.

Last, I enjoin each here to lend his aid
For my sake, and the God's, and for your land
Reft of her increase and renounced by Heaven.
It was not right, when your good king had fallen,
Although the oracle were silent still,
To leave this inquisition unperformed.
Long since ye should have purged the crime. But now
I, to whom fortune hath transferred his crown,
And given his queen in marriage,—yea, moreover,
His seed and mine had been one family,
Had not misfortune trampled on his head
Cutting him off from fair posterity,—
All this being so, I will maintain his cause
As if my father's, racking means and might
To apprehend the author of the death
Of Laius, son to Labdacus, and heir
To Polydorus and to Cadmus old,
And proud Agenor of the eldest time.

　　Once more, to all who disobey in this
May Heaven deny the produce of the ground
And offspring from their wives, and may they pine
With plagues more horrible than this to-day.
But for the rest of you Cadmean men,
Who now embrace my word, may Righteousness,
Strong to defend, and all the Gods for aye
Watch over you for blessing in your land.

　　LEADER OF CH. Under the shadow of thy curse, my lord,
I will speak. I slew him not, nor can I show
The man who slew. Phoebus, who gave the word,
Should name the guilty one.

　　OED.   Thy thought is just,
But man may not compel the Gods.

　　CH.   Again,
That failing, I perceive a second way.

　　OED. Were there a third, spare not to speak it forth.

　　CH. I know of one alone whose kingly mind
Sees all King Phoebus sees—Tirésias,—he
Infallibly could guide us in this quest.

　　OED. That doth not count among my deeds undone.

By Creon's counsel I have sent twice o'er
To fetch him, and I muse at his delay.
   Ch. The rumour that remains is old and dim.
   Oed. What rumour ? Let no tale be left untried.
   Ch. 'Twas said he perished by some wandering
       band.
   Oed. But the one witness is removed from ken.
   Ch. Well, if the man be capable of fear,
He'll not remain when he hath heard thy curse.
   Oed. Words have no terror for the soul that dares
Such doings.
   Ch.   Yet lives one who shall convict him.
For look where now they lead the holy seer,
Whom sacred Truth inspires alone of men.

Enter TIRESIAS.

   Oed. O thou whose universal thought commands
All knowledge and all mysteries, in Heaven
And on the earth beneath, thy mind perceives,
Tirésias, though thine outward eye be dark,
What plague is wasting Thebè, who in thee,
Great Sir, finds her one saviour, her sole guide.
Phoebus (albeit the messengers perchance
Have told thee this) upon our sending sent
This answer back, that no release might come
From this disaster, till we sought and found
And slew the murderers of king Laïus,
Or drave them exiles from our land. Thou, then,
Withhold not any word of augury
Or other divination which thou knowest,
But rescue Thebè, and thyself, and me,
And purge the stain that issues from the dead.
On thee we lean : and 'tis a noble thing
To use what power one hath in doing good.
   Tiresias. Ah ! terrible is knowledge to the man
Whom knowledge profits not. This well I knew,
But had forgotten. Else I ne'er had come.
   Oed. Why dost thou bring a mind so full of gloom ?
   Ti. Let me go home. Thy part and mine to-day
Will best be borne, if thou obey me in that.

OED. Disloyal and ungrateful! to deprive
The state that reared thee of thine utterance now.

TI. Thy speech, I see, is foiling thine intent;
And I would shield me from the like mishap. (*Going.*)

OED. Nay, if thou knowest, turn thee not away:
All here with suppliant hands importune thee.

TI. Yea, for ye all are blind. Never will I
Reveal my woe;—mine, that I say not, thine.

OED. So, then, thou hast the knowledge of the crime
And wilt not tell, but rather wouldst betray
This people, and destroy thy fatherland!

TI. You press me to no purpose. I'll not pain
Thee, nor myself. Thou wilt hear nought from me.

OED. How? Miscreant! Thy stubbornness would
          rouse
Wrath in a breast of stone. Wilt thou yet hold
That silent, hard, impenetrable mien?

TI. You censure me for my harsh mood. Your
          own
Dwells unsuspected with you. Me you blame!

OED. Who can be mild and gentle, when thou
          speakest
Such words to mock this people?

TI.   It will come:
Although I bury it in silence here.

OED. Must not the King be told of what will come?

TI. No word from me. At this, an if thou wilt,
Rage to the height of passionate vehemence.

OED. Ay, and my passion shall declare my thought.
'Tis clear to me as daylight, thou hast been
The arch-plotter of this deed; yea, thou hast done
All but the actual blow. Hadst thou thy sight,
I had proclaimed thee the sole murderer.

TI. Ay, say'st thou so?—I charge thee to abide
By thine own ordinance; and from this hour
Speak not to any Theban nor to me.
Thou art the vile polluter of the land.

OED. O void of shame! What wickedness is this?
What power will give thee refuge for such guilt?

TI. The might of truth is scatheless. I am free.

OED. Whence came the truth to thee ? Not from
    thine art.

TI. From thee, whose rage impelled my backward
    tongue.

OED. Speak it once more, that I may know the drift.

TI. Was it so dark ? Or wouldst thou tempt me
    further ?

OED. I cannot say 'twas clear. Speak it again.

TI. I say thou art the murderer whom thou seekest.

OED. Again that baleful word ! But thou shalt rue.

TI. Shall I add more, to aggravate thy wrath ?

OED. All is but idleness. Say what thou wilt.

TI. I tell thee thou art living unawares
In shameful commerce with thy near'st of blood,
Ignorant of the abyss wherein thou liest.

OED. Think you to triumph in offending still ?

TI. If Truth have power.

OED.   She hath, but not for thee,
Blind as thou art in eyes and ears and mind.

TI. O miserable reproach, which all who now
Behold thee, soon shall thunder forth on thee !

OED. Nursed in unbroken night, thou canst not harm
Or me, or any man who seëth the day.

TI. No, not from me proceeds thy fall ; the God,
Who cares for this, is able to perform it.

OED. Came this device from Creon or thyself ?

TI. Not Creon : thou art thy sole enemy.

OED. O wealth and sovereign power and high success
Attained through wisdom and admired of men,
What boundless jealousies environ you !
When for this rule, which to my hand the State
Committed unsolicited and free,
Creon, my first of friends, trusted and sure,
Would undermine and hurl me from my throne,
Meanly suborning such a mendicant
Botcher of lies, this crafty wizard rogue,
Blind in his art, and seeing but for gain.
Where are the proofs of thy prophetic power ?
How came it, when the minstrel-hound was here,
This folk had no deliverance through thy word ?

Her snare could not be loosed by common wit,
But needed divination and deep skill;
No sign whereof proceeded forth from thee
Procured through birds or given by God, till I,
The unknowing traveller, overmastered her,
The stranger Oedipus, not led by birds,
But ravelling out the secret by my thought:
Whom now you study to supplant, and trust
To stand as a supporter of the throne
Of lordly Creon,—To your bitter pain
Thou and the man who plotted this will hunt
Pollution forth.—But for thy reverend look
Thou hadst atoned thy trespass on the spot.

    CH. Your friends would humbly deprecate the wrath
That sounds both in your speech, my lord, and his.
That is not what we need, but to discern
How best to solve the heavenly oracle.

    TI. Though thou art king and lord, I claim no
        less
Lordly prerogative to answer thee.
Speech is my realm; Apollo rules my life,
Not thou. Nor need I Creon to protect me.
Now, then: my blindness moves thy scorn:—thou hast
Thy sight, and seest not where thou art sunk in evil,
What halls thou dost inhabit, or with whom:
Know'st not from whence thou art—nay, to thy kin,
Buried in death and here above the ground,
Unwittingly art a most grievous foe.
And when thy father's and thy mother's curse
With fearful tread shall drive thee from the land,
On both sides lashing thee,—thine eye so clear
Beholding darkness in that day,—oh, then,
What region will not shudder at thy cry?
What echo in all Cithaeron will be mute,
When thou perceiv'st, what bride-song in thy hall
Wafted thy gallant bark with flattering gale
To anchor,—where? And other store of ill
Thou seest not, that shall show thee as thou art,
Merged with thy children in one horror of birth.
Then rail at noble Creon, and contemn

My sacred utterance! No life on earth
More vilely shall be rooted out, than thine.

OED. Must I endure such words from him? Begone!
Off to thy ruin, and with speed! Away,
And take thy presence from our palace-hall!

TEI. Had you not sent for me, I ne'er had come.

OED. I knew not thou wouldst utter folly here,
Else never had I brought thee to my door.

TEI. To thee I am foolish, then; but to the pair
Who gave thee life, I was wise.

OED.   Hold, go not! who?
Who gave me being?

TEI.   To-day shall bring to light
Thy birth and thy destruction.

OED.   Wilt thou still
Speak all in riddles and dark sentences?

TEI. Methought thou wert the man to find them
out.

OED. Ay! Taunt me with the gift that makes me
great.

TEI. And yet this luck hath been thy overthrow.

OED. I care not, since I rescued this fair town.

TEI. Then I will go. Come, sirrah, guide me forth!

OED. Be it so! For standing here you vex our eye,
But, you being gone, our trouble goes with you.

TEI. I go, but I will speak. Why should I fear
Thy frown? Thou ne'er canst ruin me. The word
Wherefore I came, is this: The man you seek
With threatening proclamation of the guilt
Of Laius' blood, that man is here to-day,
An alien sojourner supposed from far,
But by-and-by he shall be certified
A true-born Theban: nor will such event
Bring him great joy; for, blind from having sight
And beggared from high fortune, with a staff
In stranger lands he shall feel forth his way;
Shown living with the children of his loins,
Their brother and their sire, and to the womb
That bare him, husband-son, and, to his father,
Parricide and corrival. Now go in,

C. S.   H

Ponder my words; and if thou find them false,
Then say my power is naught in prophecy.

> [*Exeunt severally*

CHORUS.

Whom hath the voice from Delphi's rocky throne I 1
    Loudly declared to have done
Horror unnameable with murdering hand?
    With speed of storm-swift car
    'Tis time he fled afar
With mighty footstep hurrying from the land.
    For, armed with lightning brand,
The son of Zeus assails him with fierce bounds,
Hunting with Death's inevitable hounds.

Late from divine Parnassus' snow-capped height I 2
    This utterance sprang to light,
To track by every path the man unknown.
    Through woodland caverns deep
    And o'er the rocky steep
Harbouring in caves he roams the wild alone,
    With none to share his moan,
Shunning that prophet-voice's central sound,
Which ever lives, and haunts him, hovering round.

The reverend Seer hath stirred me with strange awe. II 1
Gainsay I cannot, nor yet think him true.
I know not how to speak. My fluttering heart
In wild expectancy sees nothing clear.
Things past and future with the present doubt
Are shrouded in one mist. What quarrel lay
'Twixt Cadmus' issue and Corinthus' heir
Was never shown me, from old times till now,
By one on whose sure word I might rely
In running counter to the King's fair fame,
To wreak for Laius that mysterious death.

Zeus and Apollo scan the ways of men   II 2
With perfect vision. But of mortals here
That soothsayers are more inspired than I
What certain proof is given? A man through wit
May pass another's wisdom in the race.

But never, till I see the word fulfilled,
Will I confirm their clamour 'gainst the King.
In open day the female monster came:
Then perfect witness made his wisdom clear.
Thebè hath tried him and delights in him.
Wherefore my heart shall still believe him good.

Enter CREON.

CR. Citizens, hearing of dire calumny
Denounced on me by Oedipus the King,
I am here to make loud protest. If he think,
In this embroilment of events, one word
Or deed of mine hath wrought him injury,
I am not careful to prolong my life
Beneath such imputation. For it means
No trifling danger, but disastrous harm,
Making my life dishonoured in the state,
And meanly thought of by my friends and you.

CH. Perchance 'twas but the sudden flash of wrath,
Not the deliberate judgement of the soul.

CR. Who durst declare it, that Tirésias spake
False prophecies, set on to this by me ?

CH. Such things were said, I know not how advised.

CR. And were the eyes and spirit not distraught,
When the tongue uttered this to ruin me ?

CH. I cannot say. To what my betters do
I am blind. But see, the King comes forth again.

Enter OEDIPUS.

OED. Insolent, art thou here ? Hadst thou the face
To bring thy boldness near my palace-roof,
Proved as thou art to have contrived my death
And laid thy robber hands upon my state ?
Tell me, by heaven, had you seen in me
A coward or a fool, when you planned this ?—
Deemed you I should be blind to your attempt
Craftily creeping on, or, when perceived,
Not ward it off ? Is 't not a silly scheme,
To think to compass without troops of friends
Power, that is only won by wealth and men ?

CR. Wilt thou be counselled ? Hear as much in turn
As thou hast spoken, and then thyself be judge.

OED. I know thy tongue, but I am slow to learn
From thee, whom I have found my grievous foe.

CR. First on this very point, hear me declare—

OED. I will not hear that thou art not a villain.

CR. Thine is a shallow judgement, if thou thinkest
Self-will without true thought can bring thee gain.

OED. Thine is a shallow judgement, if thou thinkest
Thou canst abuse thy kinsman and be free.

CR. A rightful sentence. But I fain would learn
What wrong is that you speak of ?

OED.   Tell me this ;
Didst thou, or not, urge me to send and bring
The reverend-seeming prophet ?

CR.   Yea, and still
I hold that counsel firm.

OED.   How long is 't now
Since Laius—

CR.   What ? I do not catch your drift.

OED. Vanished in ruin by a dire defeat ?

CR. 'Twere long to count the years that come between.

OED. And did this prophet then profess his art ?

CR. Wise then as now, nor less in reverence.

OED. Then at that season did he mention me ?

CR. Not in my hearing.

OED.   But, I may presume,
Ye held an inquisition for the dead ?

CR. Yes, we inquired, of course : and could not hear.

OED. Why was he dumb, your prophet, in that day ?

CR. I cannot answer, for I do not know.

OED. This you can answer, for you know it well.

CR. Say what ? I will not gainsay, if I know.

OED. That, but for your advice, he had not dared
To talk of Laius' death as done by me.

CR. You know, that heard him, what he spake. But I
Would ask thee too a question in my turn.

OED. No questioning will fasten blood on me.

CR. Hast thou my sister for thine honoured queen ?

OED. The fact is patent, and denial vain.

CR. And shar'st with her dominion of this realm?
OED. All she desires is given her by my will.
CR. Then, am not I third-partner with you twain?
OED. There is your villany in breaking fealty.
CR. Not so, if thou wouldst reason with thyself
As I do. First consider one thing well:
Who would choose rule accompanied with fear
Before safe slumbers with an equal sway?
'Tis not my nature, no, nor any man's,
Who follows wholesome thoughts, to love the place
Of domination rather than the power.
Now, without fear, I have my will from thee;
But were I king, I should do much unwillingly.
How then can I desire to be a king,
When masterdom is mine without annoy?
Delusion hath not gone so far with me
As to crave more than honour joined with gain.
Now all men hail me happy, all embrace me;
All who have need of thee, call in my aid;
For thereupon their fortunes wholly turn.
How should I leave this substance for that show?
No man of sense can harbour thoughts of crime.
Such vain ambition hath no charm for me,
Nor could I bear to lend it countenance.
If you would try me, go and ask again
If I brought Phoebus' answer truly back.
Nay more, should I be found to have devised
Aught in collusion with the seer, destroy me,
Not by one vote, but two, mine own with thine.
But do not on a dim suspicion blame me
Of thy mere will. To darken a good name
Without clear cause is heinous wickedness;
And to cast off a worthy friend I call
No less a folly than to fling away
What most we love, the life within our breast.
The certainty of this will come with time;
For time alone can clear the righteous man.
An hour suffices to make known the villain.

   CH. Prudence bids hearken to such words, my lord,
For fear one fall. Swift is not sure in counsel.

OED. When he who hath designs on me is swift
In his advance, I must bethink me swiftly.
Should I wait leisurely, his work hath gained
Achievement, while my plans have missed success.

CR. What would you then ? To thrust me from the
                land ?

OED. Nay, death, not exile, is my wish for thee,
When all have seen what envy brings on men.

[CR. You'll ne'er relent nor listen to my plea.]

OED. You'll ne'er be governed or repent your guilt.

CR. Because I see thou art blind.

OED.   Not to my need.

CR. Mine must be thought of too.

OED.   You are a villain.

CR. How if thy thought be vain ?

OED.   Authority
Must be maintained.

CR.   Not when authority
Declines to evil.

OED.   O my citizens !

CR. I have a part in them no less than you.

LEADER OF CH. Cease, princes. Opportunely I be-
                hold
Jocasta coming toward you from the palace.
Her presence may attune your jarring minds.

Enter JOCASTA.

JOCASTA. Unhappy that ye are, why have ye reared
Your wordy rancour 'mid the city's harms ?
Have you no shame, to stir up private broils
In such a time as this ? Get thee within ! (*To* OED.)
And thou too, Creon ! nor enlarge your griefs
To make a mountain out of nothingness.

CR. Sister, thy husband Oedipus declares
One of two horrors he will wreak on me,
Banishment from my native land, or death.

OED. Yea, for I caught him practising, my queen,
Against our person with malignant guile.

CR. May comfort fail me, and a withering curse
Destroy me, if I e'er planned aught of this.

Jo. I pray thee, husband, listen to his plea;
Chiefly respecting his appeal to Heaven,
But also me, and these who stand by thee.

   Ch. 1. Incline to our request   I 1
Thy mind and heart, O King!
   Oed. What would you I should yield unto your
                      prayer?
   Ch. 2. Respect one ever wise,
Whose oath protects him now.
   Oed. Know ye what thing ye ask?
   Ch. 3. I know.
   Oed.   Then plainly tell.
   Ch. 4. Thy friend, who is rendered sacred by his oath,
Rob not of honour through obscure surmise.

   Oed. In asking that, you labour for my death
Or banishment. Of this be well assured.

   Ch. 5. No, by the Sun I swear,   II 1
Vaunt-courier of the host of heaven.
For may I die the last of deaths,
Unblest of God or friend,
If e'er such thought were mine.
But oh! this pining land
Afflicts my sorrow-burdened soul,
To think that to her past and present woe
She must add this, which springs to her from you.

   Oed. Then let him range, though I must die outright,
Or be thrust forth with violence from the land!
—Not for his voice, but thine, which wrings my heart:
He, wheresoe'er he live, shall have my hate.
   Cr. You show yourself as sullen when you yield,
As unendurable in your fury's height.
Such natures justly give themselves most pain.
   Oed. Let me alone, then, and begone!
   Cr.   I go,
Untainted in their sight, though thou art blind. [*Exit*

   Ch. 1. Lady, why tarriest thou   I 2
To lead thy husband in?

Jo. Not till I learn what mischief is befallen.
Ch. 2. A dim, unproved debate.
Reproach, though unfounded, stings.
Jo. From both ?
Ch. 3.   From both alike.
Jo. How caused ?
Ch. 4.   Enough for me,
Amply enough it seems, when our poor land
Is vexed already, not to wake what sleeps.

Oed. (*to* Leader of Ch.).   See where thine honest
          zeal hath landed thee,
Bating my wrath, and blunting my desire !

Ch. 5. My prince, I say it again :   II 2
Assure thee, I were lost to sense,
Infatuate, void of wholesome thought,
Could I be tempted now
To loose my faith from thee,
Who, when the land I love
Laboured beneath a wildering load,
Didst speed her forth anew with favouring gale.
Now, too, if but thou may'st, be her good guide.

Jo. Let not thy queen be left in ignorance
What cause thou hadst to lift thy wrath so high.
Oed. I'll tell thee, lady, for I honour thee
More than these citizens. 'Twas Creon there,
And his inveterate treason against me.
Jo. Accuse him, so you make the quarrel plain.
Oed. He saith I am the murderer of the King.
Jo. Speaks he from hearsay, or as one who knows ?
Oed. He keeps his own lips free : but hath suborned
A rascal soothsayer to this villany.
Jo. Hearken to me, and set your heart at rest
On that you speak of, while I make you learn
No mortal thing is touched by soothsaying.
Of that I'll give thee warrant brief and plain.
Word came to Laius once, I will not say
From Phoebus' self, but from his ministers,
The King should be destroyed by his own son,

If son were born to him from me. What followed?
Laius was slain, by robbers from abroad,
Saith Rumour, in a cross-way! But the child
Lived not three days, ere by my husband's hand
His feet were locked, and he was cast and left
By messengers on the waste mountain wold.
So Phoebus neither brought upon the boy
His father's murder, nor on Laïus
The thing he greatly feared, death by his son.
Such issue came of prophesying words.
Therefore regard them not. God can himself
With ease bring forth what for his ends he needs.

OED. What strange emotions overcloud my soul,
Stirred to her depths on hearing this thy tale!

JO. What sudden change is this? What cares op-
press thee?

OED. Methought I heard thee say, King Laïus
Was at a cross-road overpowered and slain?

JO. So ran the talk that yet is current here.

OED. Where was the scene of this unhappy blow?

JO. Phocis the land is named: the parted ways
Meet in one point from Daulia and from Delphi.

OED. And since the event how much of time hath
flown?

JO. 'Twas just ere you appeared with prospering
speed
And took the kingdom, that the tidings came.

OED. What are thy purposes against me, Zeus?

JO. Why broods thy mind upon such thoughts, my
king?

OED. Nay, ask me not! But tell me first what
height
Had Laius, and what grace of manly prime?

JO. Tall, with dark locks just sprinkled o'er with
grey:
In shape and bearing much resembling thee.

OED. O heavy fate! How all unknowingly
I laid that dreadful curse on my own head!

JO. How?
I tremble as I gaze on thee, my king!

OED. The fear appals me that the seer can see.
Tell one thing more, to make it doubly clear.

JO. I am loth to speak, but, when you ask, I will.

OED. Had he scant following, or, as princes use,
Full numbers of a well-appointed train ?

JO. There were but five in all: a herald one ;
And Laius travelled in the only car.

OED. Woe ! woe ! 'Tis clear as daylight. Who was he
That brought you this dire message, O my queen ?

JO. A home-slave, who alone returned alive.

OED. And is he now at hand within the house ?

JO. No, truly. When he came from yonder scene
And found thee king in room of Laius murdered,
He touched my hand, and made his instant prayer
That I would send him to o'erlook the flocks
And rural pastures, so to live as far
As might be from the very thought of Thebes.
I granted his desire. No servant ever
More richly merited such boon than he.

OED. Can he be brought again immediately ?

JO. Indeed he can. But why desire it so ?

OED. Words have by me been uttered, O my queen,
That give me too much cause to wish him here.

JO. Then come he shall. But I may surely claim
To hear what in thy state goes heavily.

OED. Thou shalt not lose thy rights in such an
        hour,
When I am harrowed thus with doubt and fear.
To whom more worthy should I tell my grief ?
—My father was Corinthian Polybus,
My mother, Dorian Meropè.—I lived
A prince among that people, till a chance
Encountered me, worth wonder, but, though strange,
Not worth the anxious thought it waked in me.
For at a feasting once over the wine
One deep in liquor called aloud to me,
' Hail, thou false foundling of a foster-sire ! '
That day with pain I held my passion down ;
But early on the morrow I came near
And questioned both my parents, who were fierce

In anger at the man who broached this word.
For their part I was satisfied, but still
It galled me, for the rumour would not die.
    Eluding then my parents I made way
To Delphi, where, as touching my desire,
Phoebus denied me ; but brake forth instead
With other oracles of misery
And horrible misfortune, how that I
Must know my mother's shame, and cause to appear
A birth intolerable in human view,
And do to death the author of my life.
I fled forth at the word, conjecturing now
Corinthia's region by the stars of heaven,
And wandered, where I never might behold
Those dreadful prophecies fulfilled on me.
So travelling on, I came even to the place
Where, as thou tell'st, the King of Thebè fell.
And, O my wife, I will hide nought from thee.
When I drew near the cross-road of your tale,
A herald, and a man upon a car,
Like your description, there encountered me.
And he who led the car, and he himself
The greybeard, sought to thrust me from the path.
Then in mine angry mood I sharply struck
The driver-man who turned me from the way ;
Which when the older saw, he watched for me
As I passed by, and from the chariot-seat
Smote full upon my head with the fork'd goad ;
But got more than he gave ; for, by a blow
From this right hand, smit with my staff, he fell
Instantly rolled out of the car supine.
I slew them every one. Now if that stranger
Had aught in common with king Laïus,
What wretch on earth was e'er so lost as I ?
Whom have the Heavens so followed with their
                hate ?
No house of Theban or of foreigner
Must any more receive me, none henceforth
Must speak to me, but drive me from the door !
I, I have laid this curse on mine own head !

Yea, and this arm that slew him now enfolds
His queen. O cruel stain! Am I not vile?
Polluted utterly! Yes, I must flee,
And, lost to Thebè, nevermore behold
My home, nor tread my country, lest I meet
In marriage mine own mother, and bring low
His head that gave me life and reared my youth,
My father, Polybus. Ah! right were he
Who should declare some god of cruel mood
Had sent this trouble upon my soul! Ye Powers,
Worshipped in holiness, ne'er may I see
That day, but perish from the sight of men,
Ere sins like these be branded on my name!

CH. Thy fear is ours, O king: yet lose not hope,
Till thou hast heard the witness of the deed.

OED. Ay, that is all I still have left of hope,
To bide the coming of the shepherd man.

JO. What eager thought attends his presence here?

OED. I'll tell thee. Should his speech accord with
        thine,
My life stands clear from this calamity.

JO. What word of mine agreed not with the scene?

OED. You said he spake of robbers in a band
As having slain him. Now if he shall still
Persist in the same number, I am free.
One man and many cannot be the same.
But should he tell of one lone traveller,
Then, unavoidably, this falls on me.

JO. So 'twas given out by him, be sure of that.
He cannot take it back. Not I alone
But all the people heard him speak it so.
And should he swerve in aught from his first tale,
He ne'er can show the murder of the king
Rightly accordant with the oracle.
For Phoebus said expressly he should fall
Through him whom I brought forth. But that poor
        babe
Ne'er slew his sire, but perished long before.
Wherefore henceforth I will pursue my way
Regardless of all words of prophecy.

OED. Wisely resolved. But still send one to bring
The labourer-swain, and be not slack in this.

Jo. I will, and promptly. Go we now within !
My whole desire is but to work thy will.   [*Exeunt*

CHORUS

O may my life be evermore   I 1
   Pure in each holy word and deed
   By those eternal laws decreed
That pace the sapphire-paven floor !
Children of Heaven, of Ether born,
No mortal knew their natal morn,
Nor may Oblivion's waters deep
E'er lull their wakeful spirit asleep,
Nor creeping Age o'erpower the mighty God
Who far within them holds his unprofaned abode.

Pride breeds the tyrant : monstrous birth !   I 2
   Insolent Pride, if idly nursed
   On timeless surfeit, plenty accursed,
Spurning the lowlier tract of Earth
Mounts to her pinnacle,—then falls,
Dashed headlong down sheer mountain walls
To dark Necessity's deep ground,
Where never foothold can be found.
Let wrestlers for my country's glory speed,
God, I thee pray ! Be God my helper in all need !

But if one be, whose bold disdain   II 2
Walks in a round of vapourings vain
And violent acts, regarding not
The Rule of Right, but with proud thought
Scorning the place where Gods have set their seat,
—Made captive by an Evil Doom,
Shorn of that inauspicious bloom,
Let him be shown the path of lawful gain
And taught in holier ways to guide his feet,
Nor with mad folly strain
His passionate arms to clasp things impious to retain.
Who in such courses shall defend his soul
From storms of thundrous wrath that o'er him roll ?

If honour to such lives be given,
What needs our choir to hymn the power of Heaven?

No more to Delphi, central shrine   II 2
Of Earth, I'll seek, for light divine,
Nor visit Abae's mystic fane
Nor travel o'er the well-trod plain
Where thousands throng to famed Olympia's town,
Unless, with manifest accord,
The event fulfil the oracular word.
Zeus, Lord of all! if to eternity
Thou would'st confirm thy kingdom's large renown,
Let not their vauntings high
Evade the sovereign look of the everlasting eye!
They make as though the ancient warning slept
By Laius erst with fear and trembling kept;
Apollo's glory groweth pale,
And holiest rites are prone to faint and fail.

Enter JOCASTA.

Jo. Princes of Thebes, it came into my thought
To stand before some holy altar-place
With frankincense and garlands. For the king,
Transported by the tempest of his fear,
Runs wild in grief, nor like a man of sense
Reasons of present things from what hath been.
Each tongue o'ermasters him that tells of woe.
Then since my counsels are of no avail,
To thee, for thou art nearest, Lykian God,
I bring my supplication with full hand.
O grant us absolution and relief!
For seeing him, our pilot, so distraught,
Like mariners, we are all amazed with dread.

Enter the CORINTHIAN SHEPHERD.

COR. SH. Are ye the men to tell me where to find
The mansion of the sovereign Oedipus?
Or better, where he may himself be found?

CH. Here is the roof you seek, and he, our lord,

Is there within : and, stranger, thou behold'st
The queenly mother of his royal race.

COR. SH. May she and hers be alway fortunate!
Still may she crown him with the joys of home!

JO. Be thou, too, blest, kind sir! Thy gracious tongue
Deserves no less. But tell me what request
Or what intelligence thou bring'st with thee?

COR. SH. Good tidings for thy house and husband,
                                    queen.

JO. What are they? Who hath sent thee to our hall?

COR SH. From Corinth come I, and will quickly tell
What sure will please you; though perchance 'twill
                                    grieve.

JO. What news can move us thus two ways at once?

COR. SH. 'Twas rumoured that the people of the land
Of Corinth would make Oedipus their king.

JO. Is ancient Polybus not still in power?

COR. SH. No. Death confines him in a kingly grave.

JO. Hold there! How say you? Polybus in his grave?

COR. SH. May I die for him if I speak not true!

JO. (*To an attendant*). Run thou, and tell this quickly
                to my lord!
Voices of prophecy, where are ye now?
Long time hath Oedipus, a homeless man,
Trembled with fear of slaying Polybus,
Who now lies slain by Fortune, not by him.

Enter OEDIPUS.

OED. Jocasta, my dear queen, why didst thou send
To bring me hither from our palace-hall?

JO. Hear that man's tale, and then consider well
The end of yonder dreadful prophecy.

OED. Who is the man, and what his errand here?

JO. He comes from Corinth, to make known to thee
That Polybus, thy father, is no more.

OED. How, stranger? Let me learn it from thy
                mouth.

COR. SH. If my first duty be to make this clear,
Know beyond doubt that he is dead and gone.

OED. By illness coming o'er him, or by guile?

COR. SH. Light pressure lays to rest the timeworn
            frame.
OED. He was subdued by sickness then, poor soul !
COR. SH. By sickness and the burden of his years.
OED. Ah ! my Jocasta, who again will heed
The Pythian hearth oracular, and birds
Screaming in air, blind guides ! that would have made
My father's death my deed ; but he is gone,
Hidden underneath the ground, while I stand here
Harmless and weaponless :—unless, perchance,
My absence killed him,—so he may have died
Through me. But be that as it may, the grave
That covers Polybus, hath silenced, too,
One voice of prophecy, worth nothing now.
    Jo. Did I not tell thee so, long since ?
    OED.   Thou didst.
But I was drawn to error by my fear.
    Jo. Now cast it altogether out of mind.
    OED. Must I not fear my mother's marriage-bed?
    Jo. Why should man fear, seeing his course is ruled
By fortune, and he nothing can foreknow ?
'Tis best to live at ease as best one may.
Then fear not thou thy mother's nuptial hour.
Many a man ere now in dreams hath lain
With her who bare him. He hath least annoy
Who with such omens troubleth not his mind.
    OED. That word would be well spoken, were not she
Alive that gave me birth. But since she lives,
Though you speak well, yet have I cause for fear.
    Jo. Your father's burial might enlighten you.
    OED. It doth. But I am darkened by a life.
    COR. SH. Whose being overshadows thee with fear ?
    OED. Queen Meropè, the consort of your king.
    COR. SH. What in her life should make your heart
            afraid ?
    OED. A heaven-sent oracle of dreadful sound.
    COR. SH. May it be told, or must no stranger know ?
    OED. Indeed it may. Word came from Phoebus once
That I must know my mother's shame, and shed
With these my hands my own true father's blood.

Wherefore long since my home hath been removed
Far from Corinthos :—not unhappily ;
But still 'tis sweet to see a parent's face.
  COR. SH. Did fear of this make thee so long an exile ?
  OED. Of this and parricide, my aged friend.
  COR. SH. I came with kind intent—and, dear my lord,
I fain would rid thee from this haunting dread.
  OED. Our gratitude should well reward thy love.
  COR. SH. Hope of reward from thee in thy return
Was one chief motive of my journey hither.
  OED. Return ? Not to my parents' dwelling-place !
  COR. SH. Son, 'tis too clear, you know not what you
      do.
  OED. Wherefore, kind sir ? For Heaven's sake teach
      me this.
  COR. SH. If for these reasons you avoid your home.
  OED. The fear torments me, Phoebus may prove true.
  COR. SH. Lest from your parents you receive a stain ?
  OED. That is the life-long torment of my soul.
  COR. SH. Will you be certified your fears are ground-
      less ?
  OED. How groundless, if I am my parents' child ?
  COR. SH. Because with Polybus thou hast no kin.
  OED. Why ? Was not he the author of my life ?
  COR. SH. As much as I am, and no more than I.
  OED. How can my father be no more to me
Than who is nothing ?
  COR. SH.　　　　　In begetting thee
Nor I nor he had any part at all.
  OED. Why then did he declare me for his son ?
  COR. SH. Because he took thee once a gift from me.
  OED. Was all that love unto a foundling shown ?
  COR. SH. Heirless affection so inclined his heart.
  OED. A gift from you ! Your purchase, or your
      child ?
  COR. SH. Found in Cithaeron's hollowy wilderness.
  OED. What led your travelling footstep to that
      ground ?
  COR. SH. The flocks I tended grazed the mountain
      there.

C. S.　　　　　　　　I

OED. A shepherd wast thou, and a wandering hind ?

COR. SH. Whatever else, my son, thy saviour then.

OED. From what didst thou release me or relieve ?

COR. SH. Thine instep bears memorial of the pain.

OED. Ah ! what old evil will thy words disclose ?

COR. SH. Thy feet were pierced. 'Twas I unfastened
          them.

OED. So cruel to my tender infancy !

COR. SH. From this thou hast received thy name.

OED.   By heaven
I pray thee, did my father do this thing,
Or was't my mother ?

      COR. SH.   That I dare not say.
He should know best who gave thee to my hand.

OED. Another gave me, then ? You did not find me ?

COR. SH. Another herdsman passed thee on to me.

OED. Can you describe him ? Tell us what you know.

COR. SH. Methinks they called him one of Laius'
          people.

OED. Of Laius once the sovereign of this land ?

COR. SH. E'en so. He was a shepherd of his flock.

OED. And is he still alive for me to see ?

COR. SH. You Thebans are most likely to know that.

OED. Speak, any one of you in presence here,
Can you make known the swain he tells us of,
In town or country having met with him ?
The hour for this discovery is full come.

CH. Methinks it is no other than the peasant
Whom thou didst seek before to see : but this
Could best be told by queen Jocasta there.

OED. We lately sought that one should come, my
          queen.
Know'st thou, is this of whom he speaks the same ?

Jo. What matter who ? Regard not, nor desire
Even vainly to remember aught he saith.

OED. When I have found such tokens of my birth,
I must disclose it.

Jo.   As you love your life,
By heaven I beg you, search no further here !
The sickness in my bosom is enough.

OED. Nay, never fear! Were I proved thrice a slave
And waif of bondwomen, you still are noble.

Jo. Yet hearken, I implore you: do not so.

OED. I cannot hear you. I must know this through.

Jo. With clear perception I advise the best.

OED. Thy 'best' is still my torment.

Jo. Wretched one,
Never may'st thou discover who thou art!

OED. Will some one go and bring the herdman hither?
Leave her to revel in her lordly line!

Jo. O horrible! O lost one! This alone
I speak to thee, and no word more for ever. [*Exit*

CH. Oedipus, wherefore is Jocasta gone,
Driven madly by wild grief? I needs must fear
Lest from this silence she make sorrow spring.

OED. Leave her to raise what storm she will. But I
Will persevere to know mine origin,
Though from an humble seed. Her woman's pride
Is shamed, it may be, by my lowliness.
But I, whilst I account myself the son
Of prospering Fortune, ne'er will be disgraced.
For she is my true mother: and the months,
Coheirs with me of the same father, Time,
Have marked my lowness and mine exaltation.
So born, so nurtured, I can fear no change,
That I need shrink to probe this to the root.

[OEDIPUS *remains, and gazes towards the country,*
while the CHORUS *sing.*

CHORUS.

If I wield a prophet's might,
Or have sense to search aright,
Cithaeron, when all night the moon rides high,
Loud thy praise shall be confessed,
How upon thy rugged breast,
Thou, mighty mother, nursed'st tenderly
Great Oedipus, and gav'st his being room
Within thy spacious home.

Yea, we will dance and sing
Thy glory for thy kindness to our king.
Phoebus, unto thee we cry,
Be this pleasing in thine eye!

Who, dear sovereign, gave thee birth,   2
Of the long-lived nymphs of earth?
Say, was she clasped by mountain-roving Pan?
Or beguiled she one sweet hour
With Apollo in her bower,
Who loves to trace the field untrod by man?
Or was the ruler of Cyllenè's height
The author of thy light?
Or did the Bacchic god,
Who makes the top of Helicon to nod,
Take thee for a foundling care
From his playmates that are there?

The THEBAN SHEPHERD *is seen approaching, guarded.*

OED. If haply I, who never saw his face,
Thebans, may guess, methinks I see the hind
Whose coming we have longed for. Both his age,
Agreeing with this other's wintry locks,
Accords with my conjecture, and the garb
Of his conductors is well-known to me
As that of mine own people. But methinks [*to* LEADER
        OF CHORUS]
Thou hast more perfect knowledge in this case,
Having beheld the herdman in the past.
CH. I know him well, believe me. Laïus
Had no more faithful shepherd than this man.
OED. Corinthian friend, I first appeal to you:
Was't he you spake of?
    COR. SH.   'Twas the man you see.
OED. Turn thine eyes hither, aged friend, and tell
What I shall ask thee. Wast thou Laius' slave?
    THEB. SH. I was, not bought, but bred within the
        house.
OED. What charge or occupation was thy care?
    THEB. SH. Most of my time was spent in shepherding.

OED. And where didst thou inhabit with thy flock ?

THEB. SH. 'Twas now Cithaeron, now the neighbouring tract.

OED. And hadst thou there acquaintance of this man?

THEB. SH. Following what service ? What is he you
mean ?

OED. The man you see.   Hast thou had dealings with
him ?

THEB. SH. I cannot bring him all at once to mind.

COR. SH. No marvel, good my lord.   But I will soon
Wake to clear knowledge his oblivious sense.
For sure I am he can recall the time,
When he with his two flocks, and I with one
Beside him, grazed Cithaeron's pasture wide
Good six months' space of three successive years,
From spring to rising of Arcturus ;   then
For the bleak winter-season, I drove mine
To their own folds, he his to Laius' stalls.
Do I talk idly, or is this the truth ?

THEB. SH. The time is far remote.   But all is true.

COR. SH. Well, dost remember having given me then
A child, that I might nurture him for mine ?

THEB. SH. What means thy question ?   Let me know
thy drift.

COR. SH. Friend, yonder stands the infant whom we
knew.

THEB. SH. Confusion seize thee, and thy evil tongue !

OED. Check not his speech, I pray thee, for thy words
Call more than his for chastisement, old sir.

THEB. SH. O my dread lord, wherein do I offend ?

OED. Thou wilt not answer him about the child.

THEB. SH. He knows not what he speaks.   His end
is vain.

OED. So! Thou'lt not tell to please us, but the lash
Will make thee tell.

THEB. SH.   By all that 's merciful,
Scourge not this aged frame !

OED.   Pinion him straight !

THEB. SH. Unhappy ! wherefore ?   what is 't you
would know ?

OED. Gave you this man the child of whom he asks
        you ?

THEB. SH. I gave it him. Would I had died that
        hour !

OED. Speak rightly, or your wish will soon come true.

THEB. SH. My ruin comes the sooner, if I speak.

OED. This man will balk us with his baffling prate.

THEB. SH. Not so. I said long since, ' I gave the
        child.'

OED. Whence ? Was 't your own, or from another's
        hand ?

THEB. SH. 'Twas not mine own ; another gave it me.

OED. What Theban gave it, from what home in
        Thebes ?

THEB. SH. O, I implore thee, master, ask no more !

OED. You perish, if I have to ask again.

THEB. SH. The child was of the stock of Laïus.

OED. Slave-born, or rightly of the royal line ?

THEB. SH. Ah me ! Now comes the horror to my
        tongue !

OED. And to mine ear. But thou shalt tell it me !

THEB. SH. He was given out for Laius' son : but she,
Thy queen, within the palace, best can tell.

OED. How ? Did she give it thee ?

THEB. SH.   My lord, she did.

OED. With what commission ?

THEB. SH.   I was to destroy him.

OED. And could a mother's heart be steeled to this ?

THEB. SH. With fear of evil prophecies.

OED.   What were they ?

THEB. SH. 'Twas said the child should be his father's
        death.

OED. What then possessed thee to give up the child
To this old man ?

THEB. SH.   Pity, my sovereign lord !
Supposing he would take him far away
Unto the land whence he was come. But he
Preserved him to great sorrow. For if thou
Art he this man hath said, be well assured
Thou bear'st a heavy doom.

OED.   O horrible !
Horrible ! All fulfilled, as sunlight clear !
Oh may I nevermore behold the day,
Since proved accursèd in my parentage,
In those I live with, and in him I slew !   [*Exeunt*

CHORUS.

    O mortal tribes of men,   I 1
      How near to nothingness
I count you while your lives remain !
What man that lives hath more of happiness
Than to seem blest, and, seeming, fade in night ?
O Oedipus, in this thine hour of gloom,
Musing on thee and thy relentless doom,
I call none happy who beholds the light.

    Thou through surpassing skill   I 2
      Didst rise to wealth and power,
When thou the monstrous riddling maid didst kill,
And stoodst forth to my country as a tower
To guard from myriad deaths this glorious town ;
Whence thou wert called my king, of faultless fame,
In all the world a far-resounded name,
Unparagoned in honour and renown.

But now to hear of thee, who more distressed ?   II 1
    Who more acquainted with fierce misery,
Assaulted by disasters manifest,
    Than thou in this thy day of agony ?
Most noble, most renowned !—Yet one same room
    Heard thy first cry, and in thy prime of power,
Received thee, harbouring both bride and groom,
    And bore it silently till this dread hour.
How could that furrowing of thy father's field
Year after year continue unrevealed ?

Time hath detected thine unwitting deed,   II 2
    Time, who discovers all with eyes of fire,
Accusing thee of living without heed
    In hideous wedlock husband, son, and sire.
Ah would that we, thou child of Laius born,
    Ah would that we had never seen thee nigh !

E'er since we knew thee who thou art, we mourn
    Exceedingly with cries that rend the sky.
For, to tell truth, thou didst restore our life
And gavest our soul sweet respite after strife.

Enter Messenger.

MESS. O ye who in this land have ever held
Chief honour, what an object of dire woe
Awaits your eyes, your ears ! What piercing grief
Your hearts must suffer, if as kinsmen should
Ye still regard the house of Laïus !
Not Phasis, nor the Danube's rolling flood,
Can ever wash away the stain and purge
This mansion of the horror that it hides.
—And more it soon shall give to light, not now
Unconsciously enacted. Of all ill,
Self-chosen sorrows are the worst to bear.

CH. What hast thou new to add ? the weight of grief
From that we know burdens the heart enough.

MESS. Soon spoken and soon heard is the chief sum.
Jocasta's royal head is sunk in death.

CH. The hapless queen ! What was the fatal cause ?

MESS. Her own determination. You are spared
The worst affliction, not being there to see.
Yet to the height of my poor memory's power
The wretched lady's passion you shall hear.
When she had passed in her hot mood within
The vestibule, straight to the bridal room
She rushes, tearing with both hands her hair.
Then having entered, shutting fast the door,
She called aloud on Laïus, long dead,
With anguished memory of that birth of old
Whereby the father fell, leaving his queen
To breed a dreadful brood for his own son.
And loudly o'er the bed she wailed, where she,
In twofold wedlock, hapless, had brought forth
Husband from husband, children from a child.
We could not know the moment of her death,
Which followed soon, for Oedipus with cries
Broke in, and would not let us see her end,

But held our eyes as he careered the hall,
Demanding arms, and where to find his wife,—
No, not his wife, but fatal mother-croft,
Cropped doubly with himself and his own seed.
And in his rage some god directed him
To find her :—'twas no man of us at hand.
Then with a fearful shout, as following
His leader, he assailed the folding-doors ;
And battering inward from the mortised bolts
The bending boards, he burst into the room :
Where high suspended we beheld the queen,
In twisted cordage resolutely swung.
He all at once on seeing her, wretched king !
Undid the pendent noose, and on the ground
Lay the ill-starred queen. Oh, then 'twas terrible
To see what followed—for he tore away
The tiring-pins wherewith she was arrayed,
And, lifting, smote his eyeballs to the root,
Saying, Nevermore should they behold the evil
His life inherited from that past time,
But all in dark henceforth should look upon
Features far better not beheld, and fail
To recognize the souls he had longed to know.
Thus crying aloud, not once but oftentimes
He drave the points into his eyes ; and soon
The bleeding pupils moistened all his beard,
Nor stinted the dark flood, but all at once
The ruddy hail poured down in plenteous shower.
Thus from two springs, from man and wife together,
Rose the joint evil that is now o'erflowing.
And the old happiness in that past day
Was truly happy, but the present hour
Hath pain, crime, ruin : —whatsoe'er of ill
Mankind have named, not one is absent here.

CH. And finds the sufferer now some pause of woe ?
MESS. He bids make wide the portal and display
To all the men of Thebes the man who slew
His father, who unto his mother did
What I dare not repeat, and fain would fling
His body from the land, nor calmly bide

The shock of his own curse on his own hall.
Meanwhile he needs some comfort and some guide,
For such a load of misery who can bear ?
Thyself shalt judge : for, lo, the palace-gates
Unfold, and presently thine eyes will see
A hateful sight, yet one thou needs must pity.

Enter OEDIPUS, *blind and unattended.*

LEADER OF CH. O horror of the world !
Too great for mortal eye !
More terrible than all I have known of ill !
What fury of wild thought
Came o'er thee ? Who in heaven
Hath leapt against thy hapless life
With boundings out of measure fierce and huge ?
Ah ! wretched one, I cannot look on thee :
No, though I long to search, to ask, to learn.
Thine aspect is too horrible.—I cannot !

OED. Me miserable ! Whither am I borne ?
Into what region are these wavering sounds
Wafted on aimless wings ? O ruthless Fate !
To what a height thy fury hath soared !
      CH.   Too far
For human sense to follow, or human thought
To endure the horror.

OED.   O dark cloud, descending   I 1
Unutterably on me ! invincible,
Abhorred, borne onward by too sure a wind.
Woe, woe !
Woe ! Yet again I voice it, with such pangs
Both from these piercing wounds I am assailed
And from within through memory of my grief.

CH. Nay, 'tis no marvel if thy matchless woe
Redouble thine affliction and thy moan !

OED. Ah ! Friend, thou art still constant ! Thou
            remainest   I 2
To tend me and to care for the blind man.
Alas !

I know thee well, nor fail I to perceive,
Dark though I be, thy kind familiar voice.

   CH. How dreadful is thy deed! How couldst thou
        bear
Thus to put out thine eyes? What Power impelled thee?

   OED. Apollo, dear my friends, Apollo brought to
        pass   II 1
In dreadful wise, this my calamitous woe.
But I,—no being else,—I with this hand destroyed them.
                          [Pointing to his eyes
For why should I have sight,
To whom nought now gave pleasure through the eye?

   CH. There speak'st thou truly.

   OED.   What could I see, whom hear
With gladness, whom delight in any more?
Lead me away out of the land with speed!
Be rid of the destroyer, the accursed,
Whom most of all the world the Gods abhor.

   CH. O miserable in thy calamity
And not less miserable in thy despair,
Would thou wert still in ignorance of thy birth!

   OED. My curse on him who from the cruel bond II 2
That held my feet in that high pasture-land
Freed me, and rescued me from murder there,
And saved my life! Vain kindness! Then to have died
Had spared this agony to me and mine.

   CH. Ay, would it had been so!

   OED. Then had I ne'er
Been proved a parricide, ne'er borne the shame
Of marriage-bonds incestuous! But now
I am God-abandoned, Son of the unholy,
Rival of him who gave me being. Ah woe!
What sorrow beyond sorrows hath chief place?
That sorrow Oedipus must bear!

   LEADER OF CH. I know not how to call thee wise in
        this:
Thou wert better dead than to be blind and live.

   OED. That this last act hath not been for the best
Instruct me not, nor counsel me again.

How, if I kept my sight, could I have looked
In Hades on my father's countenance,
Or mine all-hapless mother, when, toward both,
I have done deeds no death can e'er atone?
Ah! but my children were a sight of joy;—
Offspring of such a marriage! were they so?
Never, to eyes of mine! nor town, nor tower,
Nor holy shrines o' the gods, which I myself,
Dowered with the fairest life of Theban men,
Have forfeited, alas, by mine own law,
Declaring men should drive from every door
One marked by Heaven as impious and impure,
Nay worse, of Laius born! And was I then,
By mine own edict branded thus, to look
On Theban faces with unaltered eye?
Nay verily; but had there been a way
To stop the hearing-fountain through the ear,
I had not faltered, but had closed and barred
Each gate of this poor body; deaf and blind!
So thought might sweetly dwell at rest from ill.
Cithaeron! Why didst thou receive me? Why
Not slay me then and there? So had I not
Told to the world the horror of my birth.
O foster-home of Corinth and her king,
How bright the life ye cherished, filming o'er
What foulness far beneath! For I am vile,
And vile were both my parents. So 'tis proved.
O cross-road in the covert of the glen,
O thicket in the gorge where three ways met,
Bedewed by these my hands with mine own blood
From whence I sprang—have ye forgotten me?
Or doth some memory haunt you of the deeds
I did before you, and went on to do
Worse horrors here? O marriage twice accurst!
That gave me being, and then again sent forth
Fresh saplings springing from the selfsame seed,
To amaze men's eyes and minds with dire confusion
Of father, brother, son, bride, mother, wife,
Murder of parents, and all shames that are!
Silence alone befits such deeds. Then, pray you,

Hide me immediately away from men !
Kill me outright, or fling me far to sea,
Where never ye may look upon me more.
Come, lend your hand unto my misery !
Comply, and fear not, for my load of woe
Is incommunicable to all but me.

CH. With timely presence to fulfil thy need
With act and counsel, Creon comes, who now
Is regent o'er this people in thy room.

OED. Alas, what shall I say to him ? What plea
For my defence will hold ? My evil part
Toward him in all the past is clearly proved.

Enter CREON.

CR. I come not, Oedipus, to mock thy woes,
Nor to reproach thee for thine evils past.
But ye, (*to* Chorus) if all respect of mortal eye
Be dead, let awe of the universal flame
Of life's great nourisher, our lord the Sun,
Forbid your holding thus unveiled to view
This huge abomination, which nor Earth
Nor sacred Element, nor light of Heaven
Can once endure. Convey him in with speed.
Religion bids that kindred eyes and ears
Alone should witness kindred crime and woe.

OED. By Heaven, since thou hast reft away my
                          fear,
So nobly meeting my unworthiness,
I pray thee, hear me for thine own behoof.

CR. What boon dost thou desire so earnestly ?

OED. Fling me with speediest swiftness from the land,
Where nevermore I may converse with men.

CR. Doubt not I would have done it, but the God
Must be inquired of, ere we act herein.

OED. His sacred utterance was express and clear,
The parricide, the unholy, should be slain.

CR. Ay, so 'twas spoken : but, in such a time,
We needs must be advised more perfectly.

OED. Will ye then ask him for a wretch like me?

CR. Yea. For even thou methinks wilt now believe.

OED. Not only so. But I will charge thee too,
With urgent exhortation, to perform
The funeral-rite for her who lies within—
She is thy kinswoman—howe'er thou wilt.
But never let this city of my sires
Claim me for living habitant! There, there
Leave me to range the mountain, where my nurse,
Cithaeron, echoeth with my name,—Cithaeron,
Which both my parents destined for my tomb.
So my true murderers will be my death.
Yet one thing I can tell. Mine end will come
Not by disease nor ordinary chance.
I had not lived when at the point to die,
But for some terrible doom. Then let my fate
Run out its full career. But for my children
Thou, Creon, shalt provide. As for my sons,
I pray thee burden not thyself with them.
They ne'er will lack subsistence—they are men.
But my poor maidens, hapless and forlorn,
Who never had a meal apart from mine,
But ever shared my table, yea, for them
Take heedful care; and grant me, though but once,
Yea, I beseech thee, with these hands to feel,
Thou noble heart! the forms I love so well,
And weep with them our common misery.
Oh, if my arms were round them, I might seem
To have them as of old when I could see.—
What? Am I fooled once more, or do I hear
My dear ones weeping? And hath Creon sent,
Pitying my sorrows, mine own children to me
Whom most I love? Can this be truth I utter?

CR. Yea, I have done it. For I knew the joy
Thou ever hadst in this, thy comfort now.

OED. Fair be thy fortune, and, for this last deed,
Heaven guide thee on a better course than mine.
Where are ye, O my children? Come, draw near
To these my hands of brother blood with you,
Hands that have made so piteous to your sight
The darkened gaze of his once brilliant eyes,
Who all in blindness, with no thought of ill,

Became your father at that fount of life,
Where he himself took being! Oh! for you
I weep, not seeing you, when I but think
Of all the bitter passages of fate
That must attend you amongst men. For where
Can ye find fellowship, what civic throng
Shall ye resort unto, what festival,
From whence, instead of sight or sound enjoyed,
Ye will not come in tears unto your home?
And when ye reach the marriageable bloom,
My daughters, who will be the man to cast
His lot with yours, receiving for his own
All those reproaches which have marred the name
Of both my parents and your name no less?
What evil is not here? Your father slew
His father, and then eared the mother-field
Where he himself was sown, and got you from
The source of his own birth. Such taunts will fly.
And who will marry you? No man, my daughters;
But ye must wither childless and unwed.
Son of Menoeceus, who alone art left
As father to these maidens, for the pair
That gave them birth are utterly undone,
Suffer them not, being your kinswomen,
To wander desolate and poor, nor make
Their lot perforce the counterpart of mine.
But look on them with pity, left in youth
Forlorn of all protection save from thee.
Noble one, seal this promise with thy hand!
—For you, my children, were ye of an age
To ponder speech, I would have counselled you
Full carefully. Now I would have you pray
To dwell where 'tis convenient, that your life
May find more blessing than your father knew.

    Cr. Thou hast had enough of weeping. Close thee in
           thy chamber walls.
  Oed. I must yield, though sore against me.
  Cr.   Yea, for strong occasion calls.
  Oed. Know'st thou on what terms I yield it?
  Cr.   Tell me, let us hear and know.

OED. That ye send from the country.

CR.   God alone can let thee go.

OED. But the Gods long since abhor me.

CR.   Thou wilt sooner gain that boon.

OED. Then consent.

CR.   'Tis not my wont to venture promises
            too soon.

OED. Lead me now within the palace.

CR.   Come, but leave thy children.

OED.   Nay!
Tear not these from my embraces!

CR.   Hope not for perpetual sway:
Since the power thou once obtainedst ruling with un-
            questioned might
Ebbing from thy life hath vanished ere the falling of
            the night.

LEADER OF CHORUS.

Dwellers in our native Thebè, fix on Oedipus your eyes,
Who resolved the dark enigma, noblest champion and
            most wise.
Like a star his envied fortune mounted beaming far and
            wide :
Now he sinks in seas of anguish, whelmed beneath a
            raging tide.
Therefore, with the old-world sages, waiting for that
            final day,
I will call no mortal happy, while he holds his house of
            clay,
Till without one pang of sorrow, all his hours have
            passed away.

ELECTRA

THE PERSONS

An Old Man, *formerly one of the retainers of Agamemnon.*
ORESTES, *son of Agamemnon and Clytemnestra.*
ELECTRA, *sister of Orestes.*
CHORUS *of Argive Women.*
CHRYSOTHEMIS, *sister of Orestes and Electra.*
CLYTEMNESTRA.
AEGISTHUS.

PYLADES *appears with* ORESTES, *but does not speak.*

SCENE.   Mycenae : before the palace of the Pelopidae.

Agamemnon, on his return from Troy, had been murdered by his wife Clytemnestra and her paramour Aegisthus, who had usurped the Mycenean throne. Orestes, then a child, had been rescued by his sister Electra, and sent into Phocis with the one servant who remained faithful to his old master. The son of Agamemnon now returns, being of a full age, accompanied by this same attendant and his friend Pylades, with whom he has already concerted a plan for taking vengeance on his father's murderers, in obedience to the command of Apollo.

Orestes had been received in Phocis by Strophius, his father's friend. Another Phocian prince, named Phanoteus, was a friend of Aegisthus.

ELECTRA

ORESTES *and the* Old Man—PYLADES *is present.*

OLD MAN. Son of the king who led the Achaean host
Erewhile beleaguering Troy, 'tis thine to-day
To see around thee what through many a year
Thy forward spirit hath sighed for. Argolis
Lies here before us, hallowed as the scene
Of Io's wildering pain : yonder, the mart
Named from the wolf-slaying God, and there, to our
          left,
Hera's famed temple. For we reach the bourn
Of far-renowned Mycenae, rich in gold.
And Pelops' fatal roofs before us rise,
Haunted with many horrors, whence my hand,
Thy murdered sire then lying in his gore,
Received thee from thy sister, and removed
Where I have kept thee safe and nourished thee
To this bright manhood thou dost bear, to be
The avenger of thy father's bloody death.
Wherefore, Orestes, and thou, Pylades,
Dearest of friends, though from a foreign soil,
Prepare your enterprise with speed. Dark night
Is vanished with her stars, and day's bright orb
Hath waked the birds of morn into full song.
Now, then, ere foot of man go forth, ye two
Knit counsels. 'Tis no time for shy delay :
The very moment for your act is come.

OR. Kind faithful friend, how well thou mak'st appear
Thy constancy in service to our house !
As some good steed, aged, but nobly bred,
Slacks not his spirit in the day of war,
But points his ears to the fray, even so dost thou
Press on and urge thy master in the van.
Hear, then, our purpose, and if aught thy mind,

K 2

Keenly attent, discerns of weak or crude
In this I now set forth, admonish me.
  I, when I visited the Pythian shrine
Oracular, that I might learn whereby
To punish home the murderers of my sire,
Had word from Phoebus which you straight shall hear:
'No shielded host, but thine own craft, O King!
The righteous death-blow to thine arm shall bring.'
Then, since the will of Heaven is so revealed,
Go thou within, when Opportunity
Shall marshal thee the way, and gathering all
Their business, bring us certain cognizance.
Age and long absence are a safe disguise;
They never will suspect thee who thou art.
And let thy tale be that another land,
Phocis, hath sent thee forth, and Phanoteus,
Than whom they have no mightier help in war.
Then, prefaced with an oath, declare thy news,
Orestes' death by dire mischance, down-rolled
From wheel-borne chariot in the Pythian course.
So let the fable be devised; while we,
As Phoebus ordered, with luxuriant locks
Shorn from our brows, and fair libations, crown
My father's sepulchre, and thence return
Bearing aloft the shapely vase of bronze
That's hidden hard by in brushwood, as thou knowest,
And bring them welcome tidings, that my form
Is fallen ere now to ashes in the fire.
How should this pain me, in pretence being dead,
Really to save myself and win renown?
No saying bodes men ill, that brings them gain.
Oft have I known the wise, dying in word,
Return with glorious salutation home.
So lightened by this rumour shall mine eye
Blaze yet like bale-star on mine enemies.
O native earth! and Gods that hold the land,
Accept me here, and prosper this my way!
Thou, too, paternal hearth! To thee I come,
Justly to cleanse thee by behest from heaven.
Send me not bootless, Gods, but let me found

A wealthy line of fair posterity!
I have spoken. To thy charge! and with good heed
Perform it. We go forth. The Occasion calls,
Great taskmaster of enterprise to men.
   ELECTRA (*within*). Woe for my hapless lot!
   OLD M. Hark! from the doors, my son, methought
        there came
A moaning cry, as of some maid within.
   OR. Can it be poor Electra? Shall we stay,
And list again the lamentable sound?
   OLD M. Not so. Before all else begin the attempt
To execute Apollo's sovereign will,
Pouring libation to thy sire: this makes
Victory ours, and our success assured.   [*Exeunt*

Enter ELECTRA.

MONODY.

   EL. O purest light!
And air by earth alone
Measured and limitable, how oft have ye
Heard many a piercing moan,
Many a blow full on my bleeding breast,
When gloomy night
Hath slackened pace and yielded to the day!
And through the hours of rest,
Ah! well 'tis known
To my sad pillow in yon house of woe,
What vigil of scant joyance keeping,
Whiles all within are sleeping,
For my dear father without stint I groan,
Whom not in bloody fray
The War-god in the stranger-land
Received with hospitable hand,
But she that is my mother, and her groom,
As woodmen fell the oak,
Cleft through the skull with murdering stroke.
And o'er this gloom
No ray of pity, save from only me,
Goes forth on thee,

My father, who didst die
A cruel death of piteous agony.
But ne'er will I
Cease from my crying and sad mourning lay,
While I behold the sky,
Glancing with myriad fires, or this fair day.
But, like some brood-bereavèd nightingale,
With far-heard wail,
Here at my father's door my voice shall sound.
O home beneath the ground!
Hades unseen, and dread Persephonè,
And darkling Hermes, and the Curse revered,
And ye, Erinyës, of mortals feared,
Daughters of Heaven, that ever see
Who die unjustly, who are wronged i' the bed
Of those they wed,
Avenge our father's murder on his foe!
Aid us, and send my brother to my side;
Alone I cannot longer bide
The oppressive strain of strength-o'ermastering woe.

CHORUS (entering).

O sad Electra, child   I 1
Of a lost mother, why still flow
Unceasingly with lamentation wild
For him who through her treachery beguiled,
Inveigled by a wife's deceit,
Fallen at the foul adulterer's feet,
Most impiously was quelled long years ago?
Perish the cause! if I may lawfully pray so.

EL. O daughters of a noble line,
Ye come to soothe me from my troublous woe.
I see, I know:
Your love is not unrecognized of mine.
But yet I will not seem as I forgot,
Or cease to mourn my hapless father's lot.
Oh, of all love
That ever may you move,
This only boon I crave—
Leave me to rave!

CH. Lament, nor praying breath
Will raise thy sire, our honoured chief,
From that dim multitudinous gulf of death.
Beyond the mark, due grief that measureth,
Still pining with excess of pain
Thou urgest lamentation vain,
That from thy woes can bring thee no relief.
Why hast thou set thy heart on unavailing grief?

EL. Senseless were he who lost from thought
A noble father, lamentably slain!
　　　I love thy strain,
Bewildered mourner, bird divinely taught,
For 'Itys,' 'Itys,' ever heard to pine.
O Niobè, I hold thee all divine,
　　　　Of sorrows queen,
Who with all tearful mien
Insepulchred in stone
Aye makest moan.

CH. Not unto thee alone hath sorrow come,　II 1
Daughter, that thou shouldst carry grief so far
Beyond those dwellers in the palace-home
　　　Who of thy kindred are
And own one source with thee.
　　　What life hath she,
Chrysothemis, and Iphianassa bright,
　　　And he whose light
Is hidden afar from taste of horrid doom,
Youthful Orestes, who shall come
To fair Mycenae's glorious town,
Welcomed as worthy of his sire's renown,
Sped by great Zeus with kindly thought,
And to this land with happiest omen brought?

EL. Awaiting him I endlessly endure;
Unwed and childless still I go,
　　　With tears in constant flow,
Girt round with misery that finds no cure.
But he forgets his wrong and all my teaching.
What message have I sent beseeching,
But baffled flies back idly home?
Ever he longs, he saith, but, longing, will not come.

CH. Take heart, dear child! still mighty in the
sky   II 2
Is Zeus who ruleth all things and surveys.
Commit to him thy grief that surgeth high,
    And walk in safer ways,
Let not hate vex thee sore,
    Nor yet ignore
The cause of hate and sorrow in thy breast.
    Time bringeth rest:
All is made easy through his power divine.
The heir of Agamemnon's line
Who dwells by Crisa's pastoral strand
Shall yet return unto his native land;
And he shall yet regard his own
Who reigns beneath upon his Stygian throne.

EL. Meanwhile my life falls from me in despair
Years pass and patience nought avails:
    My heart within me fails:
Orphaned I pine without protecting care;
And like a sojourner all unregarded
At slave-like labour unrewarded
I toil within my father's hall
Thus meanly attired, and starved, a table-serving thrall.

CH. Sad was thy greeting when he reached the
strand,   III 1
Piteous thy crying where thy father lay
    On that fell day
When the bronze edge with dire effect was driven.
    By craft 'twas planned,
By frenzied lust the blow was given:
Mother and father of a monstrous birth,
Whether a God there wrought or mortal of the Earth.

EL. O day beyond all days that yet have rolled
Most hateful in thy course of light!
    O horror of that night!
O hideous feast, abhorr'd, not to be told!
How could I bear it, when my father's eye
Saw death advancing from the ruthless pair,
Conjoint in cruel villany,
By whom my life was plunged in black despair?

Oh, to the workers of such deeds as these
   May great Olympus' Lord
Return of evil still afford,
Nor let them wear the gloss of sovran ease!

 CH. Take thought to keep thy crying within
    bound.   III 2
Doth not thy sense enlighten thee to see
   How recklessly
Even now thou winnest undeservèd woe?
   Still art thou found
To make thy misery overflow
Through self-bred gloomy strife. But not for long
Shall one alone prevail who strives against the strong.

 EL. 'Twas dire oppression taught me my complaint
I know my rage a quenchless fire:
   But nought, however dire,
Shall visit this my frenzy with restraint,
Or check my lamentation while I live.
Dear friends, kind women of true Argive breed,
 Say, who can timely counsel give
Or word of comfort suited to my need?
   Beyond all cure shall this my cause be known.
   No counsels more! Ah leave,
Vain comforters, and let me grieve
With ceaseless pain, unmeasured in my moan.

 CH. With kind intent   IV
Full tenderly my words are meant;
Like a true mother pressing heart to heart,
I pray thee, do not aggravate thy smart.
 EL. But have my miseries a measure? Tell.
   Can it be well
To pour forgetfulness upon the dead?
   Hath mortal head
Conceived a wickedness so bold?
O never may such brightness shine for me,
   Nor let me peaceful be
With aught of good my life may still enfold,
If from wide echoing of my father's name
The wings of keen lament I must withhold.

Sure holy shame
And pious care would vanish among men,
If he, mere earth and nothingness, must lie
In darkness, and his foes shall not again
Render him blood for blood in amplest penalty.

LEADER OF CH. Less from our own desires, my child,
                we came,
Than for thy sake. But, if we speak amiss,
Take thine own course. We still will side with thee.

EL. Full well I feel that too impatiently
I seem to multiply the sounds of woe.
Yet suffer me, dear women! Mighty force
Compels me. Who that had a noble heart
And saw her father's cause, as I have done,
By day and night more outraged, could refrain?
Are my woes lessening? Are they not in bloom?—
My mother full of hate and hateful proved,
Whilst I in my own home must dwell with these,
My father's murderers, and by them be ruled,
Dependent on their bounty even for bread.
And then what days suppose you I must pass,
When I behold Aegisthus on the throne
That was my father's; when I see him wear
Such robes, and pour libations by the hearth
Where he destroyed him; lastly, when I see
Their crowning insolence,—our regicide
Laid in my father's chamber beside her,
My mother—if she still must bear the name
When resting in those arms? Her shame is dead.
She harbours with blood-guiltiness, and fears
No vengeance, but, as laughing at the wrong,
She watches for the hour wherein with guile
She killed our sire, and orders dance and mirth
That day o' the month, and joyful sacrifice
Of thanksgiving. But I within the house
Beholding, weep and pine, and mourn that feast
Of infamy, called by my father's name,
All to myself; for not even grief may flow
As largely as my spirit would desire.
That so-called princess of a noble race

O'ercrows my wailing with loud obloquy:
'Hilding! are you alone in grief? Are none
Mourning for loss of fathers but yourself?
'Fore the blest Gods! ill may you thrive, and ne'er
Find cure of sorrow from the powers below!'
So she insults: unless she hear one say
'Orestes will arrive': then standing close,
She shouts like one possessed into mine ear,
'These are your doings, this your work, I trow.
You stole Orestes from my gripe, and placed
His life with fosterers; but you shall pay
Full penalty.' So harsh is her exclaim.
And he at hand, the husband she extols,
Hounds on the cry, that prince of cowardice,
From head to foot one mass of pestilent harm.
Tongue-doughty champion of this women's-war.
I, for Orestes ever languishing
To end this, am undone. For evermore
Intending, still delaying, he wears out
All hope, both here and yonder. How, then, friends,
Can I be moderate, or feel the touch
Of holy resignation? Evil fruit
Cannot but follow on a life of ill.

CH. Say, is Aegisthus near while thus you speak?
Or hath he left the palace? We would know.

EL. Most surely. Never think, if he were by,
I could stray out of door. He is abroad.

CH. Then with less fear I may converse with thee.

EL. Ask what you will, for he is nowhere near.

CH. First of thy brother I beseech thee tell,
How deem'st thou? Will he come, or still delay?

EL. His promise comes, but still performance sleeps.

CH. Well may he pause who plans a dreadful deed.

EL. I paused not in his rescue from the sword.

CH. Fear not. He will bestead you. He is true.

EL. But for that faith my life had soon gone by.

CH. No more! I see approaching from the house
Thy sister by both parents of thy blood,
Chrysothemis; in her hand an offering,
Such as old custom yields to those below.

Enter CHRYSOTHEMIS.

CHRYSOTHEMIS. What converse keeps thee now be-
            yond the gates,
Dear sister ? why this talk in the open day ?
Wilt thou not learn after so long to cease
From vain indulgence of a bootless rage ?
I know in my own breast that I am pained
By what thou griev'st at, and if I had power,
My censure of their deeds would soon be known.
But in misfortune I have chosen to sail
With lowered canvas, rather than provoke
With puny strokes invulnerable foes.
I would thou didst the like : though I must own
The right is on thy side, and not on mine.
But if I mean to dwell at liberty,
I must obey in all the stronger will.

EL. 'Tis strange and pitiful, thy father's child
Can leave him in oblivion and subserve
The mother. All thy schooling of me springs
From her suggestion, not of thine own wit.
Sure, either thou art senseless, or thy sense
Deserts thy friends. Treason or dulness then ?
Choose !—You declared but now, if you had strength,
You would display your hatred of this pair.
Yet, when I plan full vengeance for my sire,
You aid me not, but turn me from the attempt.
What 's this but adding cowardice to evil ?
For tell me, or be patient till I show,
What should I gain by ceasing this my moan ?
I live to vex them :—though my life be poor,
Yet that suffices, for I honour him,
My father,—if affection touch the dead.
You say you hate them, but belie your word,
Consorting with our father's murderers.
I then, were all the gifts in which you glory
Laid at my feet, will never more obey
This tyrant power. I leave you your rich board
And life of luxury. Ne'er be it mine to feed
On dainties that would poison my heart's peace !

I care not for such honour as thou hast.
Nor wouldst thou care if thou wert wise.   But now,
Having the noblest of all men for sire,
Be called thy mother's offspring ; so shall most
Discern thine infamy and traitorous mind
To thy dead father and thy dearest kin.

CH. No anger, we entreat.   Both have said well,
If each would learn of other, and so do.

CHR. For my part, women, use hath seasoned me
To her discourse.   Nor had I spoken of this,·
Had I not heard a horror coming on
That will restrain her from her endless moan.

EL. Come speak it forth, this terror !   I will yield,
If thou canst tell me worse than I endure.

CHR. I'll tell thee all I know.   If thou persist
In these thy wailings, they will send thee far
From thine own land, and close thee from the day,
Where in a rock-hewn chamber thou may'st chant
Thine evil orisons in darkness drear.
Think of it, while there 's leisure to reflect ;
Or if thou suffer, henceforth blame me not.

EL. And have they so determined on my life ?

CHR. 'Tis certain ; when Aegisthus comes again.

EL. If that be all, let him return with speed !

CHR. Unhappy !   why this curse upon thyself ?

EL. If this be their intent, why, let him come !

CHR. To work such harm on thee !   What thought is
            this ?

EL. Far from mine eye to banish all your brood.

CHR. Art not more tender of the life thou hast ?

EL. Fair, to a marvel, is my life, I trow !

CHR. It would be, couldst thou be advised for good.

EL. Never advise me to forsake my kin.

CHR. I do not : only to give place to power.

EL. Thine be such flattery.   'Tis not my way.

CHR. Sure, to be wrecked by rashness is not well.

EL. Let me be wrecked in 'venging my own sire.

CHR. I trust his pardon for my helplessness.

EL. Such talk hath commendation from the vile.

CHR. Wilt thou not listen ?   Wilt thou ne'er be ruled ?

EL. No; not by thee! Let me not sink so
    low.

CHR. Then I will hie me on mine errand straight.

EL. Stay; whither art bound? For whom to spend
    those gifts?

CHR. Sent by my mother to my father's tomb
To pour libations to him.

EL.   How? To him?
Most hostile to her of all souls that are?

CHR. Who perished by her hand—so thou wouldst
    say.

EL. What friend hath moved her? Who hath cared
    for this?

CHR. Methinks 'twas some dread vision, seen by
    night.

EL. Gods of my father, O be with me now!

CHR. What? art thou hopeful from the fear I spake
    of?

EL. Tell me the dream, and I will answer thee.

CHR. I know but little of it.

EL.   Speak but that.
A little word hath ofttimes been the cause
Of ruin or salvation unto men.

CHR. 'Tis said she saw our father's spirit come
Once more to visit the abodes of light;
Then take and firmly plant upon the hearth
The sceptre which he bore of old, and now
Aegisthus bears: and out of this upsprang
A burgeoned shoot, that shadowed all the ground
Of loved Mycenae. So I heard the tale
Told by a maid who listened when the Queen
Made known her vision to the God of Day.
But more than this I know not, save that I
Am sent by her through terror of the dream.
And I beseech thee by the Gods we serve
To take my counsel and not rashly fall.
If thou repel me now, the time may come
When suffering shall have brought thee to my side.

EL. Now, dear Chrysothemis, of what thou bearest
Let nothing touch his tomb. 'Tis impious

And criminal to offer to thy sire
Rites and libations from a hateful wife.
Then cast them to the winds, or deep in dust
Conceal them, where no particle may reach
His resting-place : but lie in store for her
When she goes underground. Sure, were she not
Most hardened of all women that have been,
She ne'er had sent those loveless offerings
To grace the sepulchre of him she slew.
For think how likely is the buried king
To take such present kindly from her hand,
Who slew him like an alien enemy,
Dishonoured even in death, and mangled him,
And wiped the death-stain with his flowing locks—
Sinful purgation ! Think you that you bear
In those cold gifts atonement for her guilt ?
It is not possible. Wherefore let be.
But take a ringlet from thy comely head,
And this from mine, that lingers on my brow
Longing to shade his tomb. Ah, give it to him,
All I can give, and this my maiden-zone,
Not daintily adorned, as once erewhile.
Then, humbly kneeling, pray that from the ground
He would arise to help us 'gainst his foes,
And grant his son Orestes with high hand
Strongly to trample on his enemies ;
That in our time to come from ampler stores
We may endow him, than are ours to-day.
I cannot but imagine that his will
Hath part in visiting her sleep with fears.
But howsoe'er, I pray thee, sister mine,
Do me this service, and thyself, and him,
Dearest of all the world to me and thee,
The father of us both, who rests below.

CH. She counsels piously ; and thou, dear maid,
If thou art wise, wilt do her bidding here.

CHR. Yea, when a thing is right, it is not well
Idly to wrangle, but to act with speed.
Only, dear friends, in this mine enterprise,
Let me have silence from your lips, I pray ;

For should my mother know of it, sharp pain
Will follow yet my bold adventurous feat.

[*Exit* CHRYSOTHEMIS

CHORUS.

An erring seer am I,   I 1
Of sense and wisdom lorn,
If this prophetic Power of right,
O'ertaking the offender, come not nigh
     Ere many an hour be born.
     Yon vision of the night,
That lately breathed into my listening ear,
Hath freed me, O my daughter, from all fear.
Sweet was that bodement. He doth not forget,
The Achaean lord that gave thee being, nor yet
The bronzen-griding axe, edged like a spear,
Hungry and keen, though dark with stains of time,
That in the hour of hideous crime
Quelled him with cruel butchery:
That, too, remembers, and shall testify.

From ambush deep and dread
With power of many a hand
And many hastening feet shall spring
The Fury of the adamantine tread,
     Visiting Argive land
     Swift recompense to bring
For eager dalliance of a blood-stained pair
Unhallowed, foul, forbidden. No omen fair,—
Their impious course hath fixed this in my soul,—
Nought but black portents full of blame shall
    roll
Before their eyes that wrought or aided there.
Small force of divination would there seem
In prophecy or solemn dream,
Should not this vision of the night
Reach harbour in reality aright.

O chariot-course of Pelops, full of toil!   II
     How wearisome and sore
Hath been thine issue to our native soil!—

Since, from the golden car
Hurled to the deep afar,
        Myrtilus sank and slept,
Cruelly plucked from that fell chariot-floor,
This house unceasingly hath kept
Crime and misfortune mounting evermore.

Enter CLYTEMNESTRA.

CLYTEMNESTRA. Again you are let loose and range
            at will.
Ay, for Aegisthus is not here, who barred
Your rashness from defaming your own kin
Beyond the gates. But now he's gone from home,
You heed not me: though you have noised abroad
That I am bold in crime, and domineer
Outrageously, oppressing thee and thine.
I am no oppressor, but I speak thee ill,
For thou art ever speaking ill of me—
Still holding forth thy father's death, that I
Have done it. So I did: I know it well:
That I deny not; for not I alone
But Justice slew him; and if you had sense,
To side with Justice ought to be your part.
For who but he of all the Greeks, your sire,
For whom you whine and cry, who else but he
Took heart to sacrifice unto the Gods
Thy sister ?—having less of pain, I trow,
In getting her, than I, that bore her, knew !
Come, let me question thee ! On whose behalf
Slew he my child ? Was 't for the Argive host ?
What right had they to traffic in my flesh ?—
Menelaüs was his brother. Wilt thou say
He slew my daughter for his brother's sake ?
How then should he escape me ? Had not he,
Menelaüs, children twain, begotten of her
Whom to reclaim that army sailed to Troy ?
Was Death then so enamoured of my seed,
That he must feast thereon and let theirs live ?
Or was the God-abandoned father's heart
Tender toward them and cruel to my child ?

Doth this not argue an insensate sire ?
I think so, though your wisdom may demur.
And could my lost one speak, she would confirm it.
For my part, I can dwell on what I have done
Without regret. You, if you think me wrong,
Bring reasons forth and blame me to my face !

    EL. Thou canst not say this time that I began
And brought this on me by some taunting word.
But, so you'd suffer me, I would declare
The right both for my sister and my sire.

    CLY. Thou hast my sufferance. Nor would hearing
        vex,
If ever thus you tuned your speech to me.

    EL. Then I will speak. You say you slew him.
        Where
Could there be found confession more depraved,
Even though the cause were righteous ? But I'll prove
No rightful vengeance drew thee to the deed,
But the vile bands of him you dwell with now.
Or ask the huntress Artemis, what sin
She punished, when she tied up all the winds
Round Aulis.—I will tell thee, for her voice
Thou ne'er may'st hear ! 'Tis rumoured that my sire,
Sporting within the goddess' holy ground,
His foot disturbed a dappled hart, whose death
Drew from his lips some rash and boastful word.
Wherefore Latona's daughter in fell wrath
Stayed the army, that in quittance for the deer
My sire should slay at the altar his own child.
So came her sacrifice. The Achaean fleet
Had else no hope of being launched to Troy
Nor to their homes. Wherefore, with much constraint
And painful urging of his backward will,
Hardly he yielded ;—not for his brother's sake.
But grant thy speech were sooth, and all were done
In aid of Menelaüs ; for this cause
Hadst thou the right to slay him ? What high law
Ordaining ? Look to it, in establishing
Such precedent thou dost not lay in store
Repentance for thyself. For if by right

One die for one, thou first wilt be destroyed
If Justice find thee.—But again observe
The hollowness of thy pretended plea.
Tell me, I pray, what cause thou dost uphold
In doing now the basest deed of all,
Chambered with the blood-guilty, with whose aid
Thou slewest our father in that day. For him
You now bear children—ousting from their right
The stainless offspring of a holy sire.
How should this plead for pardon ? Wilt thou say
Thus thou dost 'venge thy daughter's injury ?
O shameful plea ? Where is the thought of honour,
If foes are married for a daughter's sake ?—
Enough. No words can move thee. Thy rash tongue
With checkless clamour cries that we revile
Our mother. Nay, no mother, but the chief
Of tyrants to us ! For my life is full
Of weariness and misery from thee
And from thy paramour. While he abroad,
Orestes, our one brother, who escaped
Hardly from thy attempt, unhappy boy !
Wears out his life, victim of cross mischance.
Oft hast thou taunted me with fostering him
To be thy punisher. And this, be sure,
Had I but strength, I had done. Now for this word,
Proclaim me what thou wilt,—evil in soul,
Or loud in cursing, or devoid of shame :
For if I am infected with such guilt,
Methinks my nature is not fallen from thine.

   CH. (*looking at* CLYTEMNESTRA). I see her fuming
            with fresh wrath : the thought
Of justice enters not her bosom now.

   CLY. What thought of justice should be mine for
           her,
Who at her age can so insult a mother ?
Will shame withhold her from the wildest deed ?

   EL. Not unashamed, assure thee, I stand here,
Little as thou mayest deem it. Well I feel
My acts untimely and my words unmeet.
But your hostility and treatment force me

Against my disposition to this course.
Harsh ways are taught by harshness.

CLY.   Brazen thing !
Too true it is that words and deeds of mine
Are evermore informing thy harsh tongue.

EL. The shame is yours, because the deeds are yours.
My words are but their issue and effect.

CLY. By sovereign Artemis, whom still I serve,
You'll rue this boldness when Aegisthus comes.

EL. See now, your anger bears you off, and ne'er
Will let you listen, though you gave me leave.

CLY. Must I not even sacrifice in peace
From your harsh clamour, when you've had your
                 say ?

EL. I have done. I check thee not. Go, sacrifice !
Accuse not me of hindering piety.

CLY. (to an attendant). Then lift for me those fruitful
                 offerings,
While to Apollo, before whom we stand,
I raise my supplication for release
From doubts and fears that shake my bosom now.
And, O defender of our house ! attend
My secret utterance. No friendly ear
Is that which hearkens for my voice. My thought
Must not be blazoned with her standing by,
Lest through her envious and wide-babbling tongue
She fill the city full of wild surmise.
List, then, as I shall speak : and grant the dreams
Whose two-fold apparition I to-night
Have seen, if good their bodement, be fulfilled :
If hostile, turn their influence on my foes.
And yield not them their wish that would by guile
Thrust me from this high fortune, but vouchsafe
That ever thus exempt from harms I rule
The Atridae's home and kingdom, in full life,
Partaking with the friends I live with now
All fair prosperity, and with my children,
Save those who hate and vex me bitterly.
Lykeian Phoebus, favourably hear
My prayer, and grant to all of us our need !

More is there, which, though I be silent here,
A God should understand. No secret thing
Is hidden from the all-seeing sons of Heaven.

Enter the Old Man.

OLD M. Kind dames and damsels, may I clearly
                know
If these be King Aegisthus' palace-halls ?
  CH. They are, sir ; you yourself have guessed aright.
  OLD M. May I guess further that in yonder dame
I see his queen ? She looks right royally.
  CH. 'Tis she,—no other,—whom your eyes behold.
  OLD M. Princess, all hail ! To thee and to thy spouse
I come with words of gladness from a friend.
  CLY. That auspice I accept. But I would first
Learn from thee who of men hath sent thee forth ?
  OLD M. Phanoteus the Phocian, with a charge of
                weight.
  CLY. Declare it, stranger. Coming from a friend,
Thou bring'st us friendly tidings, I feel sure.
  OLD M. Orestes' death. Ye have the sum in brief.
  EL. Ah me ! undone ! This day hath ruined me.
  CLY. What ? Let me hear again. Regard her not.
  OLD M. Again I say it, Orestes is no more.
  EL. Undone ! undone ! Farewell to life and hope !
  CLY. (*to* ELECTRA). See thou to thine own case ! (*To*
                Old Man) Now, stranger, tell me
In true discourse the manner of his death.
  OLD M. For that I am here, and I will tell the
                whole.
He, entering on the great arena famed
As Hellas' pride, to win a Delphian prize,
On hearing the loud summons of the man
Calling the foot-race, which hath trial first,
Came forward, a bright form, admired by all.
And when his prowess in the course fulfilled
The promise of his form, he issued forth
Dowered with the splendid meed of victory.—
To tell a few out of the many feats
Of such a hero were beyond my power.

Know then, in brief, that of the prizes set
For every customary course proclaimed
By order of the judges, the whole sum
Victoriously he gathered, happy deemed
By all; declared an Argive, and his name
Orestes, son of him who levied once
The mighty armament of Greeks for Troy.
So fared he then: but when a God inclines
To hinder happiness, not even the strong
Are scatheless. So, another day, when came
At sunrise the swift race of charioteers,
He entered there with many a rival car:—
One from Achaia, one from Sparta, two
Libyan commanders of the chariot-yoke;
And he among them fifth, with steeds of price
From Thessaly;—the sixth Aetolia sent
With chestnut mares; the seventh a Magnete man;
The eighth with milk-white colts from Oeta's vale;
The ninth from god-built Athens; and the tenth
Boeotia gave to make the number full.
Then stood they where the judges of the course
Had posted them by lot, each with his team;
And sprang forth at the brazen trumpet's blare.
Shouting together to their steeds, they shook
The reins, and all the course was filled with noise
Of rattling chariots, and the dust arose
To heaven. Now all in a confusèd throng
Spared not the goad, each eager to outgo
The crowded axles and the snorting steeds;
For close about his nimbly circling wheels
And stooping sides fell flakes of panted foam.
Orestes, ever nearest at the turn,
With whirling axle seemed to graze the stone,
And loosing with free rein the right-hand steed
That pulled the side-rope, held the near one in.
So for a time all chariots upright moved,
But soon the Oetaean's hard-mouthed horses broke
From all control, and wheeling as they passed
From the sixth circuit to begin the seventh,
Smote front to front against the Barcan car.

And when that one disaster had befallen,
Each dashed against his neighbour and was thrown,
Till the whole plain was strewn with chariot-wreck.
Then the Athenian, skilled to ply the rein,
Drew on one side, and heaving to, let pass
The rider-crested surge that rolled i' the midst.
Meanwhile Orestes, trusting to the end,
Was driving hindmost with tight rein ; but now,
Seeing him left the sole competitor,
Hurling fierce clamour through his steeds, pursued :
So drave they yoke by yoke—now this, now that
Pulling ahead with car and team.   Orestes,
Ill-fated one, each previous course had driven
Safely without a check, but after this,
In letting loose again the left-hand rein,
He struck the edge of the stone before he knew,
Shattering the axle's end, and tumbled prone,
Caught in the reins, that dragged him with sharp thongs.
Then as he fell to the earth the horses swerved,
And roamed the field.   The people when they saw
Him fallen from out the car, lamented loud
For the fair youth, who had achieved before them
Such glorious feats, and now had found such woe,—
Dashed on the ground, then tossed with legs aloft
Against the sky,—until the charioteers,
Hardly restraining the impetuous team,
Released him, covered so with blood that none,—
No friend who saw—had known his hapless form.
Which then we duly burned upon the pyre.
And straightway men appointed to the task
From all the Phocians bear his mighty frame—
Poor ashes ! narrowed in a brazen urn,—
That he may find in his own fatherland
His share of sepulture.—Such our report,
Painful to hear, but unto us, who saw,
The mightiest horror that e'er met mine eye.

   CH. Alas ! the stock of our old masters, then,
Is utterly uprooted and destroyed.

     CLY. O heavens ! what shall I say ? That this is
        well ?

Or terrible, but gainful ?   Hard my lot,
To save my life through my calamity !

   OLD M. Lady, why hath my speech disheartened
       thee ?

   CLY. To be a mother hath a marvellous power :
No injury can make one hate one's child.

   OLD M. Then it should seem our coming was in
       vain.

   CLY. In vain ?   Nay, verily ; thou, that hast
       brought
Clear evidences of his fate, who, sprung
From my life's essence, severed from my breast
And nurture, was estranged in banishment,
And never saw me from the day he went
Out from this land, but for his father's blood
Threatened me still with accusation dire ;
That sleep nor soothed at night nor sweetly stole
My senses from the day, but, all my time,
Each instant led me on the way to death !—
But this day's chance hath freed me from all fear
Of him, and of this maid : who being at home
Troubled me more, and with unmeasured thirst
Kept draining my life-blood ; but now her threats
Will leave us quiet days, methinks, and peace
Unbroken.—How then shouldst thou come in vain ?

   EL. O misery !   'Tis time to wail thy fate,
Orestes, when, in thy calamity,
Thy mother thus insults thee.   Is it well ?

   CLY. 'Tis well that he is gone, not that you live.

   EL. Hear, 'venging spirits of the lately dead !

   CLY. The avenging spirits have heard and answered
       well.

   EL. Insult us now, for thou art fortunate !

   CLY. You and Orestes are to quench my pride.

   EL. Our pride is quenched.   No hope of quenching
       thee !

   CLY. A world of good is in thy coming, stranger,
Since thou hast silenced this all-clamorous tongue.

   OLD M. Then I may go my way, seeing all is
       well.

CLY. Nay, go not yet ! That would disgrace alike
Me and the friend who sent you to our land.
But come thou in, and leave her out of door
To wail her own and loved ones' overthrow.

[*Exeunt* CLYTEMNESTRA *and* Old Man

EL. Think you the wretch in heartfelt agony
Weeps inconsolably her perished son ?
She left us with a laugh ! O misery !
How thou hast ruined me, dear brother mine,
By dying ! Thou hast torn from out my heart
The only hope I cherished yet, that thou
Living wouldst come hereafter to avenge
Thy father's woes and mine. Where must I go ?
Since I am left of thee and of my sire
Bereaved and lonely, and once more must be
The drudge and menial of my bitterest foes,
My father's murderers. Say, is it well ?
Nay, nevermore will I consort with these,
But sinking here before the palace gate,
Thus, friendless, I will wither out my life.
Hereat if any in the house be vexed,
Let them destroy me ; for to take my life
Were kindness, and to live is only pain :
Life hath not kindled my desires with joy.

CH. 1. O ever-blazing sun !   I 1
O lightning of the eternal Sire !
Can ye behold this done
And tamely hide your all-avenging fire ?
    EL. Ah me !
    CH. 2.   My daughter, why these tears?
    EL. Woe !
    CH. 3.   Weep not, calm thy fears.
    EL. You kill me.
    CH. 4.   How ?
    EL.   To breathe
A hope for one beneath
So clearly sunk in death,
'Tis to afflict me more
Already pining sore.

Ch. 5. One in a woman's toils   I 2
Was tangled, buried by her glittering coils,
Who now beneath——
El.   Ah woe!
Ch. 6. Rules with a spirit unimpaired and strong.
El. O dreadful!
Ch. 7.   Dreadful was the wrong.
El. But she was quelled.
Ch. 8.   Ay.
El.   True!
That faithful mourner knew
A brother's aid. But I
Have no man now. The one
I had, is gone, is gone.
Rapt into nothingness.

Ch. 9. Thou art wrung with sore distress.   II 1
El. I know it. Too well I know,
Taught by a life of woe,
Where horror dwells without relief.
Ch. 10. Our eyes have seen thy grief.
El. Then comfort not again——
Ch. 11. Whither now turns thy strain?
El. One utterly bereft,
Seeing no hope is left,
Of help from hands owning the same great sire.

Ch. 12. 'Tis nature's debt.   II 2
El.   To expire
On sharp-cut dragging thongs,
'Midst wildly trampling throngs
Of swiftly racing hoofs, like him,
Poor hapless one?
Ch. 13.   Vast, dim,
And boundless was the harm.
El. Yea, severed from mine arm,
By strangers kept——
Ch. 14.   O pain!
El. Hidden he must remain,
Of me unsepulchred, unmourned, unwept.

Enter CHRYSOTHEMIS.

CHR. Driven by delight, dear sister, I am come,
Reckless of dignity, with headlong speed.
For news I bear of joy and sweet relief
From ills that drew from thee thy ceaseless moan.

EL. Whence couldst thou hear of succour for my woes,
That close in darkness without hope of dawn?

CHR. Here is Orestes, learn it from my mouth,
As certainly as you now look on me.

EL. What? Art thou mad, unhappy one, to laugh
Over thine own calamity and mine?

CHR. No, by our father's hearth, I say not this
In mockery. I tell you he is come.

EL. Me miserable! Who hath given thine ear
The word that so hath wrought on thy belief?

CHR. Myself am the eyewitness; no one else
Gained my belief, but proofs I clearly saw.

EL. What sign hath so engrossed thine eye, poor girl?
What sight hath fired thee with this quenchless glow?

CHR. But list to me, I pray thee, that henceforth
Thou mayest account me clear-eyed, or a fool!

EL. By all means, if it pleasure thee, say on.

CHR. Well, I will tell thee all I saw:—I came
Unto the ancient tomb that holds our sire;
And from the topmost mound I marked a stream
Of milk fresh-flowing, and his resting-place
Ringed round with garlands of all flowers that blow.
I marvelled at the sight, and peered about,
Lest some one might be nearer than we knew.
But finding all was quiet in the spot,
I ventured closer to the tomb, and there,
Hard by the limit, I beheld a curl
Of hair new-shorn, with all the gloss of youth.
And straight it struck my heart, as with a sense
Of something seen, ah me! long, long ago,
And told me that my sight encountered here
The token of Orestes, dearest soul.
Then, clasping it, I did not cry aloud,
But straight mine eyes were filled with tears of joy.

And now as much as then I feel assured
He and none else bestowed this ornament.
To whom beyond thyself and me belongs
Such consecration ?   And I know this well,
I did it not,—nor thou. Impossible !
Thou canst not worship even the blessèd Gods
Forth of this roof, unpunished. And, most sure,
Our mother is not minded so to act,
Nor, had she done it, could we fail to know.
This offering comes then of Orestes' hand.
Take courage, dear one. Not one fate pursues
One house perpetually, but changeth still.
Ours was a sullen Genius, but perchance
This day begins the assurance of much good.

   EL. Oh how I pity thine infatuate mind !
   CHR. Why ? Dost thou find no comfort in my news ?
   EL. You know not where you roam. Far wide !
     far wide !
   CHR. Not know ? when I have seen it with mine
     eyes ?
   EL. Dear, he is dead. Look not to him, poor girl !
Salvation comes to thee no more from him.
   CHR. Oh me, unfortunate ! Who told thee this ?
   EL. He who stood by and saw his life destroyed.
   CHR. Amazement seizes me. Where is that man ?
   EL. Right welcome to the mother there within.
   CHR. Me miserable ! Who then can have decked
With all those ceremonies our father's tomb ?
   EL. I cannot but suppose some hand hath brought
These gifts in memory of Orestes dead.
   CHR. O cruel fate ! While I in ecstasy
Sped with such news, all ignorant, it seems,
Of our dire fortune ; and, arriving, find
Fresh sorrows added to the former woe.
   EL. It is so, sister ; yet if thou wilt list
To me, thou mayest disperse this heaviness.
   CHR. What ? Shall I raise the dead again to life ?
   EL. I did not mean so. I am not so fond.
   CHR. What bid you then that I have power to do ?
   EL. To endure courageously what I enjoin.

CHR. So it make profit, I will not refuse.

EL. Remember, without toil no plan may thrive!

CHR. I know it, and will aid thee to my power.

EL. Then hearken my resolve. Thou seëst now,
We have no friendly succour in the world;
But death has taken all, and we are left
Two only. I, so long as I could hear
My brother lived and flourished, still had hope
He would arise to wreak his father's blood.
But now that he is gone, to thee I turn,
To help thy sister boldly to destroy
The guilty author of our father's death,
Aegisthus.—Wherefore hide it from thee now?
—Yea, sister! Till what term wilt thou remain
Inactive? To what end? What hope is yet
Left standing? Surely thou hast cause to grieve,
Robbed of thy father's opulent heritage,
And feeling bitterly the creeping years
That find thee still a virgin and unwed.
Nay, nor imagine thou shalt ever know
That blessing. Not so careless of his life
Is King Aegisthus, as to risk the birth
Of sons from us, to his most certain fall.
But if thou wilt but follow my resolve,
First thou shalt win renown of piety
From our dead father, and our brother too,
Who rest beneath the ground, and shalt be free
For evermore in station as in birth,
And nobly matched in marriage, for the good
Draw gazers to them still. Then seest thou not
What meed of honour, if thou dost my will,
Thou shalt apportion to thyself and me?
For who, beholding us, what citizen,
What foreigner, will not extend the hand
Of admiration, and exclaim, 'See, friends,
These scions of one stock, these noble twain,
These that have saved their father's house from woe,
Who once when foes were mighty, set their life
Upon a cast, and stood forth to avenge
The stain of blood! Who will not love the pair

And do them reverence ? Who will not give
Honour at festivals, and in the throng
Of popular resort, to these in chief,
For their high courage and their bold emprise ? '
Such fame will follow us in all the world,
Living or dying, still to be renowned.
Ah, then, comply, dear sister ; give thy sire
This toil—this labour to thy brother give ;
End these my sufferings, end thine own regret :
The well-born cannot bear to live in shame.

CH. In such affairs, for those who speak and hear
Wise thoughtfulness is still the best ally.

CHR. True, noble women, and before she spake
Sound thought should have prevented the rash talk
That now hath proved her reckless. What wild aim
Beckons thee forth in arming this design
Whereto thou wouldst demand my ministry ?
Dost not perceive, thou art not man but woman,
Of strength inferior to thine enemies,—
Their Genius daily prospering more and more,
Whilst ours is dwindling into nothingness ?
Who then that plots against a life so strong
Shall quit him of the danger without harm ?
Take heed we do not add to our distress
Should some one hear of this our colloquy.
Small help and poor advantage 'twere for us
To win brief praise and then inglorious die.
Nay, death is not so hateful as when one
Desiring death is balked of that desire.
And I beseech thee, ere in utter ruin
We perish and make desolate our race,
Refrain thy rage. And I will guard for thee
In silence these thy words unrealized ;
If thou wilt learn this wisdom from long time,
Having no strength, to bend before the strong.

CH. Comply. Than prudence and a heedful mind,
No fairer treasure can be found for men.

EL. Thy words have not surprised me. Well I
                    knew
The good I offered would come back with scorn.

I, all alone and with a single hand,
Must do this. For it shall not rest undone.
 CHR. Would thou hadst been thus minded when
   our sire
Lay dying! In one act thou hadst compassed all.
 EL. My spirit was the same: my mind was less.
 CHR. Be such the life-long temper of thy mind!
 EL. Thine admonition augurs little aid.
 CHR. Yea. For the attempt would bring me certain
   bane.
 EL. I envy thee thy prudence, hate thy fear.
 CHR. Even when thou speak'st me fair, I will endure
   it.
 EL. Take heart. That never will be thine from me.
 CHR. Long time remains to settle that account.
 EL. I find no profit in thee. Go thy way.
 CHR. Profit there is, hadst thou a mind to learn.
 EL. Go to thy mother and declare all this!
 CHR. I am not so in hatred of thy life.
 EL. Yet know the shame thou wouldst prepare for
   me.
 CHR. No, no! Not shame, but care for thine estate.
 EL. Must I still follow as thou thinkest good?
 CHR. When thou hast wisdom, thou shalt be the
   guide.
 EL. 'Tis hard when error wears the garb of sense.
 CHR. Right. That is the misfortune of your case.
 EL. Why? Feel you not the justice of my speech?
 CHR. Justice may chance to bring me injury.
 EL. I care not, I, to live by such a rule.
 CHR. Well, if you do it, you will find me wise.
 EL. Well, I will do it, nought dismayed by thee.
 CHR. Speak you plain sooth? and will you not be
   counselled?
 EL. No, for bad counsel is of all most hateful.
 CHR. You take the sense of nothing that I say.
 EL. Long since, not newly, my resolve is firm.
 CHR. Then I will go. Thy heart will ne'er be brought
To praise my words, nor I thine action here.
 EL. Then go within! I will not follow thee,

Though thou desire it vehemently. None
Would be so fond to hunt on a cold trail.

CHR. If this seem wisdom to thee, then be wise
Thy way : but in the hour of misery,
When it hath caught thee, thou wilt praise my words.

[*Exit* CHRYSOTHEMIS

CHORUS.

  Wise are the birds of air   I 1
  That with true filial care
For those provide convenient food
Who gave them birth, who wrought their good.
Why will not men the like perfection prove ?
   Else, by the fires above,
   And heavenly Rectitude,
Fierce recompense they shall not long elude.
O darkling rumour, world-o'er-wandering voice
That piercest to the shades beneath the ground,
To dead Atrides waft a sound
Of sad reproach, not bidding him rejoice.

  Stained is the ancestral hall,   I 2
  Broken the battle-call,
That heretofore his children twain
In loving concord did sustain.
Alone, deserted, vexed, Electra sails,
   Storm-tossed with rugged gales,
   Lamenting evermore
Like piteous Philomel, and pining sore
For her lost father ;—might she but bring down
That two-fold Fury, caring not for death,
But ready to resign her breath.
What maid so worthy of a sire's renown ?

None who inherit from a noble race, II 1
  Complying with things base
Will let their ancient glory be defiled.
  So 'twas thy choice, dear child,
Through homeless misery to win a two-fold prize,
   Purging the sin and shame
   That cloud the Argive name,
So to be called most noble and most wise.

May'st thou surpass thy foes in wealth and power
                                                II 2
   As o'er thee now they tower !
 Since I have found thee, not in bright estate,
   Nor blessed by wayward fate,
But through thy loyalty to Heaven's eternal cause
   Wearing the stainless crown
    Of perfectest renown,
And richly dowered by the mightiest laws.

Enter ORESTES *and* PYLADES, *with the urn.*

OR. Say, dames and damsels, have we heard aright,
And speed we to the goal of our desire ?
 CH. And what desire or quest hath brought thee
   hither ?
 OR. I seek Aegisthus' dwelling all this while.
 CH. Welcome. The tongue that told thee hath no
   blame.
 OR. Which of you all will signify within.
Our joint arrival,—not unwelcome here.
 CH. This maiden, if the nearest should report.
 OR. Mistress, wilt thou go yonder and make known,
That certain Phocians on Aegisthus wait ?
 EL. Oh ! can it be that you are come to bring
Clear proofs of the sad rumour we have heard ?
 OR. I know not what ye have heard. Old Strophius
Charged me with tidings of Orestes' fate.
 EL. What, stranger ? How this terror steals on
   me !
 OR. Bearing scant remnants of his body dead
In this small vase thou seest, we bring them home.
 EL. O sorrow ! thou art here : I see full well
That burden of my heart in present view.
 OR. If thou hast tears for aught Orestes suffered,
Know that he lies within this vessel's room.
 EL. Ah, sir ! by all in Heaven, if yonder urn
Hide him, ah ! give it once into my hand,
That o'er that dust I may lament and mourn
Myself and mine own house and all our woe !
 OR. Bring it and give her, whosoe'er she be.

For not an enemy—this petition shows it—
But of his friends or kindred, is this maid.

[The urn is given into ELECTRA'S *hands*

EL. O monument of him whom o'er all else
I loved! sole relic of Orestes' life,
How cold in this thy welcome is the hope
Wherein I decked thee as I sent thee forth!
Then bright was thy departure, whom I now
Bear lightly, a mere nothing, in my hands.
Would I had gone from life, ere I dispatched
Thee from my arms that saved thee to a land
Of strangers, stealing thee from death! For then
Thou hadst been quiet on that far-off day,
And had thy portion in our father's tomb.
Now thou hast perished in the stranger land
Far from thy sister, lorn and comfortless.
And I, O wretchedness! neither have bathed
And laid thee forth, nor from the blazing fire
Collected the sad burden, as was meet:
But thou, when foreign hands have tended thee,
Com'st ā small handful in a narrow shell.
Woe for the constant care I spent on thee
Of old all vainly, with sweet toil! For never
Wast thou thy mother's darling, nay, but mine,
And I of all the household most thy nurse,
While 'sister, sister,' was thy voice to me.
But now all this is vanished in one day,
Dying in thy death. Thou hast carried all away
As with a whirlwind, and art gone. No more
My father lives: thyself art lost in death:
I am dead, who lived in thee. Our enemies
Laugh loudly, and she maddens in her joy,
Our mother most unmotherly, of whom
Thy secret missives ofttimes told me, thou
Wouldst be the punisher. But that fair hope
The hapless Genius of thy lot and mine
Hath reft away, and gives thee thus to me,—
For thy loved form thy dust and fruitless shade.
O bitterness! O piteous sight! Woe! woe!
Oh! sent on thy dire journey, dearest one,

How thou hast ruined me! Thou hast indeed,
Dear brother! Then receive me to thyself,
Hide me in this thy covering, there to dwell,
Me who am nothing, with thy nothingness,
For ever! Yea, when thou wert here above,
I ever shared with thee in all, and now
I would not have thee shut me from thy tomb.
Oh! let me die and follow thee! the dead,
My mind assures me now, have no more pain.

CH. Electra, think! Thou hadst a mortal sire,
And mortal was thy brother. Grieve not far.

OR. O me! What shall I speak, or which way
　　　turn
The desperate word? I cannot hold my tongue.

EL. What pain o'ercomes thee? Wherefore speak'st
　　　thou so?

OR. Can this be famed Electra I behold?

EL. No other. In sad case, as you may see.

OR. Ah! deep indeed was this calamity!

EL. Is't possible that thou shouldst grieve for me?

OR. O ruined form! abandoned to disgrace!

EL. 'Tis me you mean, stranger, I feel it now.

OR. Woe 's me! Untrimmed for bridal, hapless maid!

EL. Why this fixed gaze, O stranger! that deep
　　　groan?

OR. How all unknowing was I of mine ill!

EL. What thing hath passed to make it known to
　　　thee?

OR. The sight of thee attired with boundless woe.

EL. And yet thine eye sees little of my pain.

OR. Can aught be still more hateful to be seen?

EL. I have my dwelling with the murderers—

OR. Of whom? What evil would thy words disclose?

EL. Of him who gave me birth. I am their slave.

OR. Whose power compels thee to this sufferance?

EL. One called my mother, most unmotherly.

OR. How? by main force, or by degrading shames?

EL. By force and shames, and every kind of evil.

OR. And is there none to succour or prevent?

EL. None. Him I had, you give me here in dust.

M 2

Or. How mine eye pities thee this while, poor maid!

El. Know now, none ever pitied me but you.

Or. None ever came whose heart like sorrow wrung.

El. Is't possible we have some kinsman here?

Or. I will tell it, if these women here be friendly.

El. They are. They may be trusted. Only speak.

Or. Let go yon vase, that thou may'st learn the
          whole.

El. Nay, by the Gods! be not so cruel, sir!

Or. Obey me and thou shalt not come to harm.

El. Ah, never rob me of what most I love!

Or. You must not hold it.

El.   O me miserable

For thee, Orestes, if I lose thy tomb!

Or. Speak no rash word. Thou hast no right to
          mourn.

El. No right to mourn my brother who is gone?

Or. Such utterance belongs not to thy tongue.

El. Oh, am I thus dishonoured of the dead?

Or. Far from dishonour. But this ne'er was thine.

El. Is't not Orestes' body that I bear?

Or. Nay, but the idle dressing of a tale.

El. And where is his poor body's resting-place?

Or. Nowhere. Seek not the living with the dead.

El. My son, what saidst thou?

Or.   Nought but what is true.

El. Doth he yet live?

Or.   If I have life in me.

El. Art thou Orestes?

Or.   Let my signet here,

That was our father's, tell thine eyes, I am.

El. O day of days!

Or.   Time hath no happier hour.

El. Is it thy voice?

Or.   Hearken not otherwhere.

El. Have my arms caught thee?

Or.   Hold me so for aye!

El. O dearest women, Argives of my home!

Ye see Orestes, dead in craft, but now

By that same craft delivered and preserved.

CH. We see, dear daughter, and the gladsome tear
Steals from our eye to greet the bright event.

EL. Offspring of him I loved beyond all telling ! I l
Ah ! thou art come,—hast found me, eye to eye
Behold'st the face thou didst desire to see.
  OR. True, I am here ; but bide in silence still.
  EL. Wherefore ?
  OR. Hush ! speak not loud, lest one within should
        hearken.
  EL. By ever-virgin Artemis, ne'er will I
Think worthy of my fear
This useless mass of woman-cowardice
Burdening the house within,
Not peering out of door.
  OR. Yet know that women too have might in war.
Of that methinks thou hast feeling evidence.
  EL. Ah me ! thou hast unveiled
And thrust before my gaze
That burning load of my distress
No time will soothe, no remedy will heal.
  OR. I know that too.   But when we are face to
        face
With the evildoers,—then let remembrance work.

  EL. All times alike are fit with instant pain   T 2
Justly to mind me of that dreadful day ;
Even now but hardly hath my tongue been free.
  OR. Yes, that is it.   Therefore preserve this boon.
  EL. Whereby ?
  OR. Put limits to unseasonable talk.
  EL. Ah ! brother, who, when thou art come,
Could find it meet to exchange
Language for silence, as thou bidst me do ?
Since beyond hope or thought
Was this thy sight to me.
  OR. God gave me to your sight when so he willed.
  EL. O heaven of grace beyond
The joy I knew but now !
If God hath brought thee to our roof,
A miracle of bounty then is here.

OR. I hate to curb the gladness of thy spirit,
But yet I fear this ecstasy of joy.

EL. Oh! after all these years,   II
Now thou at length hast sped
Thy dearest advent on the wished-for way,
Do not, in all this woe
Thou seest surrounding me——
    OR. What means this prayer?
    EL.   Forbid me not my joy,
Nor make me lose the brightness of thy face!
    OR. Deep were my wrath at him who should attempt
        it.
    EL. Is my prayer heard?
    OR.   Why doubt it?
    EL.   Friends, I learned
A tale beyond my thought; and hearing I restrained
My passion, voiceless in my misery,
Uttering no cry. But now
I have thee safe; now, dearest, thou art come,
With thy blest countenance, which I
Can ne'er forget, even at the worst of woe.

    OR. A truce now to unnecessary words.
My mother's vileness and Aegisthus' waste,
Draining and squandering with spendthrift hand
Our patrimony, tell me not anew.
Such talk might stifle opportunity.
But teach me, as befits the present need,
What place may serve by lurking vigilance
Or sudden apparition to o'erwhelm
Our foes in the adventure of to-day.
And, when we pass within, take heedful care
Bright looks betray thee not unto our mother.
But groan as for the dire calamity
Vainly reported:—Let 's achieve success,
Then with free hearts we may rejoice and laugh.
    EL. Dear brother, wheresoe'er thy pleasure leads,
My will shall follow, since the joys I know,
Not from myself I took them, but from thee.
And ne'er would I consent thy slightest grief

Should win for me great gain. Ill should I then
Serve the divinity of this high hour!
Thou knowest how matters in the palace stand.
Thou hast surely heard, Aegisthus is from home,
And she, our mother, is within. Nor fear
She should behold me with a smiling face.
Mine ancient hate of her hath sunk too deep.
And from the time I saw thee, tears of joy
Will cease not. Wherefore should I stint their flow?
I, who in this thy coming have beheld
Thee dead and living? Strangely hast thou wrought
On me;—that should my father come alive,
I would not think the sight were miracle,
But sober truth. Since such thy presence, then,
Lead as thy spirit prompts. For I alone
Of two things surely had achievèd one,
Noble deliverance or a noble death.

 Or. Be silent; for I hear within the house
A footstep coming forth.
 El. (loudly).   Strangers, go in!
For none within the palace will reject
Your burden, nor be gladdened by the event.

Enter the Old Man.

 Old M. O lost in folly and bereft of soul!
Is't that your care for life hath ebbed away,
Or were you born without intelligence,
When fallen, not near, but in the midst of ill,
And that the greatest, ye perceive it not?
Had I not watched the doors this while, your deeds
Had gone within the palace ere yourselves.
But, as things are, my care hath fenced you round.
Now, then, have done with long-protracted talk,
And this insatiable outburst of joy,
And enter, for in such attempts as these
Delay is harmful: and 'tis more than time.
 Or. But how shall I find matters there within?
 Old M. Well. You are shielded by their ignorance.
 Or. That means you have delivered me as dead.
 Old M. Alone of dead men thou art here above.

OR. Doth this delight them, or how went the talk?

OLD M. I will report, when all is done. Meanwhile,
Know, all is well with them, even what is evil.

EL. Who is this, brother? I beseech thee, tell.

OR. Dost not perceive?

EL.   I cannot even imagine.

OR. Know'st not into whose hands thou gav'st me
      once?

EL. Whose hands? How say you?

OR.   His, who through thy care
Conveyed me secretly to Phocis' plain.

EL. What! is this he, whom I, of all the band,
Found singly faithful in our father's death?

OR. He is that man. No more!

EL.   O gladsome day!
Dear only saviour of our father's house,
How camest thou hither? Art thou he indeed,
That didst preserve Orestes and myself
From many sorrows? O dear hands, kind feet,
Swift in our service,—how couldst thou so long
Be near, nor show one gleam, but didst destroy
My heart with words, hiding the loveliest deeds?
Father!—in thee methinks I see my father.
O welcome! thou of all the world to me
Most hated and most loved in one short hour.

OLD M. Enough, dear maiden! Many nights and
      days
Are circling hitherward, that shall reveal
In clear recountment all that came between.
    But to you two that stand beside I tell,
Now is your moment, with the Queen alone,
And none of men within; but if you pause,
Know that with others of profounder skill
You'll have to strive, more than your present foes.

OR. Then, Pylades, we need no more to dwell
On words, but enter on this act with speed,
First worshipping the holy shrines o' the Gods
That were my father's, harboured at the gate.

                    [*They pass within.* ELECTRA *remains in
                         an attitude of prayer*

EL. O King Apollo! hear them graciously,
And hear me too, that with incessant hand
Honoured thee richly from my former store!
And now, fierce slayer, I importune thee,
And woo thee with such gifts as I can give,
Be kindly aidant to this enterprise,
And make the world take note, what meed of bane
Heaven still bestows on man's iniquity.

[ELECTRA *goes within*

CH. Lo, where the War-god moves   1
With soft, sure footstep, on to his design,
Breathing hot slaughter of an evil feud!
Even now the inevitable hounds that track
Dark deeds of hideous crime
Are gone beneath the covert of the domes.
Not long in wavering suspense shall hang
The dreaming presage of my wistful soul.

For lo! within is led   2
With crafty tread the avenger of the shades,
Even to his father's throne of ancient power,
And in his hand the bright new-sharpened death!
And Hermes, Maia's son,
Is leading him, and hath concealed the guile
Even to the fatal end in clouds of night.
His time of weary waiting all is o'er.

Re-enter ELECTRA.

EL. O dearest women! they are even now
About it. Only bide in silence still.
CH. What is the present scene?
EL.   She decks the vase
For burial, and they both are standing by.
CH. And wherefore hast thou darted forth?
EL.   To watch
Aegisthus' coming, that he enter not
At unawares.
CLY. (*within*). Ah! ah! Woe for the house,
Desert of friends, and filled with hands of death!
EL. A cry within! Did ye not hear it, friends?

CH. Would I had not ! I heard, and shivered through.

CLY. (*within*). Oh me ! Alas, Aegisthus ! where art
thou ?

EL. Hark ! yet again that sound !

CLY. (*within*).   O son, have pity !
Pity the womb that bare thee.

EL.   Thou hadst none
For him, nor for his father, in that day.

HALF-CH. Poor city ! hapless race !
Thy destiny to-day
Wears thee away, away.
What morn shall see thy face ?

CLY. (*within*). Oh, I am smitten !

EL.   Give a second stroke,
If thou hast power.

CLY. (*within*).   Oh me ! again, again !

EL. Would thou wert shrieking for Aegisthus too !

CH. The curse hath found, and they in earth who lie
Are living powers to-day.
Long dead, they drain away
The streaming blood of those who made them die.

Enter ORESTES *and* PYLADES.

Behold, they come, they come !
His red hand dripping as he moves
With drops of sacrifice the War-god loves.
My 'wildered heart is dumb.

EL. How is it with you, brother ?

OR.   If Apollo
Spake rightfully, the state within is well.

EL. Wretched one, is she dead ?

OR.   No more have fear
Thou shalt be slighted by thy mother's will.

CH. Cease, for I see Aegisthus near in view.

EL. In, in again, boys !

OR.   Where do ye behold
The tyrant ?

EL.   To our hand from yonder gate
He comes with beaming look.

HALF-CH. Haste, with what speed ye may,   2
Stand on the doorway stone,
That, having thus much done,
Ye may do all to-day.

OR. Fear not : we will perform it.

EL.   Speed ye now :
Follow your thought.

OR.   We are already there.

EL. Leave matters here to me. All shall go well.

                   [*Exit* ORESTES *with* PYLADES

CH. Few words, as if in gentleness, 'twere good
To utter in his ear,
That, eager and unware,
One step may launch him on the field of blood.

Enter AEGISTHUS.

AEGISTHUS. Which of you know where are the
                Phocian men
Who brought the news I hear, Orestes' life
Hath suffered shipwreck in a chariot-race ?
You, you I question, you in former time
So fearless ! You methinks most feelingly
Can tell us, for it touches you most near.

EL. I know : assure thee. Else had I not heard
The dearest of all fortunes to my heart.

AEG. Where are the strangers then ? Enlighten me.

EL. Yonder. Their hostess entertained them well.

AEG. And did they certainly report him dead ?

EL. Not only so. They showed him to our sight.

AEG. May this clear evidence be mine to see ?

EL. I envy not the sight that waits you there.

AEG. Against their wont thy words have given me
                joy.

EL. Much joy be thine, if this be joy to thee !

AEG. Silence, I say ! Wide let the gates be flung !
For all the Myceneans to behold
And all in Argolis, that if but one
Hath heretofore been buoyed on empty hopes
Fixed in Orestes, seeing him now dead,

He may accept my manage, and not wait
For our stern chastisement to teach him sense.

EL. My lesson is already learnt: at length
I am schooled to labour with the stronger will.

[The body of CLYTEMNESTRA *is disclosed
under a veil :* ORESTES *standing by*

AEG. Zeus ! Divine envy surely hath laid low
The form I here behold. But if the truth
Provoke Heaven's wrath, be it unexpressed.—Unveil !
Off with all hindrance, that mine eye may see,
And I may mourn my kinsman as I should.

OR. Thyself put forth thy hand. Not mine but thine
To look and speak with kindness to this corse.

AEG. I will, for thou advisest well ; but thou,
Call Clytemnestra, if she be within.

*[*AEGISTHUS *lifts the shroud*

OR. She is beside thee, gaze not otherwhere.

AEG. What do I see ! oh !

OR.   Why so strange ? Whom fear you ?

AEG. Who are the men into whose midmost toils
All hapless I am fallen ?

OR.   Ha ! knowest thou not
Thou hast been taking living men for dead ?

AEG. I understand that saying. Woe is me !
I know, Orestes' voice addresseth me.

OR. A prophet ! How wert thou so long deceived ?

AEG. Undone, undone ! Yet let me speak one word.

EL. Brother, by Heaven, no more ! Let him not
            speak.
When death is certain, what do men in woe
Gain from a little time ? Kill him at once !
And, killed, expose him to such burial
From dogs and vultures, as beseemeth such,
Far from our view. Nought less will solace me
For the remembrance of a life of pain.

OR. Go in and tarry not. No contest this
Of verbal question, but of life or death.

AEG. Why drive you me within ? If this you do
Be noble, why must darkness hide the deed ?
Why not destroy me out of hand ?

OR.   Command not!
Enter, and in the place where ye cut down
My father, thou shalt yield thy life to me.

AEG. Is there no help but this abode must see
The past and future ills of Pelops' race?

OR. Thine anyhow. That I can prophesy
With perfect inspiration to thine ear.

AEG. The skill you boast belonged not to your sire.

OR. You question and delay. Go in!

AEG.   Lead on.

OR. Nay, go thou first.

AEG.   That I may not escape thee?

OR. No, that thou may'st not have thy wish in death.
I may not stint one drop of bitterness.
And would this doom were given without reprieve,
If any try to act beyond the law,
To kill them. Then the wicked would be few.

LEADER OF CH. O seed of Atreus! how triumphantly
Through grief and hardness thou hast freedom found,
With full achievement in this onset crowned!

THE TRACHINIAN MAIDENS

THE PERSONS

DÊANIRA, *wife of Heracles.*

An Attendant.

HYLLUS, *son of Heracles and Dêanira.*

CHORUS *of Trachinian Maidens.*

A Messenger.

LICHAS, *the Herald.*

A Nurse.

An Old Man.

HERACLES.

IOLE, *who does not speak.*

SCENE.   Before the temporary abode of Heracles in Trachis.

This tragedy is named from the Chorus. From the subject it might have been called 'Dêanira or the Death of Heracles.'

The Centaur Nessus, in dying by the arrow of Heracles, which had been dipped in the venom of the Hydra, persuaded the bride Dêanira, whose beauty was the cause of his death, to keep some of the blood from the wound as a love-charm for her husband. Many years afterwards, when Heracles was returning from his last exploit of sacking Oechalia, in Euboea, he sent before him, by his herald Lichas, Iŏlè, the king's daughter, whom he had espoused. Dêanira, when she had discovered this, commissioned Lichas when he returned to present his master with a robe, which she had anointed with the charm,—hoping by this means to regain her lord's affection. But the poison of the Hydra did its work, and Heracles died in agony, Dêanira having already killed herself on ascertaining what she had done. The action takes place in Trachis, near the Maliac Gulf, where Heracles and Dêanira, by permission of Ceÿx, the king of the country, have been living in exile. At the close of the drama, Heracles, while yet alive, is carried towards his pyre on Mount Oeta.

THE TRACHINIAN MAIDENS

DÊANIRA. Men say,—'twas old experience gave the
    word,
—'No lot of mortal, ere he die, can once
Be known for good or evil.' But I know,
Before I come to the dark dwelling-place,
Mine is a lot, adverse and hard and sore.
Who yet at Pleuron, in my father's home,
Of all Aetolian women had most cause
To fear my bridal. For a river-god,
Swift Achelôüs, was my suitor there
And sought me from my father in three forms;
Now in his own bull-likeness, now a serpent
Of coiling sheen, and now with manlike build
But bovine front, while from the shadowy beard
Sprang fountain-waters in perpetual spray.
Looking for such a husband, I, poor girl!
Still prayed that Death might find me, ere I knew
That nuptial.—Later, to my glad relief,
Zeus' and Alcmena's glorious offspring came,
And closed with him in conflict, and released
My heart from torment. How the fight was won
I could not tell. If any were who saw
Unshaken of dread foreboding, such may speak.
But I sate quailing with an anguished fear,
Lest beauty might procure me nought but pain,
Till He that rules the issue of all strife,
Gave fortunate end—if fortunate! For since,
Assigned by that day's conquest, I have known
The couch of Heracles, my life is spent
In one continual terror for his fate.
Night brings him, and, ere morning, some fresh toil
Drives him afar. And I have borne him seed;
Which he, like some strange husbandman that farms

C. S.   N

A distant field, finds but at sowing time
And once in harvest. Such a weary life
Still tossed him to and fro,—no sooner home
But forth again, serving I know not whom.

    And when his glorious head had risen beyond
These labours, came the strongest of my fear.
For since he quelled the might of Iphitus,
We here in Trachis dwell, far from our home,
Dependent on a stranger, but where he
Is gone, none knoweth. Only this I know,
His going pierced my heart with pangs for him,
And now I am all but sure he bears some woe.
These fifteen months he hath sent me not one word.
And I have cause for fear. Ere he set forth
He left a scroll with me, whose dark intent
I oft pray Heaven may bring no sorrow down.

    ATTENDANT. Queen Dêanira, many a time ere now
Have I beheld thee with all tearful moan
Bewailing the departure of thy lord.
But, if it be permitted that a slave
Should tender counsel to the free, my voice
May venture this:—Of thy strong band of sons
Why is not one commissioned to explore
For Heracles ? and why not Hyllus first,
Whom most it would beseem to show regard
For tidings of his father's happiness ?
Ah ! here I see him bounding home, with feet
Apt for employment ! If you count me wise,
He and my words attend upon your will.

Enter HYLLUS.

    DÊ. Dear child, dear boy ! even from the lowliest
        head
Wise counsel may come forth. This woman here,
Though a bond-maiden, hath a free-born tongue.

    HYL. What word is spoken, mother ? May I know ?

    DÊ. That, with thy father lost to us so long,
'Tis shame thou dost not learn his dwelling-place.

    HYL. Yea, I have learnt, if one may trust report.

    DÊ. Where art thou told his seat is fixed, my son ?

HYL. 'Tis said that through the length of this past
      year
He wrought as bondman to a Lydian girl.

DÊ. Hath he borne that ? Then nothing can be
      strange !

HYL. Well, that is over, I am told. He is free.

DÊ. Where is he rumoured then, alive or dead ?

HYL. In rich Euboea, besieging, as they tell,
The town of Eurytus, or offering siege.

DÊ. Child, hast thou heard what holy oracles
He left with me, touching that very land ?

HYL. What were they, mother, for I never knew?

DÊ. That either he must end his being there,
Or, this one feat performed, his following time
Should grace his life with fair prosperity.
Wilt thou not then, my child, when he is held
In such a crisis of uncertain peril,
Run to his aid ?—since we must perish with him,
Or owe our lasting safety to his life.

HYL. I will go, mother. Had I heard this voice
Of prophecy, long since I had been there.
Fear is unwonted for our father's lot.
But now I know, my strength shall all be spent
To learn the course of these affairs in full.

DÊ. Go then, my son. Though late, to learn and do
What wisdom bids, hath certainty of gain.

[*Exit* HYLLUS. DÊANIRA *withdraws*

CHORUS (*entering and turning towards the East*).

Born of the starry night in her undoing,   I 1
    Lulled in her bosom at thy parting glow,
        O Sun ! I bid thee show,
What journey is Alcmena's child pursuing ?
        What region holds him now,
    'Mong winding channels of the deep,
    Or Asian plains, or rugged Western steep ?
        Declare it, thou
Peerless in vision of thy flashing ray
That lightens on the world with each new day.

N 2

Sad Dêanira, bride of battle-wooing,   I 2
Ne'er lets her tearful eyelids close in rest,
    But in love-longing breast,
Like some lorn bird its desolation rueing,
    Of her great husband's way
Still mindful, worn with harrowing fear
Lest some new danger for him should be near,
    By night and day
Pines on her widowed couch of ceaseless thought,
With dread of evil destiny distraught :

                         [*Enter* DÊANIRA.

For many as are billows of the South   II 1
Blowing unweariedly, or Northern gale,
One going and another coming on
Incessantly, baffling the gazer's eye,
Such Cretan ocean of unending toil
Cradles our Cadmus-born, and swells his fame.
    But still some power doth his foot recall
    From stumbling down to Hades' darkling hall.

Wherefore, in censure of thy mood, I bring   II 2
Glad, though opposing, counsel. Let not hope
Grow weary. Never hath a painless life
Been cast on mortals by the power supreme
Of the All-disposer, Cronos' son. But joy
And sorrow visit in perpetual round
    All mortals, even as circleth still on high
    The constellation of the Northern sky.

What lasteth in the world ? Not starry night, III
Nor wealth, nor tribulation ; but is gone
All suddenly, while to another soul
The joy or the privation passeth on.
These hopes I bid thee also, O my Queen !
Hold fast continually, for who hath seen
Zeus so forgetful of his own ?
How can his providence forsake his son ?

Dê. I see you have been told of my distress,
And that hath brought you. But my inward woe,
Be it evermore unknown to you, as now !

Such the fair garden of untrammeled ease
Where the young life grows safely. No fierce heat,
No rain, no wind disturbs it, but unharmed
It rises amid airs of peace and joy,
Till maiden turn to matron, and the night
Inherit her dark share of anxious thought,
Haunted with fears for husband or for child.
Then, imaged through her own calamity,
Some one may guess the burden of my life.

Full many have been the sorrows I have wept,
But one above the rest I tell to-day.
When my great husband parted last from home,
He left within the house an ancient scroll
Inscribed with characters of mystic note,
Which Heracles had never heretofore,
In former labours, cared to let me see,—
As bound for bright achievement, not for death.
But now, as though his life had end, he told
What marriage-portion I must keep, what shares
He left his sons out of their father's ground :
And set a time, when fifteen moons were spent,
Counted from his departure, that even then
Or he must die, or if that date were out
And he had run beyond it, he should live
Thenceforth a painless and untroubled life.
Such by Heaven's fiat was the promised end
Of Heracles' long labours, as he said ;
So once the ancient oak-tree had proclaimed
In high Dodona through the sacred Doves.
Of which prediction on this present hour
In destined order of accomplishment
The veritable issue doth depend.
And I, dear friends, while taking rest, will oft
Start from sweet slumbers with a sudden fear,
Scared by the thought, my life may be bereft
Of the best husband in the world of men.

Ch. Hush ! For I see approaching one in haste,
Garlanded, as if laden with good news.

Enter Messenger.

MESSENGER. Queen Dêanira, mine shall be the tongue
To free thee first from fear. Alcmena's child
Is living, be assured, and triumphing,
And bringing to our Gods the fruits of war.
    Dê. What mean'st thou, aged sir, by what thou
        sayest ?
    MESS. That soon thy husband, envied all around,
Will come, distinguished with victorious might.
    Dê. What citizen or stranger told thee this ?
    MESS. Your herald Lichas, where the oxen graze
The summer meadow, cries this to a crowd.
I, hearing, flew off hither, that being first
To bring thee word thereof, I might be sure
To win reward and gratitude from thee.
    Dê. And how is he not here, if all be well ?
    MESS. Crossed by no light impediment, my Queen.
For all the Maliac people, gathering round,
Throng him with question, that he cannot move.
But he must still the travail of each soul,
And none will be dismissed unsatisfied.
Such willing audience he unwillingly
Harangues, but soon himself will come in sight.
    Dê. O Zeus ! who rulest Oeta's virgin wold,
At last, though late, thou hast vouchsafed us joy.
Lift up your voices, O my women ! ye
Within the halls, and ye beyond the gate !
For now we reap the gladness of a ray,
That dawns unhoped for in this rumour's sound.

CHORUS.

With a shout by the hearth let the palace-roof ring
  From those that are dreaming of bridal ; and ye,
Young men, let your voices in harmony sing
  To the God of the quiver, the Lord of the free !
And the Paean withal from the maiden band
To Artemis, huntress of many a land,
    Let it rise o'er the glad roof-tree,

To Phoebus' own sister, with fire in each hand,
 And the Nymphs that her co-mates be!
My spirit soars. O sovereign of my soul!
I will accept the thrilling flute's control. [*They dance*
 The ivy-crownèd thyrsus, see!
 With Bacchic fire is kindling me,
 And turns my emulous tread
 Where'er the mazy dance may lead.
Euoî! Euoî!
O Paean! send us joy.
See, dearest Queen, behold!
Before thy gaze the event will now unfold.

Dê. Think not mine eye hath kept such careless
 guard,
Dear maids, that I could miss this moving train.
Herald, I bid thee hail, although so late
Appearing, if thou bringest health with thee!

Enter LICHAS, *with* Captive Women.

LICHAS. A happy welcome on a happy way,
As prosperous our achievement. Meet it is
Good words should greet bright actions, mistress mine!
 Dê. Kind friend, first tell me what I first would
 know—
Shall I receive my Heracles alive?
 LICH. I left him certainly alive and strong:
Blooming in health, not with disease oppressed.
 Dê. In Greece, or in some barbarous country?
 Tell!
 LICH. Euboea's island hath a promontory,
Where to Cenaean Zeus he consecrates
Rich altars and the tribute of the ground.
 Dê. Moved by an oracle, or from some vow?
 LICH. So vowed he when he conquered with the
 spear
The country of these women whom you see.
 Dê. And who, by Heaven, are they? Who was their
 sire?
Their case is piteous, or eludes my thought.

LICH. He took them for the service of the Gods
And his own house, when high Oechalia fell.

DÊ. Was't then before that city he was kept
Those endless ages of uncounted time?

LICH. Not so. The greater while he was detained
Among the Lydians, sold, as he declares,
To bondage. Nor be jealous of the word,
Since Heaven, my Queen, was author of the deed.
Enthrallèd so to Asian Omphalè,
He, as himself avers, fulfilled his year.
The felt reproach whereof so chafed his soul,
He bound fierce curses on himself and sware
That,—children, wife and all,—he yet would bring
In captive chains the mover of this harm.
Nor did this perish like an idle word,
But, when the stain was off him, straight he drew
Allied battalions to assault the town
Of Eurytus, whom, sole of earthly powers,
He had noted as the source of his annoy,
Because, having received him in his hall
A guest of ancient days, he burst on him
With outrage of loud voice and villanous mind,
Saying, 'with his hand upon the unerring bow,
Oechalia's princes could o'ershoot his skill;
And born to bondage, he must quail beneath
His overlord'; lastly, to crown this cry,
When at a banquet he was filled with wine,
He flung him out of door. Whereat being wroth,
When Iphitus to the Tirynthian height
Followed the track where his brood-mares had strayed,
He, while the thought and eye of the man by chance
Were sundered, threw him from the tower-crowned cliff.
In anger for which deed the Olympian King,
Father of Gods and men, delivered him
To be a bond-slave, nor could brook the offence,
That of all lives he vanquished, this alone
Should have been ta'en by guile. For had he wrought
In open quittance of outrageous wrong,
Even Zeus had granted that his cause was just.
The braggart hath no favour even in Heaven.

Whence they, o'erweening with their evil tongue,
Are now all dwellers in the house of death,
Their ancient city a captive ;—but these women
Whom thou beholdest, from their blest estate
Brought suddenly to taste of piteous woe,
Come to thy care. This task thy wedded lord
Ordained, and I, his faithful minister,
Seek to perform. But, for his noble self,
When with pure hands he hath done sacrifice
To his Great Father for the victory given,
Look for his coming, lady. This last word
Of all my happy speech is far most sweet.

CH. Now surety of delight is thine, my Queen,
Part by report and part before thine eye.

Dê. Yea, now I learn this triumph of my lord,
Joy reigns without a rival in my breast.
This needs must run with that in fellowship.
Yet wise consideration even of good
Is flecked with fear of what reverse may come.
And I, dear friends, when I behold these maids,
Am visited with sadness deep and strange.
Poor friendless beings, in a foreign land
Wandering forlorn in homeless orphanhood !
Erewhile, free daughters of a freeborn race,
Now, snared in strong captivity for life.
O Zeus of battles, breaker of the war,
Ne'er may I see thee turn against my seed
So cruelly ; or, if thou meanest so,
Let me be spared that sorrow by my death !
Such fear in me the sight of these hath wrought.
Who art thou, of all damsels most distressed ?
Single or child-bearing ? Thy looks would say,
A maid, of no mean lineage. Lichas, tell,
Who is the stranger-nymph ? Who gave her birth ?
Who was her sire ? Mine eye hath pitied her
O'er all, as she o'er all hath sense of woe.

LICH. What know I ? Why should'st thou demand ?
Perchance
Not lowest in the list of souls there born.

Dê. How if a princess, offspring of their King ?

LICH. I cannot tell. I did not question far.

DÊ. Have none of her companions breathed her
name?

LICH. I brought them silently. I did not hear.

DÊ. Yet speak it to us of thyself, poor maid!
'Tis sorrow not to know thee who thou art.

LICH. She'll ne'er untie her tongue, if she maintain
An even tenor, since nor more nor less
Would she disclose; but, poor unfortunate!
With agonizing sobs and tears she mourns
This crushing sorrow, from the day she left
Her wind-swept home. Her case is cruel, sure,—
And claims a privilege from all who feel.

DÊ. Well, let her go, and pass beneath the roof
In peace, as she desires; nor let fresh pain
From me be added to her previous woe.
She hath enough already. Come, away!
Let's all within at once, that thou mayest speed
Thy journey, and I may order all things here.

[*Exit* LICHAS, *with* Captives, *into the house.*
DÊANIRA *is about to follow them*

Re-enter Messenger.

MESS. Pause first there on the threshold, till you
learn
(Apart from those) who 'tis you take within,
And more besides that you yet know not of,
Which deeply imports your knowing. Of all this
I throughly am informed.

DÊ.   What cause hast thou
Thus to arrest my going?

MESS.   Stand, and hear.
Not idle was my former speech, nor this.

DÊ. Say, must we call them back in presence here,
Or would'st thou tell thy news to these and me?

MESS. To thee and these I may, but let those be.

DÊ. Well, they are gone. Let words declare thy drift.

MESS. That man, in all that he hath lately said,
Hath sinned against the truth: or now he's false,
Or else unfaithful in his first report.

DÊ. What ? Tell me thy full meaning clearly forth.
That thou hast uttered is all mystery.

MESS. I heard this herald say, while many thronged
To hearken, that this maiden was the cause,
Why lofty-towered Oechalia and her lord
Fell before Heracles, whom Love alone
Of heavenly powers had warmed to this emprise,
And not the Lydian thraldom or the tasks
Of rigorous Omphalè, nor that wild fate
Of rock-thrown Iphitus. Now he thrusts aside
The Love-god, contradicting his first tale.

When he that was her sire could not be brought
To yield the maid for Heracles to hold
In love unrecognized, he framed erelong
A feud about some trifle, and set forth
In arms against this damsel's fatherland
(Where Eurytus, the herald said, was king)
And slew the chief her father ; yea, and sacked
Their city. Now returning, as you see,
He sends her hither to his halls, no slave,
Nor unregarded, lady,—dream not so !
Since all his heart is kindled with desire.
I, O my Queen ! thought meet to show thee all
The tale I chanced to gather from his mouth,
Which many heard as well as I, i' the midst
Of Trachis' market-place, and can confirm
My witness. I am pained if my plain speech
Sound harshly, but the honest truth I tell.

DÊ. Ah me ! Where am I ? Whither am I
        fallen ?
What hidden woe have I unwarily
Taken beneath my roof ? O misery !
Was she unknown, as he that brought her sware ?

MESS. Nay, most distinguished both in birth and
        mien ;
Called in her day of freedom Iolè,
Eurytus' daughter,—of whose parentage,
Forsooth as ignorant, he ne'er would speak.

CH. I curse not all the wicked, but the man
Whose secret practices deform his life.

Dê. Say, maidens, how must I proceed ? The words
Now spoken have bewildered all my mind.

Ch. Go in and question Lichas, who perchance
Will tell the truth if you but tax him home.

Dê. I will ; you counsel reasonably.

Mess.   And I,
Shall I bide here till thou com'st forth ? Or how ?

Dê. Remain. For see, without my sending for him,
He issueth from the palace of himself.

Enter LICHAS.

Lich. What message must I carry to my lord ?
Tell me, my Queen. I am going, as thou seëst.

Dê. So slow in coming, and so quickly flown,
Ere one have time to talk with thee anew !

Lich. What wouldst thou ask me ? I am bent to
              hear.

Dê. And art thou bent on truth in the reply ?

Lich. By Heaven ! in all that I have knowledge of.

Dê. Then tell me, who is she thou brought'st with
              thee ?

Lich. An islander. I cannot trace her stock.

Mess. Look hither, man. Who is't to whom thou
              speakest ?

Lich. Why such a question ? What is thine intent ?

Mess. Nay, start not, but make answer if thou
              knowest.

Lich. To Dêanira, Oeneus' queenly child,
Heracles' wife,—if these mine eyes be true,—
My mistress.

Mess.   Ay, that is the very word
I longed to hear thee speak. Thy mistress, sayest ?

Lich. To whom I am bound.

Mess.   Hold there ! What punishment
Wilt thou accept, if thou art found to be
Faithless to her ?

Lich.   I faithless ! What dark speech
Hast thou contrived ?

Mess.   Not I at all. 'Tis thou
Dost wrap thy thoughts i' the dark.

LICH.   Well, I will go.
'Tis folly to have heard thee for so long.
    MESS. You go not till you answer one word more.
    LICH. One, or a thousand! You'll not stint, I see.
    MESS. Thou knowest the captive maid thou leddest
        home?
    LICH. I do. But wherefore ask?
    MESS.   Did you not say
That she, on whom you look with ignorant eye,
Was Iolè, the daughter of the King,
Committed to your charge?
    LICH.   Where? Among whom?
What witness of such words will bear thee out?
    MESS. Many and sound. A goodly company
In Trachis' market-place heard thee speak this.
    LICH. Ay.
I said 'twas rumoured. But I could not give
My vague impression for advised report.
    MESS. Impression, quotha! Did you not on oath
Proclaim your captive for your master's bride?
    LICH. My master's bride! Dear lady, by the Gods,
Who is the stranger? for I know him not.
    MESS. One who was present where he heard thee tell,
How that whole city was subdued and taken,
Not for the bondage to the Lydian girl,
But through the longing passion for this maid.
    LICH. Dear lady, let the fellow be removed.
To prate with madmen is mere foolishness.
    DÉ. Nay, I entreat thee by His name, whose fire
Lightens down Oeta's topmost glen, be not
A niggard of the truth. Thou tell'st thy tale
To no weak woman, but to one who knows
Mankind are never constant to one joy.
Whoso would buffet Love, aspires in vain.
For Love leads even Immortals at his will,
And me. Then how not others, like to me?
'Twere madness, sure, in me to blame my lord
When this hath caught him, or the woman there,
His innocent accomplice in a thing,
No shame to either, and no harm to me.

It is not so. But if from him thou learnest
The lore of falsehood, it were best unlearnt ;
Or if the instruction comes of thine own thought,
Such would-be kindness doth not prove thee kind.
Then tell me all the truth. To one free-born
The name of liar is a hateful lot.
And thou canst not be hid. Thy news was heard
By many, who will tell me. If thou fearest,
Thou hast no cause—for doubtfulness is pain,
But to know all, what harm ? His loves ere now
Were they not manifold ? And none hath borne
Reproach or evil word from me. She shall not,
Though his new passion were as strong as death ;
Since most mine eye hath pitied her, because
Her beauty was the ruin of her life,
And all unweeting, she her own bright land,
Poor hapless one ! hath ravaged and enslaved.—
Let that be as it must. But for thy part,
Though false to others, be still true to me.

CH. 'Tis fairly said. Comply. Thou ne'er wilt blame
Her faithfulness, and thou wilt earn our loves.

LICH. Yea, dear my Queen, now I have seen thee
hold
Thy mortal wishes within mortal bound
So meekly, I will freely tell thee all.
It is as he avers. This maiden's love,
Piercing through Heracles, was the sole cause,
Why her Oechalia, land of plenteous woe,
Was made the conquest of his spear. And he—
For I dare so far clear him—never bade
Concealment or denial. But myself,
Fearing the word might wound thy queenly heart,
Sinned, if thou count such tenderness a sin.
But now that all is known, for both your sakes,
His, and thine own no less, look favouringly
Upon the woman, and confirm the word
Thou here hast spoken in regard to her :—
For he, whose might is in all else supreme,
Is wholly overmastered by her love.

DÊ. Yea, so my mind is bent. I will do so.

I will not, in a bootless strife 'gainst Heaven,
Augment my misery with self-sought ill.
Come, go we in, that thou may'st bear from me
Such message as is meet, and also carry
Gifts, such as are befitting to return
For gifts new-given. Thou ought'st not to depart
Unladen, having brought so much with thee.

[*Exeunt*

CHORUS.

Victorious in her might,   I 1
    The Queen of soft delight
Still ranges onward with triumphant sway.
    What she from Kronos' son
    And strong Poseidon won,
And Pluto, King of Night, I durst not say.

    But who, to earn this bride,
    Came forth in sinewy pride
To strive, or e'er the nuptial might be known
    With fearless heart I tell
    What heroes wrestled well,
With showering blows, and dust in clouds up-
        thrown.

    One was a river bold,   I 2
    Horn-crowned, with tramp fourfold,
Bull Achelöüs, Acarnania's Fear ;
    And one from Bacchus' town,
    Own son of Zeus, came down,
With brandished mace, bent bow, and barbèd
        spear.

    Who then in battle brunt,
    Together, front to front,
Hurled, eager both to win the beauteous prize ;
    And Cypris 'mid the fray
    Alone, that dreadful day,
Sate umpire, holding promise in her eyes.

Then clashed the fist, then clanged the bow ;   II
Then horns gave crashing blow for blow,
    Whilst, as they clung,

The twining hip-throw both essay
And hurtling foreheads' fearful play,
    And groans from each were wrung.

But the tender fair one far away
    Sate watching with an eye of piteous cheer,
(A mother's heart will heed the thing I say,)
    Till won by him who freed her from her fear.
Sudden she leaves her mother's gentle side,
Borne through the waste, our hero's tender bride.

Enter DÊANIRA.

Dê. Dear friends, while yonder herald in the house
Holds converse with the captives ere he go,
I have stol'n forth to you, partly to tell
The craft my hand hath compassed, and in part,
To crave your pity for my wretchedness.
For I have taken to my hearth a maid,—
And yet, methinks, no maiden any more,
Like some fond shipmaster, taking on board
A cargo fraught with treason to my heart.
And now we two are closed in one embrace
Beneath one coverlet. Such generous meed
For faith in guarding home this dreary while
Hath the kind Heracles, our trusty spouse,
Sent in return ! Yet, oft as he hath caught
This same distemperature, I know not how
To harbour indignation against him.
But who that is a woman could endure
To dwell with her, both married to one man ?
One bloom is still advancing, one doth fade.
The budding flower is cropped ; the full-blown head
Is left to wither, while love passeth by
Unheeding. Wherefore I am sore afraid
He will be called my husband, but her mate,
For she is younger. Yet no prudent wife
Would take this angerly, as I have said.
But, dear ones, I will tell you of a way,
Whereof I have bethought me, to prevent
This heart-break. I had hidden of long time

In a bronze urn the ancient Centaur's gift,
Which I, when a mere girl, culled from the wound
Of hairy-breasted Nessus in his death.
He o'er Evenus' rolling depths, for hire,
Ferried wayfarers on his arm, not plying
Or rowing-boat, or canvas-wingèd bark.
Who, when with Heracles, a new-made bride,
I followed by my father's sending forth,
Shouldering me too, in the mid-stream, annoyed
With wanton touch. And I cried out; and he,
Zeus' son, turned suddenly, and from his bow
Sent a wing'd shaft, that whizzed into his chest
To the lungs. Then the weird Thing, with dying
                    voice
Spake to me:—'Child of agèd Oeneüs,
Since thou wert my last burden, thou shalt win
Some profit from mine act, if thou wilt do
What now I bid thee. With a careful hand
Collect and bear away the clotted gore
That clogs my wound, e'en where the monster snake
Had dyed the arrow with dark tinct of gall;
And thou shalt have this as a charm of soul
For Heracles, that never through the eye
Shall he receive another love than thine.'
Whereof bethinking me, for since his death
I kept it in a closet locked with care,
I have applied it to this robe, with such
Addition as his living voice ordained.—
The thing is done. No criminal attempts
Could e'er be mine. Far be they from my thought,
As I abhor the woman who conceives them!
But if by any means through gentle spells
And bonds on Heracles' affection, we
May triumph o'er this maiden in his heart,
My scheme is perfected. Unless you deem
Mine action wild. If so, I will desist.

  Ch. If any ground of confidence approve
Thine act, we cannot check thy counsel here.

  Dê. My confidence is grounded on belief,
Though unconfirmed as yet by actual proof.

CH. Well, do it and try. Assurance cannot come
Till action bring experience after it.
Dê. The truth will soon be known. The man e'en
    now
Is coming forth, and quickly will be there.
Screen ye but well my counsel. Doubtful deeds,
Wrapt close, will not deliver us to shame.

Enter LICHAS.

LICH. Daughter of Oeneus, tell me thy commands.
Already time rebukes our tardiness.
Dê. Even that hath been my care, Lichas, while thou
Wert talking to the stranger-maids within,
That thou shouldst take for me this finewoven web,
A present from these fingers to my lord.
And when thou giv'st it, say that none of men
Must wear it on his shoulders before him ;
And neither light of sun may look upon it,
Nor holy temple-court, nor household flame,
Till he in open station 'fore the Gods
Display it on a day when bulls are slaughtered.
So once I vowed, that should I ever see
Or hear his safe return, I would enfold
His glorious person in this robe, and show
To all the Gods in doing sacrifice
Him a fresh worshipper in fresh array.—
The truth hereof he will with ease descry
Betokened on this treasure-guarding seal.—
Now go, and be advised, of this in chief,
To act within thine office ; then of this,
To bear thee so, that from his thanks and mine
Meeting in one, a twofold grace may spring.
LICH. If this my Hermes-craft be firm and sure,
Then never will I fail thee, O my Queen !
But I will show the casket as it is
To whom I bear it, and in faithfulness
Add all the words thou sendest in fit place.
Dê. Go, then, at once. Thou hast full cognizance
How things within the palace are preserved ?
LICH. I know, and will declare. There is no flaw.

Dê. Methinks thou knowest too, for thou hast seen,
My kind reception of the stranger-maid ?

LICH. I saw, and was amazed with heart-struck joy.

Dê. What more is there to tell ?—Too rash, I fear,
Were thy report of longing on my part,
Till we can learn if we be longed for there.

[Exeunt severally

CHORUS.

O ye that haunt the strand   I 1
    Where ships in quiet land
Near Oeta's height and the warm rock-drawn well,
And ye round Melis' inland gulf who dwell,
Worshipping her who wields the golden wand,—
(There Hellas' wisest meet in council strong):
    Soon shall the flute arise
    With sound of glad surprise,
Thrilling your sense with no unwelcome song,
But tones that to the harp of Heavenly Muse belong.

Zeus' and Alcmena's son,—   I 2
    All deeds of glory done,—
Speeds now triumphant to his home, whom we
Twelve weary months of blind expectancy
Lost in vast distance, from our country gone.
While, sadly languishing, his loving wife,
    Still flowing down with tears,
    Pined with unnumbered fears.
But Ares, lately stung to furious strife,
Frees him for ever from the toilsome life.

O let him come to-day !   II
    Ne'er may his vessel stay,
But glide with feathery sweep of many an oar,
Till from his altar by yon island shore
Even to our town he wind his prosperous way,
    In mien returning mild,
    And inly reconciled,
With that anointing in his heart ingrained,
Which the dark Centaur's wizard lips ordained.

o 2

Enter Dêanira.

Dê. O how I fear, my friends, lest all too far
I have ventured in my action of to-day!
  Ch. What ails thee, Dêanira, Oeneus' child?
  Dê. I know not, but am haunted by a dread,
Lest quickly I be found to have performed
A mighty mischief, through bright hopes betrayed.
  Ch. Thou dost not mean thy gift to Heracles?
  Dê. Indeed I do. Now I perceive how fond
Is eagerness, where actions are obscure.
  Ch. Tell, if it may be told, thy cause of fear.
  Dê. A thing is come to pass, which should I tell,
Will strike you with strange wonder when you learn.
For, O my friends, the stuff wherewith I dressed
That robe, a flock of soft and milkwhite wool,
Is shrivelled out of sight, not gnawn by tooth
Of any creature here, but, self-consumed,
Frittered and wasting on the courtyard-stones.
    To let you know the circumstance at full,
I will speak on. Of all the Centaur-Thing,
When labouring in his side with the fell point
O' the shaft, enjoined me, I had nothing lost,
But his vaticination in my heart
Remained indelible, as though engraved
With pen of iron upon brass. 'Twas thus:—
I was to keep this unguent closely hid
In dark recesses, where no heat of fire
Or warming ray might reach it, till with fresh
Anointing I addressed it to an end.
So I had done. And now this was to do,
Within my chamber covertly I spread
The ointment with piece of wool, a tuft
Pulled from a home-bred sheep; and, as ye saw,
I folded up my gift and packed it close
In hollow casket from the glaring sun.
But, entering in, a fact encounters me
Past human wit to fathom with surmise.
For, as it happened, I had tossed aside
The bit of wool I worked with, carelessly,

Into the open daylight, 'mid the blaze
Of Helios' beam. And, as it kindled warm,
It fell away to nothing, crumbled small,
Like dust in severing wood by sawyers strewn.
So, on the point of vanishing, it lay.
But, from the place where it had lain, brake forth
A frothy scum in clots of seething foam,
Like the rich draught in purple vintage poured
From Bacchus' vine upon the thirsty ground.
And I, unhappy, know not toward what thought
To turn me, but I see mine act is dire.
For wherefore should the Centaur, for what end,
Show kindness to the cause for whom he died?
That cannot be. But seeking to destroy
His slayer, he cajoled me. This I learn
Too late, by sad experience, for no good.
And, if I err not now, my hapless fate
Is all alone to be his murderess.
For, well I know, the shaft that made the wound
Gave pain to Cheiron, who was more than man;
And wheresoe'er it falls, it ravageth
All the wild creatures of the world. And now
This gory venom blackly spreading bane
From Nessus' angry wound, must it not cause
The death of Heracles? I think it must.
   Yet my resolve is firm, if aught harm him,
My death shall follow in the self-same hour.
She cannot bear to live in evil fame,
Who cares to have a nature pure from ill.

CH. Horrid mischance must needs occasion fear.
But Hope is not condemned before the event.

Dê. In ill-advised proceeding not even Hope
Remains to minister a cheerful mind.

CH. Yet to have erred unwittingly abates
The fire of wrath; and thou art in this case.

Dê. So speaks not he who hath a share of sin,
But who is clear of all offence at home.

CH. 'Twere well to say no more, unless thou hast aught
To impart to thine own son: for he is here,
Who went erewhile to find his father forth.

HYLLUS (*re-entering*).

O mother, mother!
I would to heaven one of three things were true:
Either that thou wert dead, or, living, wert
No mother to me, or hadst gained a mind
Furnished with better thoughts than thou hast now!

 Dê. My son! what canst thou so mislike in me?

 Hyl. I tell thee thou this day hast been the death
Of him that was thy husband and my sire.

 Dê. What word hath passed thy lips? my child, my
   child!

 Hyl. A word that must be verified. For who
Can make the accomplished fact as things undone?

 Dê. Alas, my son! what saidst thou? Who hath
   told
That I have wrought a deed so full of woe?

 Hyl. 'Twas I myself that saw with these mine eyes
My father's heavy state:—no hearsay word.

 Dê. And where didst thou come near him and stand
   by?

 Hyl. Art thou to hear it? On, then, with my tale!
When after sacking Eurytus' great city
He marched in triumph with first-fruits of war,—
There is a headland, last of long Euboea,
Surf-beat Cenaeum,—where to his father Zeus
He dedicates high altars and a grove.
There first I saw him, gladdened from desire.
And when he now addressed him to the work
Of various sacrifice, the herald Lichas
Arrived from home, bearing thy fatal gift,
The deadly robe: wherewith invested straight,
As thou hadst given charge, he sacrificed
The firstlings of the spoil, twelve bulls entire,
Each after each. But the full count he brought
Was a clear hundred of all kinds of head.
 Then the all-hapless one commenced his prayer
In solemn gladness for the bright array.
But presently, when from the holy things,
And from the richness of the oak-tree core,

There issued flame mingled with blood, a sweat
Rose on his flesh, and close to every limb
Clung, like stone-drapery from the craftsman's hand,
The garment, glued unto his side. Then came
The tearing pangs within his bones, and then
The poison feasted like the venomed tooth
Of murderous basilisk.—When this began,
He shouted on poor Lichas, none to blame
For thy sole crime, 'What guile is here, thou knave ?
What was thy fraud in fetching me this robe ? '
He, all-unknowing, in an evil hour
Declared his message, that the gift was thine.
Whereat the hero, while the shooting spasm
Had fastened on the lungs, seized him by the foot
Where the ankle turns i' the socket, and, with a thought,
Hurl'd on a surf-vex'd reef that showed i' the sea :
And rained the grey pulp from the hair, the brain
Being scattered with the blood.   Then the great throng
Saddened their festival with piteous wail
For one in death and one in agony.
And none had courage to approach my sire,—
Convulsed upon the ground, then tossed i' the air
With horrid yells and crying, till the cliffs
Echoed round, the mountain-promontories
Of Locris, and Euboea's rugged shore.
Wearied at length with flinging on the earth,
And shrieking oft with lamentable cry,
Cursing the fatal marriage with thyself
The all-wretched, and the bond to Oeneus' house,
That prize that was the poisoner of his peace,
He lifted a wild glance above the smoke
That hung around, and 'midst the crowd of men
Saw me in tears, and looked on me and said,
' O son, come near ; fly not from my distress,
Though thou shouldst be consumèd in my death,
But lift and bear me forth ; and, if thou mayest,
Set me where no one of mankind shall see me.
But if thy heart withhold thee, yet convey me
Out of this land as quickly as ye may.
Let me not die where I am now.' We then,

Thus urgently commanded, laid him down
Within our bark, and hardly to this shore
Rowed him convulsed and roaring.—Presently,
He will appear, alive or lately dead.

Such, mother, is the crime thou hast devised
And done against our sire, wherefore let Right
And Vengeance punish thee!—May I pray so?
I may: for thou absolv'st me by thy deed,
Thou that hast slain the noblest of the Earth,
Thy spouse, whose like thou ne'er wilt see again.

[*Exit* DÈANIRA.

CH. Why steal'st thou forth in silence? Know'st
       thou not
Thy silence argues thine accuser's plea?

HYL. Let her go off. Would that a sudden flood
Might sweep her far and swiftly from mine eye!
Why fondle vainly the fair-sounding name
Of mother, when her acts are all unmotherly?
Let her begone for me: and may she find
Such joy as she hath rendered to my sire!

[*Exit* HYLLUS

CHORUS.

See where falls the doom, of old   I 1
   By the unerring Voice foretold,—
'When twelve troublous years have rolled,
  Then shall end your long desire:
  Toil on toil no more shall tire
  The offspring of the Eternal Sire.'
  Lo! the destined Hour is come!
  Lo! it hath brought its burden home.
For when the eyes have looked their last
How should sore labour vex again?
How, when the powers of will and thought are past,
Should life be any more enthralled to pain?

  And if Nessus' withering shroud,   I 2
  Wrought by destiny and craft,
  Steep him in a poisonous cloud
  Steaming from the venomed shaft,

Which to Death in hideous lair
The many-wreathed Hydra bare,
How shall he another day
Feel the glad warmth of Helios' ray ?—
Enfolded by the Monster-Thing
Of Lerna, while the cruel sting
Of the shagg'd Centaur's murderous-guileful tongue
Breaks forth withal to do him painful wrong.

And she, poor innocent, who saw   II 1
    Checkless advancing to the gate
    A mighty harm unto her state,—
This rash young bridal without fear of law,—
Gave not her will to aught that caused this woe,
    But since it came through that strange mind's
       conceiving,—
    That ruined her in meeting,—deeply grieving,
She mourns with dewy tears in tenderest flow.
The approaching hour appeareth great with woe :
Some guile-born misery doth Fate foreshow.

The springs of sorrow are unbound,   II 2
    And such an agony disclose,
    As never from the hands of foes
To afflict the life of Heracles was found.
O dark with battle-stains, world-champion spear,
    That from Oechalia's highland leddest then
    This bride that followed swiftly in thy train,
How fatally overshadowing was thy fear !
But these wild sorrows all too clearly come
From Love's dread minister, disguised and dumb.

CH. 1. Am I a fool, or do I truly hear
Lament new-rising from our master's home ?
Tell !
    CH. 2. Clearly from within a wailing voice
Peals piteously. The house hath some fresh woe.
    CH. 3. Mark !
How strangely, with what cloud upon her brow,
Yon aged matron with her tidings moves !

Enter Nurse.

NURSE. Ah! mighty, O my daughters! was the grief
Sprung from the gift to Heracles conveyed!

LEADER OF CH. What new thing is befallen? Why
   speak'st thou so?

NUR. Our Queen hath found her latest journey's end.
Even now she is gone, without the help of feet.

CH. Not dead?

NUR.   You know the whole.

CH.   Dead! hapless Queen!

NUR. The truth hath twice been told.

CH.   O tell us how!
What was her death, poor victim of dire woe?

NUR. Most ruthless was the deed.

CH.   Say, woman, say!
What was the sudden end?

NUR.   Herself she slew.

CH. What rage, what madness, clutched
The mischief-working brand?
How could her single thought
Contrive the accomplishment of death on death?

NUR. Chill iron stopped the sources of her breath.

CH. And thou, poor helpless crone, didst see this
   done?

NUR. Yea, I stood near and saw.

CH.   How was it? Tell!

NUR. With her own hand this violence was given.

CH. What do I hear?

NUR.   The certainty of truth.

CH. A child is come,
From this new bridal that hath rushed within,
A fresh-born Fury of woe!

NUR. Too true. But hadst thou been at hand to see
Her action, pity would have wrung thy soul.

CH. Could this be ventured by a woman's hand?

NUR. Ay, and in dreadful wise, as thou shalt hear.
When all alone she had gone within the gate,
And passing through the court beheld her boy
Spreading the couch that should receive his sire,

Ere he returned to meet him,—out of sight
She hid herself, and fell at the altar's foot,
And loudly cried that she was left forlorn ;
And, taking in her touch each household thing
That formerly she used, poor lady, wept
O'er all ; and then went ranging through the rooms,
Where, if there caught her eye the well-loved form
Of any of her household, she would gaze
And weep aloud, accusing her own fate
And her abandoned lot, childless henceforth !
When this was ended, suddenly I see her
Fly to the hero's room of genial rest.
With unsuspected gaze o'ershadowed near,
I watched, and saw her casting on the bed
The finest sheets of all. When that was done,
She leapt upon the couch where they had lain
And sat there in the midst. And the hot flood
Burst from her eyes before she spake :—' Farewell,
My bridal bed, for never more shalt thou
Give me the comfort I have known thee give.'
Then with tight fingers she undid her robe,
Where the brooch lay before the breast, and bared
All her left arm and side. I, with what speed
Strength ministered, ran forth to tell her son
The act she was preparing. But meanwhile,
Ere we could come again, the fatal blow
Fell, and we saw the wound. And he, her boy,
Seeing, wept aloud. For now the hapless youth
Knew that himself had done this in his wrath,
Told all too late i' the house, how she had wrought
Most innocently, from the Centaur's wit.
So now the unhappy one, with passionate words
And cries and wild embracings of the dead,
Groaned forth that he had slain her with false breath
Of evil accusation, and was left
Orphaned of both, his mother and his sire.

    Such is the state within. What fool is he
That counts one day, or two, or more to come !
To-morrow is not, till the present day
In fair prosperity have passed away.   [*Exit*

CHORUS.

Which shall come first in my wail,   I 1
Which shall be last to prevail,
Is a doubt that will never be done.

Trouble at home may be seen,   I 2
Trouble is looked for with teen ;
And to have and to look for are one.

Would some fair wind   II 1
But waft me forth to roam
Far from the native region of my home,
Ere death me find, oppressed with wild affright
Even at the sudden sight
Of him, the valiant son of Zeus most High !
Before the house, they tell, he fareth nigh,
A wonder beyond thought,
With torment unapproachable distraught.

Hark ! . . . .   II 2
The cause then of my cry
Was coming all too nigh :
(Doth the clear nightingale lament for nought ?)
Some step of stranger folk is this way brought.
As for a friend they love
Heavy and slow with noiseless feet they move.
Which way ? which way ? Ah me ! behold him
          come.
His pallid lips are dumb.
Dead, or at rest in sleep ? What shall I say ?
          [HERACLES *is brought in on a litter, accom-*
                    panied by HYLLUS *and an* Old Man

HYL. Oh, woe is me !
My father, piteous woe for thee !
Oh, whither shall I turn my thought ! Ah me !
  OLD M. Hush ! speak not, O my child,
Lest torment fierce and wild
Rekindle in thy father's rugged breast,
And break this rest

Where now his life is held at point to fall.
With firm lips clenched refrain thy voice through all.
    HYL. Yet tell me, doth he live,
Old sir ?
    OLD M. Wake not the slumberer,
Nor kindle and revive
The terrible recurrent power of pain,
My son !
    HYL. My foolish words are done,
But my full heart sinks 'neath the heavy strain.

    HERACLES. O Father, who are these ?
What countrymen ? Where am I ? What far land
Holds me in pain that ceaseth not ? Ah me !
Again that pest is rending me. Pain, pain !
    OLD M. Now thou may'st know
'Twas better to have lurked in silent shade
And not thus widely throw
The slumber from his eyelids and his head.
    HYL. I could not brook
All speechless on his misery to look.

MONODY.

    HER. O altar on the Euboean strand,
High-heaped with offerings from my hand,
What meed for lavish gifts bestowed
From thy new sanctuary hath flowed !
Father of Gods ! thy cruel power
Hath foiled me with an evil blight.
Ah ! would mine eyes had closed in night
Ere madness in a fatal hour
Had burst upon them with a blaze,
No help or soothing once allays !

What hand to heal, what voice to charm,
Can e'er dispel this hideous harm ?
Whose skill save thine,
Monarch Divine ?
Mine eyes, if such I saw,
Would hail him from afar with trembling awe.

Ah ! ah !
O vex me not, touch me not, leave me to rest,
To sleep my last sleep on Earth's gentle breast.
You touch me, you press me, you turn me again,
You break me, you kill me ! O pain ! O pain !
You have kindled the pang that had slumbered still.
It comes, it hath seized me with tyrannous will !

Where are ye, men, whom over Hellas wide
This arm hath freed, and o'er the ocean-tide,
And through rough brakes, from every monstrous
          thing ?
Yet now in mine affliction none will bring
A sword to aid, a fire to quell this fire,
O most unrighteous ! nor to my desire
Will come and quench the hateful life I hold
With mortal stroke ! Ah ! is there none so bold ?

OLD M. Son of our hero, this hath mounted past
My feeble force to cope with. Take him thou !
Fresher thine eye and more the hope thou hast
Than mine to save him.
HYL.   I support him now
Thus with mine arm : but neither fleshly vest
Nor inmost spirit can I lull to rest
From torture. None may dream
To wield this power, save he, the King supreme.

HER. Son !
Where art thou to lift me and hold me aright ?
It tears me, it kills me, it rushes in might,
This cruel, devouring, unconquered pain
Shoots forth to consume me. Again ! again !
O Fate ! O Athena !—O son, at my word
Have pity and slay me with merciful sword !

Pity thy father, boy ; with sharp relief
Smite on my breast, and heal the wrathful grief
Wherewith thy mother, God-abandoned wife,
Hath wrought this ruin on her husband's life.
O may I see her falling, even so
As she hath thrown me, to like depth of woe !

Sweet Hades, with swift death,
Brother of Zeus, release my suffering breath!

CH. Horror hath caught me as I hear this woe,
Racking our mighty one with mightier pain.

HER. Many hot toils and hard beyond report,
With sturdy thews and sinews I have borne.
But no such labour hath the Thunderer's wife
Or sour Eurystheus ever given, as this,
Which Oeneus' daughter of the treacherous eye
Hath fastened on my back, this amply-woven
Net of the Furies, that is breaking me.
For, glued unto my side, it hath devoured
My flesh to the bone, and lodging in the lungs
It drains the vital channels, and hath drunk
The fresh life-blood, and ruins all my frame,
Foiled in the tangle of a viewless bond.
Yet me nor War-host, nor Earth's giant brood,
Nor Centaur's monstrous violence could subdue,
Nor Hellas, nor the Stranger, nor all lands
Where I have gone, cleansing the world from harms.
But a soft woman without manhood's strain
Alone and weaponless hath conquered me.
Son, let me know thee mine true-born, nor rate
Thy mother's claim beyond thy sire's, but bring
Thyself from out the chambers to my hand
Her body that hath borne thee, that my heart
May be assured, if lesser than my pain
It will distress thee to behold her limbs
With righteous torment agonized and torn.
Nay, shrink not, son, but pity me, whom all
May pity—me, who, like a tender girl,
Am heard to weep aloud! This none could say
He knew in me of old; for, murmuring not,
I went with evil fortune, silent still.
Now, such a foe hath found the woman in me!

Ay, but come near; stand by me, and behold
What cause I have for crying. Look but here!
Here is the mystery unveiled. O see!
Ye people, gaze on this poor quivering flesh,
Look with compassion on my misery!

Ah me!
Ah! ah! Again!
Even now the hot convulsion of disease
Shoots through my side, and will not let me rest
From this fierce exercise of wearing woe.
Take me, O King of Night!
O sudden thunderstroke.
Smite me! O sire, transfix me with the dart
Of thy swift lightning! Yet again that fang
Is tearing; it hath blossomed forth anew,
It soars up to the height!

             O breast and back,
O shrivelling arms and hands, ye are the same
That crushed the dweller of the Némean wild,
The lion unapproachable and rude,
The oxherd's plague, and Hydra of the lake
Of Lerna, and the twi-form prancing throng
Of Centaurs,—insolent, unsociable,
Lawless, ungovernable:—the tuskèd pest
Of Erymanthine glades; then underground
Pluto's three-headed cur—a perilous fear,
Born from the monster-worm; and, on the verge
Of Earth, the dragon, guarding fruits of gold.
These toils and others countless I have tried,
And none hath triumphed o'er me. But to-day,
Jointless and riven to tatters, I am wrecked
Thus utterly by imperceptible woe;
I, proudly named Alcmena's child, and His
Who reigns in highest heaven, the King supreme!

    Ay, but even yet, I tell ye, even from here,
Where I am nothingness and cannot move,
She who hath done this deed shall feel my power.
Let her come near, that, mastered by my might,
She may have this to tell the world, that, dying,
As living, I gave punishment to wrong.

    CH. O Hellas, how I grieve for thy distress!
How thou wilt mourn in losing him we see!

    HYL. My father, since thy silence gives me leave,
Still hear me patiently, though in thy pain!
For my request is just. Lend me thy mind

Less wrathfully distempered than 'tis now;
Else thou canst never know, where thou art keen
With vain resentment and with vain desire.

HER. Speak what thou wilt and cease, for I in pain
Catch not the sense of thy mysterious talk.

HYL. I come to tell thee of my mother's case,
And her involuntary unconscious fault.

HER. Base villain! hast thou breathed thy mother's
name,
Thy father's murderess, in my hearing too!

HYL. Her state requires not silence, but full speech.

HER. Her faults in former time might well be told.

HYL. So might her fault to-day, couldst thou but
know.

HER. Speak, but beware base words disgrace thee
not.

HYL. List! She is dead even now with new-given
wound.

HER. By whom? Thy words flash wonder through
my woe.

HYL. Her own hand slaughtered her; no foreign
stroke.

HER. Wretch! to have reft this office from my hands.

HYL. Even your rash spirit were softened, if you
knew.

HER. This bodes some knavery. But declare thy
thought!

HYL. She erred with good intent. The whole is said.

HER. Good, O thou villain, to destroy thy sire!

HYL. When she perceived that marriage in her home,
She erred, supposing to enchain thy love.

HER. Hath Trachis a magician of such might?

HYL. Long since the Centaur Nessus moved her mind
To work this charm for heightening thy desire.

HER. O horror, thou art here! I am no more.
My day is darkened, boy! Undone, undone!
I see our plight too plainly: woe is me!
Come, O my son!—thou hast no more a father,—
Call to me all the brethren of thy blood,
And poor Alcmena, wedded all in vain

Unto the Highest, that ye may hear me tell
With my last breath what prophecies I know.

HYL. Thy mother is not here, but by the shore
Of Tiryns hath obtained a dwelling-place;
And of thy sons, some she hath with her there,
And some inhabit Thebè's citadel.
But we who are with thee, sire, if there be aught
That may by us be done, will hear, and do.

HER. Then hearken thou unto this task, and show
If worthily thou art reputed mine.
Now is time to prove thee. My great father
Forewarned me long ago that I should die
By none who lived and breathed, but from the will
Of one now dwelling in the house of death.
And so this Centaur, as the voice Divine
Then prophesied, in death hath slain me living.
And in agreement with that ancient word
I now interpret newer oracles
Which I wrote down on going within the grove
Of the hill-roving and earth-couching Selli,—
Dictated to me by the mystic tongue
Innumerous, of my Father's sacred tree;
Declaring that my ever instant toils
Should in the time that now hath being and life
End and release me. And I look'd for joy.
But the true meaning plainly was my death.—
No labour is appointed for the dead.—
Then, since all argues one event, my son,
Once more thou must befriend me, and not wait
For my voice goading thee, but of thyself
Submit and second my resolve, and know
Filial obedience for thy noblest rule.

HYL. I will obey thee, father, though my heart
Sinks heavily in approaching such a theme.

HER. Before aught else, lay thy right hand in
        mine.

HYL. Why so intent on this assurance, sire?

HER. Give it at once and be not froward, boy.

HYL. There is my hand: I will gainsay thee nought.

HER. Swear by the head of him who gave me life.

HYL. Tell me the oath, and I will utter it.

HER. Swear thou wilt do the thing I bid thee do.

HYL. I swear, and make Zeus witness of my troth.

HER. But if you swerve, pray that the curse may
come.

HYL. It will not come for swerving :—but I pray.

HER. Now, dost thou know on Oeta's topmost height
The crag of Zeus ?

HYL.   I know it, and full oft
Have stood there sacrificing.

HER.   Then even there,
With thine own hand uplifting this my body,
Taking what friends thou wilt, and having lopped
Much wood from the deep-rooted oak and rough
Wild olive, lay me on the gathered pile,
And burn all with the touch of pine-wood flame.
Let not a tear of mourning dim thine eye ;
But silent, with dry gaze, if thou art mine,
Perform it. Else my curse awaits thee still
To weigh thee down when I am lost in night.

HYL. How cruel, O my father, is thy tongue !

HER. 'Tis peremptory. Else, if thou refuse,
Be called another's and be no more mine.

HYL. Alas that thou shouldst challenge me to this,
To be thy murderer, guilty of thy blood !

HER. Not I, in sooth : but healer of my pain,
And sole preserver from a life of woe.

HYL. How can it heal to burn thee on the pyre ?

HER. If this act frighten thee, perform the rest.

HYL. Mine arms shall not refuse to carry thee.

HER. And wilt thou gather the appointed wood ?

HYL. So my hand fire it not. In all but this,
Not scanting labour, I will do my part.

HER. Enough. 'Tis well. And having thus much
given
Add one small kindness to a list so full.

HYL. How great soe'er it were, it should be done.

HER. The maid of Eurytus thou knowest, I ween.

HYL. Of Iolè thou speak'st, or I mistake.

HER. Of her. This then is all I urge, my son.

When I am dead, if thou wouldst show thy duty,
Think of thine oath to me, and, on my word,
Make her thy wife : nor let another man
Take her, but only thou ; since she hath lain
So near this heart. Obey me, O my boy!
And be thyself the maker of this bond.
To spurn at trifles after great things given,
Were to confound the meed already won.

HYL. Oh, anger is not right, when men are ill !
But who could bear to see thee in this mind ?

HER. You murmur, as you meant to disobey.

HYL. How can I do it, when my mother's death
And thy sad state sprang solely from this girl ?
Who, not possessed with furies, could choose this ?
Far better, father, for me too to die,
Than to live still with my worst enemy.

HER. This youth withdraws his reverence in my
                                                        death.
But, if thou yield'st not to thy father's hest,
The curse from Heaven shall dog thy footsteps still.

HYL. Ah ! thou wilt tell me that thy pain is come.

HER. Yea, for thou wak'st the torment that had slept.

HYL. Ay me ! how cross and doubtful is my way !

HER. Because you will reject your father's word.

HYL. Must I be taught impiety from thee ?

HER. It is not impious to content my heart.

HYL. Then you require this with an absolute will ?

HER. And bid Heaven witness to my strong com-
                                                        mand.

HYL. Then I will do it, for the act is thine.
I will not cast it off. Obeying thee,
My sire, the Gods will ne'er reprove my deed.

HER. Thou endest fairly. Now, then, O my son,
Add the performance swiftly, that, before
Some spasm or furious onset of my pain
Have seized me, ye may place me on the pyre.
Come, loiter not, but lift me. Now my end
Is near, the last cessation of my woe.

HYL. Since thy command is urgent, O my sire !
We tarry not, but bear thee to the pyre.

HER. Stubborn heart, ere yet again
Wakes the fierce rebound of pain,
While the evil holds aloof,
Thou, with bit of diamond proof,
Curb thy cry, with forcèd will
Seeming to do gladly still!

HYL. Lift him, men, and hate not me
For the evil deeds ye see,
Since the Heavens' relentless sway
Recks not of the righteous way.
He who gave life and doth claim
From his seed a Father's name
Can behold this hour of blame.
Though the future none can tell,
Yet the present is not well:
Sore for him who bears the blow,
Sad for us who feel his woe,
Shameful to the Gods, we trow.

CH. Maidens from the palace-hall,
Come ye forth, too, at our call!
Mighty deaths beyond belief,
Many an unknown form of grief,
Ye have seen to-day; and nought
But the power of Zeus hath wrought.

PHILOCTETES

THE PERSONS

ODYSSEUS.
NEOPTOLEMUS.
CHORUS *of Mariners.*
PHILOCTETES.
Messenger, *disguised as a Merchantman.*
HERACLES, *appearing from the sky.*

SCENE. A desert shore of the Island of Lemnos.

It was fated that Troy should be taken by Neoptolemus, the son of Achilles, assisted by the bow of Heracles in the hands of Philoctetes.

Now Philoctetes had been rejected by the army because of a trouble in his foot, which made his presence with them insufferable; and had been cast away by Odysseus on the island of Lemnos.

But when the decree of fate was revealed by prophecy, Odysseus undertook to bring Philoctetes back, and took with him Neoptolemus, whose ambition could only be gratified through the return of Philoctetes with the bow.

Philoctetes was resolutely set against returning, and at the opening of the drama Neoptolemus is persuaded by Odysseus to take him with guile.

But when Philoctetes appears, the youth's ingenuous nature is so wrought upon through pity and remorse, that his sympathy and native truthfulness at length overcome his ambition.

When the inward sacrifice is complete, Heracles appears from heaven, and by a few words changes the mind of Philoctetes, so that all ends well.

PHILOCTETES

ODYSSEUS. NEOPTOLEMUS.

ODYSSEUS. This coast of sea-girt Lemnos, where we
    stand,
Is uninhabited, untrodden of men.
And here, O noble son of noblest sire,
Achilles-born Neoptolemus, I erewhile,—
Ordered by those who had command,—cast forth
Trachinian Philoctetes, Poeas' son,
His foot dark-dripping with a rankling wound;
When with wild cries, that frighted holy rest,
Filling the camp, he troubled every rite,
That none might handle sacrifice, or pour
Wine-offering, but his noise disturbed our peace.
    But why these words? No moment this for talk,
Lest he discern my coming, and I lose
The scheme, wherewith I think to catch him soon.
Now most behoves thy service, to explore
This headland for a cave with double mouth,
Whose twofold aperture, on wintry days,
Gives choice of sunshine, and in summer noons
The breeze wafts slumber through the airy cell.
Then, something lower down, upon the left,
Unless 'tis dried, thine eye may note a spring.
Go near now silently, and make me know
If still he persevere, and hold this spot,
Or have roamed elsewhere, that informed of this
I may proceed with what remains to say,
And we may act in concert.
    NEOPTOLEMUS.   Lord Odysseus,
Thy foremost errand will not task me far.
Methinks I see the cave whereof thou speakest.
    OD. Where? let me see it. Above there, or below?

NEO. Yonder, above. And yet I hear no tread.

[NEOPTOLEMUS *climbs up to the cave*

OD. Look if he be not lodged in slumber there.

NEO. I find no inmate, but an empty room.

OD. What ? no provision for a dwelling-place ?

NEO. A bed of leaves for some one harbouring here.

OD. Nought else beneath the roof ? Is all forlorn ?

NEO. A cup of wood, some untaught craftsman's
          skill,
And, close at hand, these embers of a fire.

OD. That store is his. I read the token clear.

NEO. Oh ! and these festering rags give evidence,
Steeped as with dressing some malignant sore.

OD. The man inhabits here : I know it now.
And sure he 's not far off. How can he range,
Whose limb drags heavy with an ancient harm ?
But he 's gone, either to bring forage home,
Or where he hath found some plant of healing power.
Send therefore thine attendant to look forth,
Lest unawares he find me. All our host
Were not so fair a prize for him as I.

NEO. My man is going, and shall watch the path.
What more dost thou require of me ? Speak on.

OD. Son of Achilles, know that thou art come
To serve us nobly, not with strength alone,
But, faithful to thy mission, if so be,
To do things strange, unwonted to thine ear.

NEO. What dost thou bid me ?

OD.   'Tis thy duty now
To entrap the mind of Poeas' son with words.
When he shall ask thee, who and whence thou art,
Declare thy name and father. 'Tis not that
I charge thee to conceal. But for thy voyage,
'Tis homeward, leaving the Achaean host,
With perfect hatred hating them, because
They who had drawn thee with strong prayers from
          home,
Their hope for taking Troy, allowed thee not
Thy just demand to have thy father's arms,
But, e'er thy coming, wrongly gave them o'er

Unto Odysseus : and thereon launch forth
With boundless execration against me.
That will not pain me : but if thou reject
This counsel, thou wilt trouble all our host ;
Since, if his bow shall not be ta'en, thy life
Will ne'er be crowned through Troy's discomfiture.

   Now let me show, why thine approach to him
Is safe and trustful as mine cannot be.
Thou didst sail forth, not to redeem thine oath,
Nor by constraint, nor with the foremost band.
All which reproaches I must bear : and he,
But seeing me, while master of his bow,
Will slay me, and my ruin will be thine.
This point then craves our cunning, to acquire
By subtle means the irresistible bow.—
Thy nature was not framed, I know it well,
For speaking falsehood, or contriving harm.
Yet, since the prize of victory is so dear,
Endure it.—We'll be just another day.
But now, for one brief hour, devote thyself
To serve me without shame, and then for aye
Hereafter be the pearl of righteousness.

   NEO. The thing that, being named, revolts mine
      ear,
Son of Laërtes, I abhor to do.
'Tis not my nature, no, nor, as they tell,
My father's, to work aught by craft and guile.
I'll undertake to bring him in by force,
Not by deceit. For, sure, with his one foot,
He cannot be a match for all our crew.
Being sent, my lord, to serve thee, I am loth
To seem rebellious. But I rather choose
To offend with honour, than to win by wrong.

   OD. Son of a valiant sire, I, too, in youth,
Had once a slow tongue and an active hand.
But since I have proved the world, I clearly see
Words and not deeds give mastery over men.

   NEO. What then is thy command ? To lie ? No
      more ?

   OD. To entangle Philoctetes with deceit.

NEO. Why through deceit ?   May not persuasion
       fetch him ?
OD. Never.   And force as certainly will fail.
NEO. What lends him such assurance of defence ?
OD. Arrows, the unerring harbingers of Death.
NEO. Then to go near him is a perilous thing.
OD. Unless with subtlety, as I have said.
NEO. And is not lying shameful to thy soul ?
OD. Not if by lying I can save my soul.
NEO. How must one look in speaking such a
       word ?
OD. Where gain invites, this shrinking is not good.
NEO. What gain I through his coming back to
       Troy ?
OD. His arms alone have power to take Troy-town.
NEO. Then am not I the spoiler, as ye said ?
OD. Thou without them, they without thee, are
       powerless.
NEO. If it be so, they must be sought and won.
OD. Yea, for in this two prizes will be thine.
NEO. What ?   When I learn them, I will not refuse.
OD. Wisdom and valour joined in one good name.
NEO. Shame, to the winds !   Come, I will do this
       thing.
OD. Say, dost thou bear my bidding full in mind ?
NEO. Doubt not, since once for all I have em-
       braced it.
OD. Thou, then, await him here.   I will retire,
For fear my hated presence should be known,
And take back our attendant to the ship.
And then once more, should ye appear to waste
The time unduly, I will send again
This same man hither in disguise, transformed
To the strange semblance of a merchantman ;
From dark suggestion of whose crafty tongue,
Thou, O my son, shalt gather timely counsel.
   Now to my ship.   This charge I leave to thee.
May secret Hermes guide us to our end,
And civic Pallas, named of victory,
The sure protectress of my devious way

CHORUS (*entering*).

Strange in the stranger land,   I 1
What shall I speak ? What hide
From a heart suspicious of ill ?
Tell me, O master mine !
Wise above all is the man,
Peerless in searching thought,
Who with the Zeus-given wand
Wieldeth a Heaven-sent power.
This unto thee, dear son,
Fraught with ancestral might,
This to thy life hath come.
Wherefore I bid thee declare,
What must I do for thy need ?

NEO. Even now methinks thou longest to espy
Near ocean's marge the place where he doth lie.
Gaze without fear. But when the traveller stern,
Who from this roof is parted, shall return,
Advancing still as I the signal give,
To serve each moment's mission thou shalt strive.

CH. That, O my son, from of old   I 2
Hath been my care, to take note
What by thy beck'ning is told ;
Still thy success to promote.
But for our errand to-day
Behoves thee, master, to say
Where is the hearth of his home ;
Or where even now doth he roam ?
O tell me, lest all unaware
He spring like a wolf from his lair
And I by surprise should be ta'en,
Where doth he move or remain,
Here lodging, or wandering away ?

NEO. Thou seëst yon double doorway of his cell,
Poor habitation of the rock.
CH. 2.   But tell
Where is the pain-worn wight himself abroad ?
NEO. To me 'tis clear, that, in his quest for food,

Here, not far off, he trails yon furrowed path.
For, so 'tis told, this mode the sufferer hath
Of sustenance, oh hardness! bringing low
Wild creatures with wing'd arrows from his bow;
Nor findeth healer for his troublous woe.

   Cн. I feel his misery.   II 1
  With no companion eye,
  Far from all human care,
  He pines with fell disease;
  Each want he hourly sees
  Awakening new despair.
  How can he bear it still?
  O cruel Heavens! O pain
  Of that afflicted mortal train
  Whose life sharp sorrows fill!

  Born in a princely hall,   II 2
  Highest, perchance, of all,
  Now lies he comfortless
  Alone in deep distress,
  'Mongst rough and dappled brutes,
  With pangs and hunger worn;
  While from far distance shoots,
  On airy pinion borne,
  The unbridled Echo, still replying
  To his most bitter crying.

NEO. At nought of this I marvel—for if I
Judge rightly, there assailed him from on high
That former plague through Chrysa's cruel sting:
And if to-day he suffer anything
With none to soothe, it must be from the will
Of some great God, so caring to fulfil
The word of prophecy, lest he should bend
On Troy the shaft no mortal may forfend,
Before the arrival of Troy's destined hour,
When she must fall, o'er-mastered by their power.

 Cн. 1. Hush, my son!   III 1
 NEO.   Why so?
 Cн. 1.   A sound
Gendered of some mortal woe,

Started from the neighbouring groun[d]
Here, or there ? Ah ! now I know.
Hark ! 'tis the voice of one in pain,
Travelling hardly, the deep strain
Of human anguish, all too clear,
That smites my heart, that wounds mine ear.

    CH. 2. From far it peals. But thou, my son ! III 2
    NEO. What ?
    CH. 2.   Think again. He moveth nigh :
He holds the region : not with tone
Of piping shepherd's rural minstrelsy,
But belloweth his far cry,
Stumbling perchance with mortal pain,
    Or else in wild amaze,
    As he our ship surveys
Unwonted on the inhospitable main.

Enter PHILOCTETES.

PHILOCTETES. Ho !
What men are ye that to this desert shore,
Harbourless, uninhabited, are come
On shipboard ? Of what country or what race
Shall I pronounce ye ? For your outward garb
Is Grecian, ever dearest to this heart
That hungers now to hear your voices' tune.
Ah ! do not fear me, do not shrink away
From my wild looks : but, pitying one so poor,
Forlorn and desolate in nameless woe,
Speak, if with friendly purpose ye are come.
Oh answer ! 'Tis not meet that I should lose
This kindness from your lips, or ye from mine.

    NEO. Then know this first, O stranger, as thou
             wouldest,
That we are Greeks.

    PHI.   O dear, dear name ! Ah me !
In all these years, once, only once, I hear it !
My son, what fairest gale hath wafted thee ?
What need hath brought thee to the shore ? What
           mission ?

Declare all this, that I may know thee well.

NEO. The sea-girt Scyros is my native home.
Thitherward I make voyage :—Achilles' son,
Named Neoptolemus.—I have told thee all.

PHI. Dear is that shore to me, dear is thy father.
O ancient Lycomedes' foster-child,
Whence cam'st thou hither ? How didst thou set forth ?

NEO. From Troy we made our course in sailing hither.

PHI. How ? Sure thou wast not with us, when at first
We launched our vessels on the Troyward way ?

NEO. Hadst thou a share in that adventurous toil ?

PHI. And know'st thou not whom thou behold'st in
            me,
Young boy ?

NEO.   How should I know him whom I ne'er
Set eye on ?

PHI.   Hast not even heard my name,
Nor echoing rumour of my ruinous woe ?

NEO. Nay, I know nought of all thy questioning.

PHI. How full of griefs am I, how Heaven-abhorred,
When of my piteous state no faintest sound
Hath reached my home, or any Grecian land !
But they, who pitilessly cast me forth,
Keep silence and are glad, while this my plague
Blooms ever, and is strengthened more and more.
Boy, great Achilles' offspring, in this form
Thou seest the man, of whom, methinks, erewhile
Thou hast been told, to whom the Herculean bow
Descended, Philoctetes, Poeas' son ;
Whom the two generals and the Ithacan king
Cast out thus shamefully forlorn, afflicted
With the fierce malady and desperate wound
Made by the cruel basilisk's murderous tooth.
With this for company they left me, child !
Exposed upon this shore, deserted, lone.

    From seaward Chrysa came they with their fleet
And touched at Lemnos. I had fallen to rest
From the long tossing, in a shadowy cave
On yonder cliff by the shore. Gladly they saw,
And left me, having set forth for my need,

Poor man, some scanty rags, and a thin s.
Of provender. Such food be theirs, I pray!
Imagine, O my son, when they were gone,
What wakening, what arising, then was mine;
What weeping, what lamenting of my woe!
When I beheld the ships, wherewith I sailed,
Gone, one and all! and no man in the place,
None to bestead me, none to comfort me
In my sore sickness. And where'er I looked,
Nought but distress was present with me still.
No lack of that, for one thing!—Ah! my son,
Time passed, and there I found myself alone
Within my narrow lodging, forced to serve
Each pressing need. For body's sustenance
This bow supplied me with sufficient store,
Wounding the feathered doves, and when the shaft,
From the tight string, had struck, myself, ay me!
Dragging this foot, would crawl to my swift prey.
Then water must be fetched, and in sharp frost
Wood must be found and broken,—all by me.
Nor would fire come unbidden, but with flint
From flints striking dim sparks, I hammered forth
The struggling flame that keeps the life in me.
For houseroom with the single help of fire
Gives all I need, save healing for my sore.

Now learn, my son, the nature of this isle.
No mariner puts in here willingly.
For it hath neither moorage, nor sea-port,
For traffic or kind shelter or good cheer.
Not hitherward do prudent men make voyage.
Perchance one may have touched against his will.
Many strange things may happen in long time.
These, when they come, in words have pitied me,
And given me food, or raiment, in compassion.
But none is willing, when I speak thereof,
To take me safely home. Wherefore I pine
Now this tenth year, in famine and distress,
Feeding the hunger of my ravenous plague.

Such deeds, my son, the Atridae, and the might
Of sage Odysseus, have performed on me.

c. s.   Q

Wherefore may all the Olympian gods, one day,
Plague them with stern requital for my wrong!

CH. Methinks my feeling for thee, Poeas' child,
Is like that of thy former visitants.

NEO. I, too, a witness to confirm his words,
Know them for verities, since I have found
The Atridae and Odysseus evil men.

PHI. Art thou, too, wroth with the all-pestilent sons
Of Atreus? Have they given thee cause to grieve?

NEO. Would that my hand might ease the wrath I
feel!
Then Sparta and Mycenae should be ware
That Scyros too breeds valiant sons for war.

PHI. Brave youth! I love thee. Tell me the great
cause
Why thou inveighest against them with such heat?

NEO. O son of Poeas, hardly shall I tell
What outrage I endured when I had come;
Yet I will speak it. When the fate of death
O'ertook Achilles——

PHI.   Out, alas! no more!
Hold, till thou first hast made me clearly know,
Is Peleus' offspring dead?

NEO.   Alas! he is,
Slain by no mortal, felled by Phoebus' shaft:
So men reported—

PHI.   Well, right princely was he!
And princely is he who slew him. Shall I mourn
Him first, or wait till I have heard thy tale?

NEO. Methinks thou hast thyself enough to mourn,
Without the burden of another's woe.

PHI. Well spoken. Then renew thine own complaint,
And tell once more wherein they insulted thee.

NEO. There came to fetch me, in a gallant ship,
Odysseus and the fosterer of my sire,
Saying, whether soothly, or in idle show,
That, since my father perished, it was known
None else but I should take Troy's citadel.
Such words from them, my friend, thou may'st believe,
Held me not long from making voyage with speed,

Chiefly through longing for my father's corse,
To see him yet unburied,—for I ne'er
Had seen him. Then, besides, 'twas a fair cause,
If, by my going, I should vanquish Troy.
One day I had sailed, and on the second came
To sad Sigeum with wind-favoured speed,
When straightway all the host, surrounding me
As I set foot on shore, saluted me,
And swore the dead Achilles was in life,
Their eyes being witness, when they looked on me.
He lay there in his shroud: but I, unhappy,
Soon ending lamentation for the dead,
Went near to those Atridae, as to friends,
To obtain my father's armour and all else
That had been his. And then,—alas the while,
That men should be so hard !—they spake this word :
'Seed of Achilles, thou may'st freely take
All else thy father owned, but for those arms,
Another wields them now, Laërtes' son.'
Tears rushed into mine eyes, and in hot wrath
I straightway rose, and bitterly outspake :
'O miscreant ! What ? And have ye dared to give
Mine arms to some man else, unknown to me ?'
Then said Odysseus, for he chanced to be near,
'Yea, child, and justly have they given me these.
I saved them and their master in the field.'
Then in fierce anger all at once I launched
All terms of execration at his head,
Bating no word, being maddened by the thought
That I should lose this heirloom,—and to him !
He, at this pass, though not of wrathful mood,
Stung by such utterance, made rejoinder thus:
'Thou wast not with us here, but wrongfully
Didst bide afar. And, since thou mak'st so bold,
I tell thee, never shalt thou, as thou sayest,
Sail with these arms to Scyros.'—Thus reviled,
With such an evil echo in mine ear,
I voyage homeward, robbed of mine own right
By that vile offset of an evil tree.
Yet less I blame him than the men in power.

For every multitude, be it army or state,
Takes tone from those who rule it, and all taint
Of disobedience from bad counsel springs.
I have spoken. May the Atridae's enemy
Be dear to Heaven, as he is loved by me!

> CH. Mother of mightiest Zeus,   1
>   Feeder of all that live,
>   Who from thy mountainous breast
>   Rivers of gold dost give!
> To thee, O Earth, I cried that shameful day,
> When insolence from Atreus' sons went forth
> Full on our lord: when they bestowed away
> His father's arms to crown Odysseus' worth;
> Thou, whom bull-slaughtering lions yokèd bear,
>   O mighty mother, hear!

PHI. Your coming is commended by a grief
That makes you kindly welcome. For I feel
A chord that vibrates to your voice, and tells,
Thus have Odysseus and the Atridae wrought.
Full well I know, Odysseus' poisoned tongue
Shrinks from no mischief nor no guileful word
That leads to bad achievement in the end.
This moves not my main marvel, but if one
Saw this and bore it,—Aias of the shield.
          NEO. Ah, friend, he was no more. Had he but
                    lived,
This robbery had ne'er been wrought on me.
          PHI. What? Is he too departed?
          NEO.   He is dead.
The light no more beholds him.
          PHI.   Oh! alas!
But Tydeus' offspring, and the rascal birth
Laërtes bought of Sisyphus, they live:
I know it. For their death were to be wished.
          NEO. Yea, be assured, they live and flourish high
Exalted in the host of Argive men.
          PHI. And Nestor, my old friend, good aged man,
Is he yet living? Oft he would prevent
Their evils, by the wisdom of his thought.

NEO. He too is now in trouble, having lost
Antilochus, the comfort of his age.

PHI. There, there! In one brief word thou hast
          revealed
The mournful case of twain, whom I would last
Have chosen to hear of as undone. Ah me!
Where must one look? when these are dead, and he,
Odysseus, lives,—and in a time like this,
That craves their presence, and his death for theirs.

NEO. He wrestles cleverly; but, O my friend,
Even ablest wits are ofttimes snared at last.

PHI. Tell me, I pray, what was become of him,
Patroclus, whom thy father loved so well?

NEO. He, too, was gone. I'll teach thee in a word
One truth for all. War doth not willingly
Snatch off the wicked, but still takes the good.

PHI. True! and to prove thy saying, I will inquire
The fate of a poor dastard, of mean worth,
But ever shrewd and nimble with his tongue.

NEO. Whom but Odysseus canst thou mean by this?

PHI. I meant not him. But there was one Thersites,
Who ne'er made conscience to stint speech, where all
Cried 'Silence!' Is he living, dost thou know?

NEO. I saw him not, but knew he was alive.

PHI. He must be: for no evil yet was crushed.
The Heavens will ever shield it. 'Tis their sport
To turn back all things rancorous and malign
From going down to the grave, and send instead
The good and true. Oh, how shall we commend
Such dealings, how defend them? When I praise
Things god-like, I find evil in the Gods.

NEO. I, O thou child of a Trachinian sire,
Henceforth will take good care, from far away
To look on Troy and Atreus' children twain.
Yea, where the trickster lords it o'er the just,
And goodness languishes and rascals rule,
—Such courses I will nevermore endure.
But rock-bound Scyros henceforth shall suffice
To yield me full contentment in my home.
Now, to my vessel! And thou, Poeas' child,

Farewell, right heartily farewell! May Heaven
Grant thy desire, and rid thee of thy plague!
Let us be going, that when God shall give
Fair voyage, that moment we may launch away.

    PHI. My son, are ye now setting forth?

    NEO.   Our time
Bids us go near and look to sail erelong.

    PHI. Now, by thy father, by thy mother,—nay,
By all thy love e'er cherished in thy home,
Suppliant I beg thee, leave me not thus lone,
Forlorn in all my misery which thou seest,
In all thou hast heard of here surrounding me!
Stow me with other freightage. Full of care,
I know, and burdensome the charge may prove.
Yet venture! Surely to the noble mind
All shame is hateful and all kindness blest.
And shame would be thy meed, didst thou fail here;
But, doing this, thou shalt have glorious fame,
When I return alive to Oeta's vale.
Come, 'tis the labour not of one whole day.
So thou durst take me, fling me where thou wilt
O' the ship, in hold, prow, stern, or wheresoe'er
I least may trouble those on board with me.
Ah! by great Zeus, the suppliant's friend, comply,
My son, be softened! See, where I am fall'n
Thus on my knees before thee, though so weak,
Crippled and powerless. Ah! forsake me not
Thus far from human footstep. Take me, take me!
If only to thy home, or to the town
Of old Chalcodon in Euboea.—From thence
I have not far to Oeta, and the ridge
Of Trachis, and Spercheius' lordly flood.
So thou shalt bless my father with my sight.
And yet long since I fear he may be gone.
For oft I sent him suppliant prayers by men
Who touched this isle, entreating him to fetch
And bear me safely home with his own crew.
But either he is dead, or else, methinks,
It well may be, my messengers made light
Of my concerns, and hastened onward home.

But now in thee I find both messenger
And convoy, thou wilt pity me and save.
For, well thou knowest, danger never sleeps,
And fear of dark reverse is always nigh.
Mortals, when free, should look where mischief lurks,
And in their happiest hour consider well
Their life, lest ruin unsuspected come.

      CH. Pity him, O my king!   2
         Many a crushing woe
         He telleth, such as I pray
         None of my friends may know.
And if, dear master, thou mislikest sore
Yon cruel-hearted lordly pair, I would,
Turning their plan of evil to his good,
On swift ship bear him to his native shore,
    Meeting his heart's desire; and free thy path
         From fear of heavenly wrath.

NEO. Thou mak'st small scruple here; but be
         advised:
Lest, when this plague on board shall weary thee,
Thy voice should alter from this liberal tone.
CH. No, truly! Fear not thou shalt ever have
Just cause to utter such reproach on me.
NEO. Then sure 'twere shame, should I more
         backward prove
Than thou, to labour for the stranger's need.
Come, if thou wilt, let us make voyage, and he,
Let him set forth with speed. Our ship shall take
         him.
He shall not be refused. Only may Heaven
Lead safely hence and to our destined port!
PHI. O morning full of brightness! Kindest friend,
Sweet mariners, how can I make you feel,
In act, how dearly from my heart I love you!
Ye have won my soul. Let us be gone, my son,—
First having said farewell to this poor cave,
My homeless dwelling-place, that thou may'st know,
How barely I have lived, how firm my heart!
Methinks another could not have endured

The very sight of what I bore. But I
Through strong necessity have conquered pain.
  CH. Stay: let us understand. There come two men,
A stranger, with a shipmate of thy crew.
When ye have heard them, ye may then go in.

Enter Messenger, *disguised as a merchantman.*

  MERCHANTMAN. Son of Achilles, my companion here,
Who with two more remained to guard thy ship,
Agreed to help me find thee where thou wert,
Since unexpectedly, through fortune's will,
I meet thee, mooring by the self-same shore.
For like a merchantman, with no great sail,
Making my course from Ilion to my home,
Grape-clustered Peparethos, when I heard
The mariners declare that one and all
Were of thy crew, I would not launch again,
Without a word, till we had told our news.—
Methinks thou knowest nought of thine own case,
What new devices of the Argive chiefs
Surround thee; nor devices only now,
But active deeds, no longer unperformed.
  NEO. Well, stranger, for the kindness thou hast
          shown,—
Else were I base,—my heart must thank thee still.
But tell me what thou meanest, that I may learn
What new-laid plot thou bring'st me from the camp.
  MER. Old Phoenix, Acamas and Demophon
Are gone in thy pursuit with ships and men.
  NEO. To bring me back with reasons or perforce?
  MER. I know not. What I heard, I am here to
          tell.
  NEO. How? And is this in act? Are they set forth
To please the Atridae, Phoenix and the rest?
  MER. The thing is not to do, but doing now.
  NEO. What kept Odysseus back, if this be so,
From going himself? Had he some cause for fear?
  MER. He and the son of Tydeus, when our ship
Hoist sail, were gone to fetch another man.
  NEO. For whom could he himself be sailing forth?

MER. For some one,—but first tell me, whispering
                    low
Whate'er thou speakest,—who is this I see ?
NEO. (*speaking aloud*). This, sir, is Philoctetes the
                    renowned.
MER. (*aside to* NEOPTOLEMUS). Without more ques-
                    tion, snatch thyself away
And sail forth from this land.
PHI.   What saith he, boy ?
Through what dark traffic is the mariner
Betraying me with whispering in thine ear ?
NEO. I have not caught it, but whate'er he speaks
He must speak openly to us and thee.
MER. Seed of Achilles, let me not offend
The army by my words ! Full many a boon,
Being poor, I reap from them for service done.
NEO. The Atridae are my foes ; the man you see
Is my fast friend, because he hates them sore.
Then, if you come in kindness, you must hide
Nothing from him or me of all thou hast heard.
MER. Look what thou doest, my son !
NEO.   I mark it well.
MER. Thou shalt be answerable.
NEO.   Content : but speak.
MER. Then hear me. These two men whom I have
                    named,
Diomedes and Odysseus, are set forth
Engaged on oath to bring this man by force
If reasons fail. The Achaeans every one
Have heard this plainly from Odysseus' mouth.
He was the louder and more confident.
NEO. Say, for what cause, after so long a time,
Can Atreus' sons have turned their thoughts on him,
Whom long they had cast forth ? What passing touch
Of conscience moved them, or what stroke from Heaven,
Whose wrath requites all wicked deeds of men ?
MER. Methinks thou hast not heard what I will now
Unfold to thee. There was a princely seer,
A son of Priam, Helenus by name,
Whom he for whom no word is bad enough,

Crafty Odysseus, sallying forth alone
One night, had taken, and in bonds displayed
'Fore all the Achaeans, a right noble prey.
He, 'mid his other prophecies, foretold
No Grecian force should sack Troy's citadel,
Till with fair reasons they had brought this man
From Lemnos isle, his lonely dwelling-place.

When thus the prophet spake, Laërtes' son
Straight undertook to fetch this man, and show him
To all the camp:—he hoped, with fair consent:
But else, perforce.—And, if he failed in this,
Whoever would might smite him on the head.

My tale is told, dear youth. I counsel speed
To thee and to the friend for whom thou carest.

Phi. Ah me, unhappy! has that rascal knave
Sworn to fetch me with reasons to their camp?
As likely might his reasons bring me back,
Like his begetter, from the house of death.

Mer. You talk of what I know not. I will go
Shipward. May God be with you for all good. [*Exit*

Phi. Is not this terrible, Laërtes' son
Should ever think to bring me with soft words
And show me from his deck to all their host?
No! Sooner will I listen to the tongue
Of the curs'd basilisk that thus hath maim'd me
        Ay, but he'll venture anything in word
Or deed. And now I know he will be here.
Come, O my son, let us be gone, while seas
And winds divide us from Odysseus' ship.
Let us depart. Sure timely haste brings rest
And quiet slumber when the toil is done.

Neo. Shall we not sail when this south-western wind
Hath fallen, that now is adverse to our course?

Phi. All winds are fair to him who flies from woe.

Neo. Nay, but this head-wind hinders them no
                less.

Phi. No head-wind hinders pirates on their way,
When violence and rapine lead them on.

Neo. Well, then, let us be going, if you will;

When you have taken from within the cave
What most you need and value.
PHI.   Though my all
Be little, there is that I may not lose.
  NEO. What can there be that we have not on board ?
  PHI. A leaf I have found, wherewith I still the
        rage
Of my sore plague, and lull it quite to rest.
  NEO. Well, bring it forth.—What ? Is there some-
        thing more ?
  PHI. If any of these arrows here are fallen,
I would not leave them for a casual prey.
  NEO. How ? Do I see thee with the marvellous
        bow ?
  PHI. Here in my hand. The world hath only one.
  NEO. And may one touch and handle it, and gaze
With reverence, as on a thing from Heaven ?
  PHI. Thou mayest, my son. This and whate'er of
        mine
May stead thee, 'tis thy privilege to enjoy.
  NEO. In very truth I long for it, but so,
That longing waits on leave. Am I permitted ?
  PHI. Thou art, my son,—and well thou speakest,—
        thou art.
Thou, that hast given me light and life, the joy
Of seeing Mount Oeta and my father's home,
With all I love there, and his aged head,—
Thou that hast raised me far above my foes
Who triumphed ! Thou may'st take it in thine hand,
And,—when thou hast given it back to me,—may'st
        vaunt
Alone of mortals for thine excellence
To have held this in thy touch. I, too, at first,
Received it as a boon for kindness done.
  NEO. Well, go within.
  PHI.   Nay, I must take thee too.
My sickness craves thee for its comforter.

        [PHILOCTETES *and* NEOPTOLEMUS *go into*
         the cave

CHORUS.

In fable I have heard,   I 1
Though sight hath ne'er confirmed the word,
How he who attempted once the couch supreme,
To a whirling wheel by Zeus the all-ruler bound,
Tied head and heel, careering ever round,
Atones his impious unsubstantial dream.
Of no man else, through eye or ear,
Have I discerned a fate more full of fear
Than yonder sufferer's of the cureless wound :
Who did no violence, defrauded none :—
A just man, had he dwelt among the just
Unworthily behold him thrust
Alone to hear the billows roar
That break around a rugged shore !
How could he live, whose life was thus consumed with
          moan ?

Where neighbour there was none :   I 2
No arm to stay him wandering lone,
Unevenly, with stumbling steps and sore ;
No friend in need, no kind inhabitant,
To minister to his importunate want,
No heart whereto his pangs he might deplore.
None who, whene'er the gory flow
Was rushing hot, might healing herbs bestow,
Or cull from teeming Earth some genial plant
To allay the anguish of malignant pain
And soothe the sharpness of his poignant woe.
Like infant whom the nurse lets go,
With tottering movement here and there,
He crawled for comfort, whensoe'er
His soul-devouring plague relaxed its cruel strain.

Not fed with foison of all-teeming Earth   II 1
Whence we sustain us, ever-toiling men,
But only now and then
With wingèd things, by his wing'd shafts brought low,
He stayed his hunger from his bow.

Poor soul, that never through ten years of dearth
Had pleasure from the fruitage of the vine,
But seeking to some standing pool,
    Nor clear nor cool,
Foul water heaved to head for lack of heartening wine.

But now, consorted with the hero's child,   II 2
He winneth greatness and a joyful change;
Over the water wild
Borne by a friendly bark beneath the range
Of Oeta, where Spercheius fills
Wide channels winding among lovely hills
Haunted of Melian nymphs, till he espies
The roof-tree of his father's hall,
    And high o'er all
Shines the bronze shield of him, whose home is in the
    skies.

[NEOPTOLEMUS *comes out of the cave, followed
by* PHILOCTETES *in pain*

NEO. Prithee, come on ! Why dost thou stand aghast,
Voiceless, and thus astonied in thine air ?
PHI. Oh ! oh !
NEO.   What ?
PHI.   Nothing. Come my son, fear nought.
NEO. Is pain upon thee ? Hath thy trouble come ?
PHI. No pain, no pain ! 'Tis past ; I am easy now.
Ye heavenly powers !
NEO.   Why dost thou groan aloud,
And cry to Heaven ?
PHI.   To come and save. Kind Heaven !
Oh, oh !
NEO. What is 't ? Why silent ? Wilt not speak ?
I see thy misery.
PHI.   Oh ! I am lost, my son !
I cannot hide it from you. Oh ! it shoots,
It pierces. Oh unhappy ! Oh ! my woe !
I am lost, my son, I am devoured. Oh me !
Oh ! Oh ! Oh ! Oh ! Pain ! pain ! Oh pain ! oh pain !
Child, if a sword be to thine hand, smite hard,
Shear off my foot ! heed not my life ! Quick, come !

NEO. What hath so suddenly arisen, that thus
Thou mak'st ado and groanest o'er thyself ?

PHI. Thou knowest.

NEO.   What know I ?

PHI.   O ! thou knowest, my son !

NEO. I know not.

PHI.   How ? Not know ? Ah me ! Pain, pain !

NEO. Thy plague is a sore burden, heavy and sore.

PHI. Sore ? 'Tis unutterable. Have pity on me !

NEO. What shall I do ?

PHI.   Do not in fear forsake me.
This wandering evil comes in force again,
Hungry as ere it fed.

NEO.   O hapless one !
Thrice hapless in thy manifold distress !
What wilt thou ? Shall I raise thee on mine arm ?

PHI. Nay, but receiving from my hand the bow,
As late thou didst desire me, keep it safe
And guard it, till the fury of my pain
Pass over me and cease. For when 'tis spent,
Slumber will seize me, else it ne'er would end.
I must sleep undisturbed. But if meanwhile
They come,—by Heaven I charge thee, in no wise,
Willingly nor perforce, let them have this !
Else thou wilt be the slayer of us both ;
Of me thy suppliant, and of thyself.

NEO. Fear not my care. No hand shall hold these
                                         arms
But thine and mine. Give, and Heaven bless the deed !

PHI. I give them; there, my son! But look to Heaven
And pray no envy smite thee, nor such bane
In having them, as fell on me and him
Who bore them formerly.

NEO.   O grant it, Gods !
And grant us fair and happy voyage, where'er
Our course is shaped and righteous Heaven shall guide.

PHI. Ah ! but I fear, my son, thy prayer is vain :
For welling yet again from depths within,
This gory ooze is dripping. It will come !
I know it will. O, foot, torn helpless thing,

What wilt thou do to me? Ah! ah! It comes,
It is at hand. 'Tis here! Woe's me, undone!
I have shown you all. Stay near me. Go not far:
Ah! ah!
O island king, I would this agony
Might cleave thy bosom through and through! Woe,
　　　　　　　　　　woe!
Woe! Ah! ye two commanders of the host,
Agamemnon, Menelaüs, O that ye,
Another ten years' durance in my room
Might nurse this malady! O Death, Death, Death!
I call thee daily—wilt thou never come?
Will it not be?—My son, thou noble boy,
If thou art noble, take and burn me there
Aloft in yon all-worshipped Lemnian fire!
Yea, when the bow thou keep'st was my reward,
I did like service for the child of Heaven.
How now, my son?
What say'st? Art silent? Where—where art thou,
　　　　　　　　boy?
　　NEO. My heart is full, and groaning o'er thy woes.
　　PHI. Nay, yet have comfort. This affliction oft
Goes no less swiftly than it came. I pray thee,
Stand fast and leave me not alone!
　　NEO.　　　　　　　　　　Fear nought.
We will not stir.
　　PHI. Wilt thou remain?
　　NEO.　　　　　　　　　　Be sure of it.
　　PHI. I'll not degrade thee with an oath, my son.
　　NEO. Rest satisfied. I may not go without thee.
　　PHI. Thy hand, to pledge me that!
　　NEO.　　　　　　　　There, I will stay.
　　PHI. Now, now, aloft!
　　NEO.　　　　　　　Where mean'st thou?
　　PHI.　　　　　　　　　Yonder aloft!
　　NEO. Whither? Thou rav'st. Why starest thou at
　　　　　　the sky?
　　PHI. Now, let me go.
　　NEO.　　　　　Where?
　　PHI.　　　　　　　Let me go, I say!

NEO. I will not.
PHI.   You will kill me. Let me go!
NEO. Well, thou know'st best. I hold thee not.
PHI.   O Earth,
I die: receive me to thy breast! This pain
Subdues me utterly; I cannot stand.

NEO. Methinks he will be fast in slumber soon.
That head sinks backward, and a clammy sweat
Bathes all his limbs, while from his foot hath burst
A vein, dark-bleeding. Let us leave him, friends,
In quietness, till he hath fallen to sleep.

CHORUS.

Lord of the happiest life,   1
Sleep, thou that know'st not strife,
      That know'st not grief,
Still wafting sure relief,
      Come, saviour, now!
Thy healing balm is spread
Over this pain-worn head;
Quench not the beam that gives calm to his brow.

Look, O my lord, to thy path,
Either to go or to stay:
How is my thought to proceed?
What is our cause for delay?
Look! Opportunity's power,
Fitting the task to the hour,
Giveth the race to the swift.

NEO. He hears not. But I see that to have ta'en
His bow without him were a bootless gain.
He must sail with us. So the god hath said.
Heaven hath decreed this garland for his head:
And to have failed with falsehood were a meed
Of shameful soilure for a shameless deed.

CH. God shall determine the end:—
      But for thine answer, friend,
            Waft soft words low!
      All sick men's sleep, we know,

       Hath open eye;
       Their quickly ruffling mind
       Quivers in lightest wind,
Sleepless in slumber new danger to spy.

       Think, O my lord, of thy path,
       Secretly look forth afar,
       What wilt thou do for thy need?
       How with the wise wilt thou care?
       If toward the nameless thy heart
       Chooseth this merciful part,
       Huge are the dangers that drift.

The wind is fair, my son, the wind is fair,
The man is dark and helpless, stretched in night.
(O kind, warm sleep that calmest human care!)
Powerless of hand and foot and ear and sight,
Blind, as one lying in the house of death.
(Think well if here thou utterest timely breath.)
This, O my son, is all my thought can find,
Best are the toils that without frightening bind.

  NEO. Hush! One word more were madness. He
     revives.
His eye hath motion. He uplifts his head.
  PHI. Fair daylight following sleep, and ye, dear
     friends,
Faithful beyond all hope in tending me!
I never could have dreamed that thou, dear youth,
Couldst thus have borne my sufferings and stood
     near
So full of pity to relieve my pain.
Not so the worthy generals of the host;—
This princely patience was not theirs to show.
Only thy noble nature, nobly sprung,
Made light of all the trouble, though oppressed
With fetid odours and unceasing cries.
And now, since this my plague would seem to yield
Some pause and brief forgetfulness of pain,
With thine own hand, my son, upraise me here,
And set me on my feet, that, when my strength

c. s.   R

After exhaustion shall return again,
We may move shoreward and launch forth with speed.

NEO. I feel unhoped-for gladness when I see
Thy painless gaze, and hear thy living breath,
For thine appearance and surroundings both
Were deathlike. But arise! Or, if thou wilt,
These men shall raise thee. For they will not shrink
From toil which thou and I at once enjoin.

PHI. Right, right, my son! But lift me thine own self,
As I am sure thou meanest. Let these be,
Lest they be burdened with the noisome smell
Before the time. Enough for them to bear
The trouble on board.

NEO.   I will; stand up, endure!
PHI. Fear not. Old habit will enable me.

NEO. O me!
What shall I do? Now 'tis my turn to exclaim!

PHI. What canst thou mean? What change is here,
my son?

NEO. I know not how to shift the troublous word.
'Tis hopeless.

PHI.   What is hopeless? Speak not so,
Dear child!

NEO.   But so my wretched lot hath fallen.

PHI. Ah! Can it be, the offence of my disease
Hath moved thee not to take me now on board?

NEO. All is offence to one who hath forced himself
From the true bent to an unbecoming deed.

PHI. Nought misbecoming to thyself or sire
Doest thou or speak'st, befriending a good man.

NEO. My baseness will appear. That wrings my
soul.

PHI. Not in thy deeds. But for thy words, I fear me!

NEO. O Heaven! Must double vileness then be mine
Both shameful silence and most shameful speech?

PHI. Or my discernment is at fault, or thou
Mean'st to betray me and make voyage without me.

NEO. Nay, not without thee, there is my distress!
Lest I convey thee to thy bitter grief.

PHI. How ? How, dear youth ? I do not understand.

NEO. Here I unveil it. Thou art to sail to Troy,
To join the chieftains and the Achaean host.

PHI. What do I hear ? Ah !

NEO.   Grieve not till you learn.

PHI. Learn what ? What wilt thou make of me ?
            What mean'st thou ?

NEO. First to release thee from this plague, and then
With thee to go and take the realm of Troy.

PHI. And is this thine intent ?

NEO.   'Tis so ordained
Unchangeably. Be not dismayed ! 'Tis so.

PHI. Me miserable ! I am betrayed, undone !
What guile is here ? My bow ! give back my bow !

NEO. I may not. Interest, and duty too,
Force me to obey commandment.

PHI.   O thou fire,
Thou terror of the world ! Dark instrument
Of ever-hateful guile !—What hast thou done ?
How thou hast cheated me ! Art not ashamed
To look on him that sued to thee for shelter ?
O heart of stone, thou hast stolen my life away
With yonder bow !—Ah, yet I beg of thee,
Give it me back, my son, I entreat thee, give !
By all thy father worshipped, rob me not
Of life !—Ah me ! Now he will speak no more,
But turns away, obdúrate to retain it.
O ye, my comrades in this wilderness,
Rude creatures of the rocks, O promontories,
Creeks, precipices of the hills, to you
And your familiar presence I complain
Of this foul trespass of Achilles' son.
Sworn to convey me home, to Troy he bears me.
And under pledge of his right hand hath ta'en
And holds from me perforce my wondrous bow,
The sacred gift of Zeus-born Heracles,
Thinking to wave it midst the Achaean host
Triumphantly for his. In conquering me
He vaunts as of some valorous feat, and knows not
He is spoiling a mere corse, an empty dream,

B 2

The shadow of a vapour. In my strength
He ne'er had vanquished me. Even as I am,
He could not, but by guile. Now, all forlorn,
I am abused, deceived. What must I do?
Nay, give it me. Nay, yet be thy true self!
Thou art silent. I am lost. O misery!
Rude face of rock, back I return to thee
And thy twin gateway, robbed of arms and food,
To wither in thy cave companionless :——
No more with these mine arrows to destroy
Or flying bird or mountain-roving beast.
But, all unhappy! I myself must be
The feast of those on whom I fed, the chase
Of that I hunted, and shall dearly pay
In bloody quittance for their death, through one
Who seemed all ignorant of sinful guile.
Perish,—not till I am certain if thy heart
Will change once more,—if not, my curse on thee!

CH. What shall we do, my lord? We wait thy word
Or to sail now, or yield to his desire.

NEO. My heart is pressed with a strange pity for him,
Not now beginning, but long since begun.

PHI. Ay, pity me, my son! by all above,
Make not thy name a scorn by wronging me!

NEO. O! I am troubled sore. What must I do?
Would I had never left mine island home!

PHI. Thou art not base, but seemest to have learnt
Some baseness from base men. Now, as 'tis meet,
Be better guided—leave me mine arms, and go.

NEO. (*to Chorus*). What shall we do?

Enter ODYSSEUS.

ODYSSEUS.   What art thou doing, knave?
Give me that bow, and haste thee back again.

PHI. Alas! What do I hear? Odysseus' voice?

OD. Be sure of that, Odysseus, whom thou seest.

PHI. Oh, I am bought and sold, undone! 'Twas he
That kidnapped me, and robbed me of my bow.

OD. Yea. I deny it not. Be sure, 'twas I.

PHI. Give back, my son, the bow; release it!

OD.　　　　　　　　　　　　　　　　　That,
Though he desire it, he shall never do.
Thou too shalt march along, or these shall force thee.

PHI. They force me! O thou boldest of bad men!
They force me?

OD.　　　　　　If thou com'st not willingly.

PHI. O Lemnian earth and thou almighty flame,
Hephaestos' workmanship, shall this be borne,
That he by force must drag me from your care?

OD. 'Tis Zeus, I tell thee, monarch of this isle,
Who thus hath willed. I am his minister.

PHI. Wretch, what vile words thy wit hath power to
　　　　　　say!
The gods are liars when invoked by thee.

OD. Nay, 'tis their truth compels thee to this voyage.

PHI. I will not have it so.

OD.　　　　　　　　I will. Thou shalt.

PHI. Woe for my wretchedness! My father, then,
Begat no freeman, but a slave in me.

OD. Nay, but the peer of noblest men, with whom
Thou art to take and ravage Troy with might.

PHI. Never,—though I must suffer direst woe,—
While this steep Lemnian ground is mine to tread!

OD. What now is thine intent?

PHI.　　　　　　　　　Down from the crag
This head shall plunge and stain the crag beneath.

OD. (to the Attendants.) Ay, seize and bind him.
　　　　　　Baffle him in this.

PHI. Poor hands, for lack of your beloved string,
Caught by this craven! O corrupted soul!
How thou hast undermined me, having taken
To screen thy quest this youth to me unknown,
Far worthier of my friendship than of thine,
Who knew no better than to obey command.
Even now 'tis manifest he burns within
With pain for his own error and my wrong.
But, though unwilling and inapt for ill,
Thy crafty, mean, and cranny-spying soul
Too well hath lessoned him in sinful lore.

Now thou hast bound me, O thou wretch, and thinkest
To take me from this coast, where thou didst cast me
Outlawed and desolate, a corpse 'mongst men.
  Oh!
I curse thee now, as ofttimes in the past:
But since Heaven yields me nought but bitterness,
Thou livest and art blithe, while 'tis my pain
To live on in my misery, laughed to scorn
By thee and Atreus' sons, those generals twain
Whom thou art serving in this chase.   But thou
With strong compulsion and deceit was driven
Troyward, whilst I, poor victim, of free will
Took my seven ships and sailed there, yet was thrown
Far from all honour,—as thou sayest, by them,
But, as they turn the tale, by thee.—And now
Why fetch me hence and take me ? To what end ?
I am nothing, dead to you this many a year.
How, O thou Heaven-abhorred ! am I not now
Lame and of evil smell ? how shall ye vaunt
Before the gods drink-offering or the fat
Of victims, if I sail among your crew ?
For this, as ye professed, was the chief cause
Why ye disowned me.   Perish !—So ye shall,
For the wrong done me, if the Heavens be just.
And that they are, I know.   Else had ye ne'er
Sailed on this errand for an outcast wretch,
Had they not pricked your heart with thoughts of me.
Oh, if ye pity me, chastising powers,
And thou, the Genius of my land, revenge,
Revenge this crime on all their heads at once !
My life is pitiable ; but if I saw
Their ruin, I would think me well and strong.
  CH. How full of bitterness is his resolve,
Wrathfully spoken with unbending will !
  OD. I might speak long in answer, did the time
Give scope, but now one thing is mine to say.
I am known to vary with the varying need ;
And when 'tis tried, who can be just and good,
My peer will not be found for piety.
But though on all occasions covetous

Of victory, this once I yield to thee,
And willingly. Unhand him there. Let go!
Leave him to stay. What further use of thee,
When we have ta'en these arms? Have we not Teucer,
Skilled in this mystery? Yea, I may boast
Myself thine equal both in strength and aim
To wield them. Fare thee well, then! Thou art free
To roam thy barren isle. We need thee not.
Let us be going! And perchance thy gift
May bring thy destined glory to my brow.

PHI. What shall I do? Alas, shalt thou be seen
Graced with mine arms amongst Achaean men?

OD. No more! I am going.

PHI.   O Achilles' child!
Wilt thou, too, vanish? Must I lose thy voice?

OD. Come on, and look not, noble though thou be,
Lest thou undo our fortune.

PHI.   Mariners,
Must ye, too, leave me thus disconsolate?
Will ye not pity me?

CH.   Our captain's here.
Whate'er he saith to thee, that we too speak.

NEO. My chief will call me weakling, soft of heart;
But go not yet, since our friend bids you stay,
Till we have prayed, and all be ready on board.
Meanwhile, perchance, he may conceive some thought
That favours our design. We two will start;
And ye, be swift to speed forth at our call. [Exit

MONODY.

PHI. O cavern of the hollow rock,   I I
Frosty and stifling in the seasons' change!
How I seem fated never more to range
From thy sad covert, that hath felt the shock
Of pain on pain, steeped with my wretchedness.
Now thou wilt be my comforter in death!
Grief-haunted harbour, choked with my distress!
Tell me, what hope is mine of daily food,
Who will be careful for my good?

I fail. Ye cowering creatures of the sky,
      Oh, as ye fly,
Snatch me, borne upward on the blast's sharp breath !
  CH. 1. Thou child of misery !
       No mightier power hath this decreed,
       But thine own will and deed
       Hath bound thee thus in grief,
Since, when kind Heaven had sent relief
And shown the path of wisdom firm and sure,
Thou still hast chosen this evil to endure.

PHI. O hapless life, sore bruised with pain !   I 2
No more with living mortal may I dwell,
But ever pining in this desert cell
With lonely grief, all famished must remain
And perish ; for what food is mine to share,
When this strong arm no longer wields my bow,
Whose fleet shafts flew to smite the birds of air
I was o'erthrown by words, words dark and blind,
Low-creeping from a traitorous mind !
O might I see him, whose unrighteous thought
       This ruin wrought,
Plagued for no less a period with like woe !
  CH. 2. Not by our craft thou art caught,
But Destiny divine hath wrought
       The net that holds thee bound.
       Aim not at us the sound
Of thy dread curse with dire disaster fraught.
On others let that light ! 'Tis our true care
Thou should'st not scorn our love in thy despair.

PHI. Now, seated by the shore   II 1
    Of heaving ocean hoar,
    He mocks me, waving high
    The sole support of my precarious being,
    The bow which none e'er held but I.
O treasure of my heart, torn from this hand,
That loved thy touch,—if thou canst understand,
How sad must be thy look in seeing
Thy master destined now no more,
Like Heracles of yore,

To wield thee with an archer's might !
But in the grasp of an all-scheming wight,
O bitter change ! thou art plied ;
And swaying ever by his side,
Shalt view his life of dark malignity,
Teeming with guileful shames, like those he wrought on
        me.
  CH. 3. Nobly to speak for the right
        Is manly and strong ;
        But not with an envious blight
        To envenom the tongue ;
        He to serve all his friends of the fleet,
        One obeying a many-voiced word,
        Through the minist'ring craft of our lord
        Hath but done what was meet.

PHI. Come, legions of the wild,   II 2
      Of aspect fierce or mild,
    Fowl from the fields of air,
    And beasts that roam with bright untroubled
        gaze,
    No longer bounding from my lair
    Fly mine approach ! Now freely without fear
    Ye may surround my covert and come near,
    Treading the savage rock-strewn ways.
    The might I had is no more mine,
    Stolen with those arms divine.
    This fort hath no man to defend.
    Come satisfy your vengeful jaws, and rend
    These quivering tainted limbs !
    Already hovering death bedims
    My fainting sense. Who thus can live on air,
    Tasting no gift of earth that breathing mortals
        share ?
  CH. 4. Ah ! do not shrink from thy friend,
        If love thou reverest,
        But know 'tis for thee to forfend
        The fate which thou fearest.
        The lot thou hast here to deplore,
        Is sad evermore to maintain,

And hardship in sickness is sore,
But sorest in pain.

PHI. Kindest of all that e'er before   III
Have trod this shore,
Again thou mind'st me of mine ancient woe!
Why wilt thou ruin me? What wouldst thou do?
  CH. 5. How mean'st thou?
  PHI.   If to Troy, of me abhorred,
Thou e'er hast hoped to lead me with thy lord.
  CH. 6. So I judge best.
  PHI.   Begone at once, begone!
  CH. 7. Sweet is that word, and swiftly shall be done!
Let us be gone, each to his place on board.
          [The Chorus make as if they were going
  PHI. Nay, by dear Zeus, to whom all suppliants moan,
Leave me not yet!
  CH. 8.   Keep measure in thy word.
  PHI. Stay, by Heaven, stay!
  CH. 9. What wilt thou say?
  PHI. O misery! O cruel power
That rul'st this hour!
I am destroyed. Ah me!
O poor torn limb, what shall I do with thee
Through all my days to be?
Ah, strangers, come, return, return!
  CH. 10. What new command are we to learn
Crossing thy former mind?
  PHI. Ah! yet be kind.
Reprove not him, whose tongue, with grief distraught,
Obeys not, in dark storms, the helm of thought!

  CH. 11. Come, poor friend, the way we call.
  PHI. Never, learn it once for all!
Not though he, whom Heaven obeys,
Blast me with fierce lightning's blaze!
Perish Troy, and all your host,
That have chosen, to their cost,
To despise and cast me forth,
Since my wound obscured my worth!
Ah, but, strangers, if your sense

Hath o'er-mastered this offence,
Yield but one thing to my prayer!

CH. 12. What wouldst thou have?

PHI.   Some weapon bare,
Axe or sword or sharpened dart,
Bring it to content my heart.

CH. 13. What is thy new intent?

PHI. To sever point by point
This body, joint from joint.
On bloody death my mind is bent.

CH. 14. Wherefore?

PHI.   To see my father's face.

CH. 15. Where upon earth?

PHI.   He hath no place
Where sun doth shine, but in the halls of night.
O native country, land of my delight,
Would I were blest one moment with thy sight!
Why did I leave thy sacred dew
And loose my vessels from thy shore,
To join the hateful Danaän crew
And lend them succour? Oh, I am no more!

LEADER OF CH. Long since thou hadst seen me
                    nearing yonder ship,
Had I not spied Odysseus and the son
Of great Achilles hastening to our side.

OD. Wilt thou not tell me why thou art hurrying
This backward journey with reverted speed?

NEO. To undo what I have wrongly done to-day.

OD. Thy words appal me. What is wrongly done?

NEO. When in obeying thee and all the host——

OD. Thou didst what deed that misbecame thy life?

NEO. I conquered with base stratagem and fraud——

OD. Whom? What new plan is rising in thy mind?

NEO. Not new. But to the child of Poeas here——

OD. What wilt thou do? I quake with strange alarm.

NEO. From whom I took these weapons, back
                    again——

OD. O Heaven! thou wilt not give them! Mean'st
        thou this?

NEO. Yea, for I have them through base sinful means.

OD. I pray thee, speak'st thou thus to anger me?

NEO. If the truth anger thee, the truth is said.

OD. Achilles' son! What word is fallen from thee?

NEO. Must the same syllables be thrice thrown forth?

OD. Once was too much. Would they had ne'er been
          said!

NEO. Enough. Thou hast heard my purpose clearly
          told.

OD. I know what power shall thwart thee in the deed.

NEO. Whose will shall hinder me?

OD.   The Achaean host,
And I among them.

NEO.   Thou'rt sharp-witted, sure!
But little wit or wisdom show'st thou here.

OD. Neither thy words nor thy design is wise.

NEO. But if 'tis righteous, that is better far.

OD. How righteous, to release what thou hast ta'en
By my device?

NEO.   I sinned a shameful sin,
And I will do mine utmost to retrieve it.

OD. How? Fear'st thou not the Achaeans in this
          act?

NEO. In doing right I fear not them nor thee.

OD. I call thy power in question.

NEO.   Then I'll fight,
Not with Troy's legions, but with thee.

OD.   Come on!
Let fortune arbitrate.

NEO.   Thou seest my hand
Feeling the hilt.

OD.   And me thou soon shalt see
Doing the like and dallying not!—And yet
I will not touch thee, but will go and tell
The army, that shall wreak this on thy head. [*Exit*

NEO. Thou show'st discretion: which if thou pre-
          serve,
Thou may'st maintain a path exempt from pain.
Ho! son of Poeas, Philoctetes, come
And leave thy habitation in the rock.

PHI. What noise again is troubling my poor cave?
Why do ye summon me? What crave ye, sirs?
Ha! 'tis some knavery. Are ye come to add
Some monster evil to my mountainous woe?

NEO. Fear not, but hearken to what now I speak.

PHI. I needs must fear thee, whose fair words erewhile
Brought me to bitter fortune.

NEO.   May not men
Repent and change?

PHI.   Such wast thou in thy talk,
When thou didst rob me of my bow,—so bright
Without, so black within.

NEO.   Ah, but not now,
Assure thee! Only let me hear thy will,
Is 't constant to remain here and endure,
Or to make voyage with us?

PHI.   Stop, speak no more!
Idle and vain will all thine utterance be.

NEO. Thou art so resolved?

PHI.   More firmly than I say.

NEO. I would I might have brought thee to my mind,
But since my words are out of tune, I have done.

PHI. Thou wert best. No word of thine can touch
my soul
Or win me to thy love, who by deceit
Hast reft my life away. And then thou com'st
To school me,—of noblest father, basest son!
Perish, the Atridae first of all, and then
Laërtes' child, and thou!

NEO.   Curse me no more,
But take this hallowed weapon from my hand.

PHI. What words are these? Am I again deceived?

NEO. No, by the holiest name of Zeus on high!

PHI. O voice of gladness, if thy speech be true!

NEO. The deed shall prove it. Only reach thy hand,
And be again sole master of thy bow.

                              [ODYSSEUS *appears*

OD. But I make protest, in the sight of Heaven,
For Atreus' sons, and all the Achaean host.

PHI. Dear son, whose voice disturbs us ? Do I hear
Odysseus ?

OD.   Ay, and thou behold'st him nigh,
And he shall force thee to the Trojan plain,
Howe'er Achilles' offspring make or mar.

PHI. This shaft shall bear thee sorrow for that boast.

NEO. Let it not fly, by Heaven !

PHI.   Dear child, let go
Mine arm !

NEO.   I will not.   [*Exit* ODYSSEUS

PHI.   Ah ! Why hast thou robbed
My bow of bringing down mine enemy ?

NEO. This were ignoble both for thee and me.

PHI. One thing is manifest, the first o' the host,
Lying forerunners of the Achaean band,
Are brave with words, but cowards with the steel.

NEO. Well, now the bow is thine. Thou hast no cause
For blame or anger any more 'gainst me.

PHI. None. Thou hast proved thy birthright,
                              dearest boy.
Not from the loins of Sisyphus thou camest,
But from Achilles, who in life was held
Noblest of men alive, and now o' the dead.

NEO. It gladdens me that thou shouldst speak in
                              praise
Both of my sire and me. But hear me tell
The boon for which I sue thee.—Mortal men
Must bear such evils as high Heaven ordains ;
But those afflicted by self-chosen ills,
Like thine to-day, receive not from just men
Or kind indulgence or compassionate thought.
And thou art restive grown, and wilt not hearken,
But though one counsel thee with kind'st intent,
Wilt take him for a dark malignant foe.
Yet, calling Zeus to witness for my soul,
Once more I will speak. Know this, and mark it well :
Thou bear'st this sickness by a heavenly doom,
Through coming near to Chrysa's sentinel,
The lurking snake, that guards the sky-roofed fold.
And from this plague thou ne'er shall find reprieve

While the same Sun-god rears him from the east
And droops to west again, till thou be come
Of thine own willing mind to Troia's plain,
Where our physicians, sons of Phoebus' child,
Shall soothe thee from thy sore, and thou with me
And with this bow shalt take Troy's citadel.
How do I know this ? I will tell thee straight.
We have a Trojan captive, Helenus,
Both prince and prophet, who hath clearly told
This must be so ; yea, and ere harvest-time
This year, great Troy must fall ; else if his words
Be falsified, who will may slay the seer.
Now, since thou know'st of this, yield thy consent ;
For glorious is the gain, being singled forth
From all the Greeks as noblest, first to come
To healing hands, and then to win renown
Unrivalled, vanquishing all-tearful Troy.

    PHI. Oh how I hate my life ! Why must it keep
This breathing form from sinking to the shades ?
How can I prove a rebel to his mind
Who thus exhorts me with affectionate heart ?
And yet, oh misery ! must I give way ?
Then how could I endure the light of heaven ?
With whom could I exchange a word ? Ay me !
Eyes that have seen each act of my sad life,
How could ye bear it, to behold the sons
Of Atreus, my destroyers, comrades now
And friends ! Laërtes' wicked son, my friend !
And less I feel the grief of former wrong
Than shudder with expectance of fresh harm
They yet may work on me. For when the mind
Hath once been mother of an evil brood,
It nurses nought but evils. Yea, at thee
I marvel. Thou should'st ne'er return to Troy,
Nor suffer me to go, when thou remember'st
What insult they have done thee, ravishing
Thy father's rights from thee. And wilt thou then
Sail to befriend them, pressing me in aid ?
Nay, do not, son ; but, even as thou hast sworn,
Convey me home, and thou, in Scyros dwelling,

Leave to their evil doom those evil men.
So thou shalt win a twofold gratitude
From me and from my father, and not seem,
Helping vile men, to be as vile as they.

NEO. 'Tis fairly spoken. Yet I would that thou,
Relying on my word and on Heaven's aid,
Would'st voyage forth from Lemnos with thy friend.

PHI. Mean'st thou to Troy, and to the hateful sons
Of Atreus, me, with this distressful limb ?

NEO. Nay, but to those that will relieve the pain
Of thy torn foot and heal thee of thy plague.

PHI. Thy words are horrible. What mean'st thou,
          boy ?

NEO. The act I deem the noblest for us both.

PHI. Wilt thou speak so ? Where is thy fear of
          Heaven ?

NEO. Why should I fear, when I see certain gain?

PHI. Gain for the sons of Atreus, or for me ?

NEO. Methinks a friend should give thee friendly
          counsel.

PHI. Friendly, to hand me over to my foes ?

NEO. Ah, be not hardened in thy misery !

PHI. I know thou wilt ruin me by what thou speakest.

NEO. Not I. The case is dark to thee, I see.

PHI. I know the Atreidae cast me on this rock.

NEO. But how, if they should save thee afterward ?

PHI. They ne'er shall make me see Troy with my will.

NEO. Hard is my fortune, then, if by no sleight
Of reasoning I can draw thee to my mind.
For me, 'twere easiest to end speech, that thou
Might'st live on as thou livest in hopeless pain.

PHI. Then leave me to my fate !—But thou hast
          touched
My right hand with thine own, and given consent
To bear me to my home. Do this, dear son !
And do not linger to take thought of Troy.
Enough that name hath echoed in my groans.

NEO. If thou wilt, let us be going.

PHI.   Nobly hast thou said the word.

NEO. Lean thy steps on mine.
PHI.   As firmly as my foot will strength afford.
NEO. Ah! but how shall I escape Achaean anger?
PHI.   Do not care!
NEO. Ah! but should they spoil my country!
PHI.   I to shield thee will be there.
NEO. How to shield me, how to aid me?
PHI.   With the shafts of Heracles
I will scare them.
NEO. Give thy blessing to this isle, and come in
        peace.

HERACLES *appears from above.*

HERACLES. First, son of Poeas, wait till thou hast
        heard
The voice of Heracles, and weighed his word.
Him thou beholdest from the Heavenly seat
Come down, for thee leaving the blest retreat,
To tell thee all high Zeus intends, and stay
Thy purpose in the journey of to-day.

    Then hear me, first how after my long toils
By strange adventure I have found and won
Immortal glory, which thine eyes perceive;
And the like lot, I tell thee, shall be thine,
After these pains to rise to glorious fame.
Sailing with this thy comrade to Troy-town,
First thou shalt heal thee from thy grievous sore,
And then, being singled forth from all the host
As noblest, thou shalt conquer with that bow
Paris, prime author of these years of harm,
And capture Troy, and bear back to thy hall
The choicest guerdon, for thy valour's meed,
To Oeta's vale and thine own father's home.
But every prize thou tak'st be sure thou bear
Unto my pyre, in memory of my bow.
    This word, Achilles' offspring, is for thee
No less. For, as thou could'st not without him,
So, without thee, he cannot conquer Troy.
Then, like twin lions hunting the same hill,

C. S.   S

Guard thou him, and he thee! and I will send
Asclepius Troyward to relieve thy pain.
For Ilion now a second time must fall
Before the Herculean bow. But, take good heed,
Midst all your spoil to hold the gods in awe.
For our great Father counteth piety
Far above all. This follows men in death,
And fails them not when they resign their breath.

   PHI. Thou whom I have longed to see,
     Thy dear voice is law to me.
   NEO. I obey with gladdened heart.
   HER. Lose no time: at once depart!
     Bright occasion and fair wind
     Urge your vessel from behind.

   PHI. Come, let me bless the region ere I go.
     Poor house, sad comrade of my watch, farewell!
     Ye nymphs of meadows where soft waters flow,
     Thou ocean headland, pealing thy deep knell,
     Where oft within my cavern as I lay
     My hair was moist with dashing south-wind's spray,
     And ofttimes came from Hermes' foreland high
     Sad replication of my storm-vext cry;
     Ye fountains and thou Lycian water sweet,—
     I never thought to leave you, yet my feet
     Are turning from your paths,—we part for aye.
     Farewell! and waft me kindly on my way,
     O Lemnian earth enclosed by circling seas,
     To sail, where mighty Fate my course decrees,
     And friendly voices point me, and the will
     Of that heroic power, who doth this act fulfil.

   CH. Come now all in one strong band;
     Then, ere loosing from the land,
     Pray we to the nymphs of sea
     Kind protectresses to be,
     Till we touch the Trojan strand.

OEDIPUS AT COLONOS

THE PERSONS

OEDIPUS, *old and blind.*
ANTIGONE, *his daughter, a young girl.*
ISMENE, *his daughter, a young girl.*
CHORUS *of Village Guardians.*
An Athenian.
THESEUS, *King of Athens.*
CREON, *Envoy from Thebes.*
POLYNICES, *the elder son of Oedipus.*
Messenger.

SCENE. Colonos.

OEDIPUS had remained at Thebes for some time after his fall. But he was afterwards banished by the command of Creon, with the consent of his own sons. Their intention at first was to lay no claim to the throne. But by-and-by ambition prevailed with Eteocles, the younger-born, and he persuaded Creon and the citizens to banish his elder brother. Polynices took refuge at Argos, where he married the daughter of Adrastus, and levied an army of auxiliaries to support his pretensions to the throne of Thebes. Before going into exile Oedipus had cursed his sons.

Antigone after a while fled forth to join her father and support him in his wanderings. Ismenè also once brought him secret intelligence.

Years have now elapsed, and the Delphian oracle proclaims that if Oedipus dies in a foreign land the enemies of Thebes shall overcome her.

In ignorance of this fact, Oedipus, now aged as well as blind, and led by his daughter Antigone, appears before the grove of the Eumenides, at Colonos, in the neighbourhood of Athens. He has felt an inward intimation, which is strengthened by some words of the oracle received by him long since at Delphi, that his involuntary crimes have been atoned for, and that the Avenging Deities will now receive him kindly and make his cause their own.

After some natural hesitation on the part of the village-councillors of Colonos, Oedipus is received with princely magnanimity by Theseus, who takes him under his protection of Athens, and defends him against the machinations of Creon.

Thus the blessing of the Gods, which Oedipus carried with him, is secured to Athens, and denied to Thebes. The craft of Creon and the prayers of Polynices alike prove unavailing. Then the man of many sorrows, whose essential nobleness has survived them all, passes away mysteriously from the sight of men.

The scene is laid at Colonos, a suburb of Athens much frequented by the upper classes, especially the Knights (see Thuc. viii. 67); and before the sacred grove of the Eumenides, or Gentle Goddesses, a euphemistic title for the Erinyes, or Goddesses of Vengeance.

OEDIPUS AT COLONOS

OEDIPUS. ANTIGONE.

OEDIPUS. Antigone, child of the old blind sire,
What land is here, what people? Who to-day
Shall dole to Oedipus, the wandering exile,
Their meagre gifts? Little I ask, and less
Receive with full contentment; for my woes,
And the long years ripening the noble mind,
Have schooled me to endure.—But, O my child,
If thou espiest where we may sit, though near
Some holy precinct, stay me and set me there,
Till we may learn where we are come. 'Tis ours
To hear the will of strangers and to obey.

ANTIGONE. Woe-wearied father, yonder city's wall
That shields her, looks far distant; but this ground
Is surely sacred, thickly planted over
With olive, bay and vine, within whose bowers
Thick-fluttering song-birds make sweet melody.
Here then repose thee on this unhewn stone.
Thou hast travelled far to-day for one so old.

    OED. Seat me, my child, and be the blind man's
      guard.
    ANT. Long time hath well instructed me in that.
    OED. Now, canst thou tell me where we have set our
      feet?
    ANT. Athens I know, but not the nearer ground.
    OED. Ay, every man that met us in the way
Named Athens.
    ANT.   Shall I go, then, and find out
The name of the spot?
    OED.   Yes, if 'tis habitable.
    ANT. It is inhabited. Yet I need not go.
I see a man even now appproaching here.

OED. How ? Makes he towards us ? Is he drawing
        nigh ?
ANT. He is close beside us. Whatsoe'er thou findest
Good to be spoken, say it. The man is here.

Enter an Athenian.

OED. O stranger, learning from this maid, who sees
Both for herself and me, that thou art come
With timely light to clear our troubled thought—
ATHENIAN. Ere thou ask more, come forth from
        where thou sittest !
Ye trench on soil forbidden human tread.
OED. What soil ? And to what Power thus conse-
        crate ?
ATH. None may go near, nor dwell there. 'Tis pos-
        sessed
By the dread sisters, children of Earth and Night.
OED. What holy name will please them, if I pray ?
ATH. ' All-seeing Gentle Powers ' the dwellers here
Would call them. But each land hath its own rule.
OED. And gently may they look on him who now
Implores them, and will never leave this grove !
ATH. What saying is this ?
OED.   The watchword of my doom.
ATH. Yet dare I not remove thee, till the town
Have heard my purpose and confirm the deed.
OED. By Heaven, I pray thee, stranger, scorn me not,
Poor wanderer that I am, but answer me.
ATH. Make clear thy drift. Thou'lt get no scorn
        from me.
OED. Then, pray thee, tell me how ye name the place
Where now I sit.
ATH.   The region all around
Is sacred. For 'tis guarded and possessed
By dread Poseidon, and the Titan mind
That brought us fire—Prometheus. But that floor
Whereon thy feet are resting, hath been called
The brazen threshold of our land, the stay
Of glorious Athens, and the neighbouring fields
Are fain to honour for their patron-god

Thee, O Colonos, first of Knights, whose name
                              [*Pointing to a statue*
They bear in brotherhood and own for theirs.
Such, friend, believe me, is this place, not praised
In story, but of many a heart beloved.

   OED. Then is the land inhabited of men ?
   ATH. By men, who name them from Colonos there.
   OED. Have they a lord, or sways the people's voice ?
   ATH. Lord Theseus, child of Aegeus, our late king.
   OED. Will some one of your people bring him hither ?
   ATH. Wherefore ? What urgent cause requires his
        presence ?
   OED. He shall gain mightily by granting little.
   ATH. Who can gain profit from the blind ?
   OED.   The words
These lips shall utter, shall be full of sight.
   ATH. Well, thou look'st nobly, but for thy hard
        fate.
This course is safe. Thus do. Stay where I found
        thee,
Till I go tell the neighbour townsmen here
Not of the city, but Colonos. They
Shall judge for thee to abide or to depart.   [*Exit*
   OED. Tell me, my daughter, is the man away ?
   ANT. He is gone, father. I alone am near.
Speak what thou wilt in peace and quietness.

   OED. Dread Forms of holy Fear, since in this land
Your sanctuary first gave my limbs repose,
Be not obdúrate to my prayer, nor spurn
The voice of Phoebus, who that fateful day,
When he proclaimed my host of ills to come,
Told me of rest after a weary time,
Where else but here ? ' When I should reach my bourne,
And find repose and refuge with the Powers
Of reverend name, my troubled life should end
With blessing to the men who sheltered me,
And curses on their race who banished me
And sent me wandering forth.' Whereof he vouched me
Sure token, or by earthquake, or by fire
From heaven, or thundrous voices. And I know

Some aëry message from your shrine hath drawn me
With wingèd whisper to this grove. Not else
Had ye first met me coming, nor had I
Sate on your dread unchiselled seat of stone,
With dry cold lips greeting your sober shrine.
Then give Apollo's word due course, and give
Completion to my life, if in your sight
These toils and sorrows past the human bound
Seem not too little. Kindly, gentle powers,
Offspring of primal darkness, hear my prayer!
Hear it, Athenai, of all cities queen,
Great Pallas' foster-city! Look with ruth
On this poor shadow of great Oedipus,
This fading semblance of his kingly form.

ANT. Be silent now. There comes an aged band
With jealous looks to know thine errand here.

OED. I will be silent, and thine arm shall guide
My footstep under covert of the grove
Out of the path, till I make sure what words
These men will utter. Warily to observe
Is the prime secret of the prudent mind.   [*Exeunt*

CHORUS (*entering*).

Keep watch! Who is it? Look!   1
Where is he? Vanished! Gone! Oh where?
    Most uncontrolled of men!
    Look well, inquire him out,
    Search keenly in every nook!
    —Some wanderer is the aged wight,
    A wanderer surely, not a native here.
    Else never had he gone within
    The untrodden grove
Of these—unmarried, unapproachable in might,
    —Whose name we dare not breathe,
    But pass their shrine
    Without a look, without a word,
Uttering the unheard voice of reverential thought.
    But now, one comes, they tell, devoid of awe,
    Whom, peering all around this grove
    I find not, where he abideth.

OED. (*behind*). Behold me! For I 'see by sound,'
As mortals say.

CH. Oh, Oh!

With horror I see him, with horror hear him speak.

OED. Pray you, regard me not as a transgressor!

CH. Defend us, Zeus! Who is that aged wight?

OED. Not one of happiest fate,
Or enviable, O guardians of this land!
'Tis manifest; else had I not come hither
Led by another's eyes, not moored my bark
On such a slender stay.

CH. Alas! And are thine eyes   2
Sightless? O full of misery,
  As thou look'st full of years!
  But not, if I prevail,
  Shalt thou bring down this curse.
  Thou art trespassing. Yet keep thy foot
  From stumbling in that verdant, voiceless dell,
  Where running water as it fills
  The hallowed bowl,
Mingles with draughts of honey. Stranger, hapless one!
  Avoid that with all care.
  Away! Remove!
  Distance impedes the sound. Dost hear,
Woe-burdened wanderer? If aught thou carest to bring
  Before our council, leave forbidden ground,
  And there, where all have liberty,
  Speak,—but till then, avaunt thee!

OED. Daughter, what must I think, or do?

ANT.   My sire!
We must conform us to the people's will,
Yielding ere they compel.

OED.   Give me thy hand.

ANT. Thou hast it.

OED.   —Strangers, let me not
Be wronged, when I have trusted you
And come from where I stood!

CH. Assure thee, from this seat
No man shall drag thee off against thy will.

OED. Farther ?

CH.   Advance thy foot.

OED.   Yet more ?

CH.   Assist him onward,
Maiden, thou hast thy sight.

ANT. Come, follow, this way follow with thy darkened
                 steps,
Father, the way I am leading thee.

CH. Content thee, sojourning in a strange land,
O man of woe !
To eschew whate'er the city holds in hate,
And honour what she loves !

OED.   Then do thou lead me, child,
Where with our feet secure from sin
We may be suffered both to speak and hear.
Let us not war against necessity.

CH. There ! From that bench of rock
Go not again astray.

OED. Even here ?

CH.   Enough, I tell thee.

OED.   May I sit ?

CH. Ay, crouch thee low adown
Crooking thy limbs, upon the stone.

ANT. Father, this task is mine.—
Sink gently down into thy resting-place,

OED. Woe is me !

ANT. Supporting on this loving hand
Thy reverend aged form.

OED. Woe, for my cruel fate !   [OEDIPUS *is seated*

CH. Now thou unbendest from thy stubborn ways,
O man of woe !
Declare, what mortal wight thou art,
That, marked by troublous fortune, here art led.
What native country, shall we learn, is thine ?

OED. O strangers, I have none !
But do not—

CH.   What dost thou forbid, old sir ?

OED. Do not, oh, do not ask me who I am,
Nor probe me with more question.

CH.   What dost thou mean ?
OED. My birth is dreadful.
CH.   Tell it forth.
OED. What should I utter, O my child ? Woe is me !
CH. Thy seed, thy father's name, stranger, pronounce!
OED. Alas ! What must I do ? My child !
ANT. Since no resource avails thee, speak !
OED. I will.   I cannot hide it further.
CH. Ye are long about it.   Haste thee !
OED.   Know ye of one
Begotten of Laius ?
CH.   Horror ! Horror ! Oh !
OED. Derived from Labdacus ?
CH.   O Heaven !
OED. Fate-wearied Oedipus ?
CH.   Art thou he ?
OED. Fear not my words.
CH.   Oh ! Oh !
OED. Unhappy me !
CH.   Oh !
OED.   Daughter, what is coming ?
CH. Away ! Go forth.   Leave ye the land.   Begone !
OED. And where, then, is the promise thou hast given ?
CH. No doom retributive attends the deed
That wreaks prevenient wrong.
Deceit, matched with deceit, makes recompense
Of evil, not of kindness.   Get thee forth !
Desert that seat again, and from this land
Unmooring speed thee away, lest on our state
Thou bring some further bale !

MCNODY.

ANT. O strangers, full of reverent care !
Since ye cannot endure my father here,
Aged and blind,
Because ye have heard a rumour of the deeds
He did unknowingly,—yet, we entreat you,
Strangers, have pity on me, the hapless girl,
Who pray for mine own sire and for none else,
—Pray, looking in your eyes with eyes not blind,

As if a daughter had appeared to you.
Pleading for mercy to the unfortunate.
We are in your hands as in the hand of God,
Helpless. O then accord the unhoped-for boon!
By what is dear to thee, thy veriest own,
I pray thee,—chattel or child, or holier name!
Search through the world, thou wilt not find the man
Who could resist the leading of a God.

CH. Daughter of Oedipus, be well assured
We view with pity both thy case and his,
But fear of Heavenly wrath confines our speech
To that we have already said to you.
OED. What profit lives in fame and fair renown
By unsubstantial rumour idly spread?
When Athens is extolled with peerless praise
For reverence, and for mercy!—She alone
The sufferer's shield, the exile's comforter!
What have I reaped hereof? Ye have raised me up
From yonder seat, and now would drive me forth
Fearing a name! For there is nought in me
Or deeds of mine to make you fear. My life
Hath more of wrong endured than of wrong done,
Were it but lawful to disclose to you
Wherefore ye dread me,—not my sin but theirs,
My mother's and my sire's. I know your thought.
Yet never can ye fasten guilt on me,
Who, though I had acted with the clear'st intent,
Were guiltless, for my deed requited wrong.
But as it was, all blindly I went forth
On that dire road, while they who planned my death
Planned it with perfect knowledge. Therefore, sirs,
By Heaven I pray you, as ye have bid me rise,
Protect your suppliant without fail; and do not
In jealous reverence for the blessed Gods
Rob them of truest reverence, but know this:—
God looks upon the righteousness of men
And their unrighteousness, nor ever yet
Hath one escaped who wrought iniquity.
Take part, then, with the Gods, nor overcloud

The golden fame of Athens with dark deeds;
But as ye have pledged your faith to shelter me,
Defend me and rescue, not rejecting me
Through mere abhorrence of my ruined face.
For on a holy mission am I come,
Sent with rich blessings for your neighbours here.
And when the head and sovereign of your folk
Is present, ye shall learn the truth at full.
Till then, be gracious to me, and not perverse.

CH. Thy meaning needs must strike our hearts with
          awe,
Old wanderer! so weighty are the words
That body it forth. Therefore we are content
The Lord of Athens shall decide this case.

OED. And where is he who rules this country, sirs?
CH. He keeps his father's citadel. But one
Is gone to fetch him, he who brought us hither.
OED. Think you he will consider the blind man,
And come in person here to visit him?
CH. Be sure he will,—when he hath heard thy name.
OED. And who will carry that?
CH.   'Tis a long road;
But rumour from the lips of wayfarers
Flies far and wide, so that he needs must hear;
And hearing, never doubt but he will come.
So noised in every land hath been thy name,
Old sovereign,—were he sunk in drowsiness,
That sound would bring him swiftly to thy side.
OED. Well, may he come to bless his city and me!
When hath not goodness blessed the giver of good?

ANT. O Heavens! What shall I say, what think, my
          father?
OED. Daughter Antigone, what is it?
ANT.   I see
A woman coming toward us, mounted well
On a fair Sicilian palfrey, and her face
With brow-defending hood of Thessaly
Is shadowed from the sun. What must I think?
Is it she or no? Can the eye so far deceive?

It is. 'Tis not. Unhappy that I am,
I know not.—Yes, 'tis she. For drawing near
She greets me with bright glances, and declares
Beyond a doubt, Ismenè's self is here.

    ŒD. What say'st thou, daughter ?
    ANT.   That I see thy child,
My sister. Soon her voice will make thee sure.

Enter ISMENE.

ISMENE. Father and sister !—names for ever dear !
Hard hath it been to find you, yea, and hard
I feel it now to look on you for grief.
    ŒD. Child, art thou here ?
    ISM.   Father ! O sight of pain !
    ŒD. Offspring and sister !
    ISM.   Woe for thy dark fate !
    ŒD. Hast thou come, daughter ?
    ISM.   On a troublous way.
    ŒD. Touch me, my child !
    ISM.   I give a hand to both.
    ŒD. To her and me ?
    ISM.   Three linked in one sad knot.
    ŒD. Child, wherefore art thou come ?
    ISM.   In care for thee.
    ŒD. Because you missed me ?
    ISM.   Ay, and to bring thee tidings,
With the only slave whom I could trust.
    ŒD.   And they,
Thy brethren, what of them ? Were they not there
To take this journey for their father's good ?
    ISM. Ask not of them. Dire deeds are theirs to-day.
    ŒD. How in all points their life obeys the law
Of Egypt, where the men keep house and weave
Sitting within-doors, while the wives abroad
Provide with ceaseless toil the means of life.
So in your case, my daughters, they who should
Have ta'en this burden on them, bide at home
Like maidens, while ye take their place, and lighten
My miseries by your toil. Antigone,
E'er since her childhood ended, and her frame

Was firmly knit, with ceaseless ministry
Still tends upon the old man's wandering,
Oft in the forest ranging up and down
Fasting and barefoot through the burning heat
Or pelting rain, nor thinks, unhappy maid,
Of home or comfort, so her father's need
Be satisfied. And thou, that camest before,
Eluding the Cadmeans, and didst tell me
What words Apollo had pronounced on me,
And when they banished me, stood'st firm to shield me,
What news, Ismenè, bring'st thou to thy sire
To-day? What mission sped thee forth? I know
Thou com'st not idly, but with fears for me.

Ism. Father, I will not say what I endured
In searching out the place that sheltered thee.
To tell it o'er would but renew the pain.
But of the danger now encompassing
Thine ill-starred sons,—of that I came to speak.
At first they strove with Creon and declared
The throne should be left vacant and the town
Freed from pollution,—paying deep regard
In their debate to the dark heritage
Of ruin that o'ershadowed all thy race.
Far different is the strife which holds them now,
Since some great Power, joined to their sinful mind,
Incites them both to seize on sovereign sway.
Eteocles, in pride of younger years,
Robbed elder Polynices of his right,
Dethroned and banished him. To Argos then
Goes exiled Polynices, and obtains
Through intermarriage a strong favouring league,
Whose word is, 'Either Argos vanquishes
The seed of Cadmus or exalts their fame.'
This, father, is no tissue of empty talk,
But dreadful truth, nor can I tell where Heaven
Is to reveal his mercy to thy woe.

Oed. And hadst thou ever hoped the Gods would
care
For mine affliction, and restore my life?

Ism. I hope it now since this last oracle.

OED. What oracle hath been declared, my child ?

ISM. That they shall seek thee forth, alive or dead,
To bring salvation to the Theban race.

OED. Who can win safety through such help as mine ?

ISM. 'Tis said their victory depends on thee.

OED. When shrunk to nothing, am I indeed a man?

ISM. Yea, for the Gods uphold thee, who then
destroyed.

OED. Poor work, to uphold in age who falls when
young !

ISM. Know howsoe'er that Creon will be here
For this same end, ere many an hour be spent.

OED. For what end, daughter ? Tell me in plain
speech.

ISM. To set thee near their land, that thou may'st be
Beyond their borders, but within their power.

OED. What good am I, thus lying at their gate ?

ISM. Thine inauspicious burial brings them woe.

OED. There needs no oracle to tell me one that.

ISM. And therefore they would place thee near their
land,
Where thou mays't have no power upon thyself.

OED. Say then, shall Theban dust o'ershadow me ?

ISM. The blood of kindred cleaving to thy hand,
Father, forbids thee.

OED.   Never, then, henceforth,
Shall they lay hold on me !

ISM.   If that be true,
The brood of Cadmus shall have bale.

OED.   What cause
Having appeared, will bring this doom to pass ?

ISM. Thy wrath, when they are marshalled at thy
tomb.

OED. From whom hast thou heard this ?

ISM.   Sworn messengers
Brought such report from Delphi's holy shrine.

OED. Hath Phoebus so pronounced my destiny ?

ISM. So they declare who brought the answer back.

OED. Did my sons hear ?

ISM.   They know it, both of them.

OED. Villains, who, being informed of such a word,
Turned not their thoughts toward me, but rather chose
Ambition and a throne!

ISM.   It wounds mine ear
To hear it spoken, but the news I bring
Is to that stern effect.

OED.   Then I pray Heaven
The fury of their fate-appointed strife
May ne'er be quenched, but that the end may come
According to my wish upon them twain
To this contention and arbitrament
Of battle which they now assay and lift
The threatening spear! So neither he who wields
The sceptred power should keep possession still,
Nor should his brother out of banishment
Ever return:—who, when their sire—when I
Was shamefully thrust from my native land,
Checked not my fall nor saved me, but, for them,
I was driven homeless and proclaimed an exile.
Ye will tell me 'twas in reason that the State
Granted this boon to my express desire
Nay; for in those first hours of agony,
When my heart raged, and it seemed sweetest to me
To die the death, and to be stoned with stones,
No help appeared to yield me that relief.
But after lapse of days, when all my pain
Was softened, and I felt that my hot spirit
Had run to fierce excess of bitterness
In wreaking mine offence—then, then the State
Drove me for ever from the land, and they,
Their father's sons, who might have saved their father,
Cared not to help him, but betrayed by them,
For lack of one light word, I wandered forth
To homeless banishment and beggary.
But these weak maidens to their nature's power
Have striven to furnish me with means to live
And dwell securely, girded round with love.
My sons have chosen before their father's life
A lordly throne and sceptred sovereignty.
But never shall they win me to their aid,

Nor shall the Theban throne for which they strive
Bring them desired content. That well I know,
Comparing with my daughter's prophecies
Those ancient oracles which Phoebus once
Spake in mine ear. Then let them send to seek me
Creon, or who is strongest in their State.
For if ye, strangers, will but add your might
To the protection of these awful Powers,
The guardians of your soil, to shelter me,
Ye shall acquire for this your State a saviour
Mighty to save, and ye shall vex my foes.

CH. Thou art worthy of all compassion, Oedipus,
Thyself and these thy daughters. Now, moreover,
Since thou proclaim'st thyself our country's saviour
I would advise thee for the best.

OED.   Kind sir,
Be my good guide. I will do all thou biddest.

CH. Propitiate then these holy powers, whose grove
Received thee when first treading this their ground.

OED. What are the appointed forms? Advise me,
          sirs.

CH. First see to it that from some perennial fount
Clean hands provide a pure drink-offering.

OED. And when I have gotten this unpolluted
          draught?

CH. You will find bowls, formed by a skilful hand,
Whose brims and handles you must duly wreathe.

OED. With leaves or flocks of wool, or in what way?

CH. With tender wool ta'en from a young ewe-lamb.

OED. Well, and what follows to complete the rite?

CH. Next, make libation toward the earliest dawn.

OED. Mean'st thou from those same urns whereof thou
          speakest?

CH. From those three vessels pour three several
          streams,
Filling the last to the brim.

OED.   With what contents
Must this be filled? Instruct me.

CH.   Not with wine,
But water and the treasure of the bee.

OED. And when leaf-shadowed Earth has drunk of
this,
What follows ?
CH.   Thou shalt lay upon her then
From both thy hands a row of olive-twigs—
Counting thrice nine in all—and add this prayer—
OED. That is the chief thing,—that I long to
hear.
CH. As we have named them Gentle, so may they
From gentle hearts accord their suppliant aid ;—
Be this thy prayer, or whoso prays for thee,
Spoken not aloud, but so that none may hear ;
And in departing, turn not. This being done,
I can stand by thee without dread. But else,
I needs must fear concerning thee.
OED.   My daughters,
Have ye both heard our friends who inhabit here ?
ANT. Yea, father ; and we wait for thy command.
OED. I cannot go. Two losses hinder me,
Two evils, want of strength and want of sight.
Let one of you go and perform this service.
One soul, methinks, in paying such a debt
May quit a million, if the heart be pure.
Haste, then, to do it. Only leave me not
Untended. For I cannot move alone
Nor without some one to support me and guide.
ISM. I will be ministrant. But let me know
Where I must find the place of offering.
CH. Beyond this grove. And, stranger maid, if
aught
Seem wanting, there is one at hand to show it.
ISM. Then to my task. Meantime, Antigone,
Watch by our sire. We must not make account
Of labour that supplies a parent's need.   [*Exit*

CH. Thy long since slumbering woe I would not wake
again,   I 1
But yet I long to learn.
OED.   What hidden lore ?
CH.   The pain

That sprang against thy life with spirit-mastering
          force.

OED. Ah, sirs, as ye are kind, re-open not that source
Of unavoided shame.

CH.   Friend, we would hear the tale
Told truly, whose wide voice doth hourly more prevail.

OED. Misery!

CH.   Be not loth!

OED.   O bitterness!

CH.   Consent.
For all thou didst require we gave to thy content.

OED. Oh, strangers, I have borne an all-too-willing
          brand,   I 2
Yet not of mine own choice.

CH.   Whence? We would understand.

OED. Nought knowing of the curse she fastened
          on my head
Thebè in evil bands bound me.

CH.   Thy mother's bed,
Say, didst thou fill? mine ear still echoes to the noise.

OED. 'Tis death to me to hear, but, these, mine only
          joys,
Friends, are my curse.

CH.   O Heaven!

OED.   The travail of one womb
Hath gendered all you see, one mother, one dark doom.

CH. How? Are they both thy race, and—   II 1

OED.   Sister branches too,
Nursed at the self-same place with him from whom
          they grew.

CH. O horror!

OED. Ay, not one, ten thousand charged me then!

CH. O sorrow!

OED.   Never done, an ever-sounding strain.

CH. O crime!

OED.   By me ne'er wrought.

CH.   But how?

OED.   The guerdon fell.
Would I had earned it not from those I served too well.

CH. But, hapless, didst thou slay—   II 2
OED.   What seek ye more to know?
CH. Thy father?
OED.   O dismay! Ye wound me, blow on blow.
CH. Thy hand destroyed him.
OED.   Yes. Yet lacks there not herein
A plea for my redress.
CH.   How canst thou clear that sin?
OED. I'll tell thee. For the deed, 'twas proved
          mine,—Oh 'tis true!
Yet by Heaven's law I am freed :—I wist not whom I
    slew.

CH. Enough. For lo! where Aegeus' princely son,
Theseus, comes hither, summoned at thy word.

Enter THESEUS.

THESEUS. From many voices in the former time
Telling thy cruel tale of sight destroyed
I have known thee, son of Laius, and to-day
I know thee anew, in learning thou art here.
Thy raiment, and the sad change in thy face,
Proclaim thee who thou art, and pitying thee,
Dark-fated Oedipus, I fain would hear
What prayer or supplication thou preferrest
To me and to my city, thou and this
Poor maid who moves beside thee. Full of dread
Must be that fortune thou canst name, which I
Would shrink from, since I know of mine own youth,
How in strange lands a stranger as thou art
I bore the brunt of perilous circumstance
Beyond all others; nor shall any man,
Like thee an alien from his native home,
Find me to turn my face from succouring him.
I am a man and know it. To-morrow's good
Is no more mine than thine or any man's.
  OED. Thy noble spirit, Theseus, in few words
Hath made my task of utterance brief indeed.
Thou hast told aright my name and parentage
And native city. Nought remains for me

But to make known mine errand, and our talk
Is ended.

THE. Tell me plainly thy desire.

OED. I come to offer thee this woe-worn frame,
As a free boon,—not goodly in outward view.
A better gift than beauty is that I bring.

THE. What boon dost thou profess to have brought
with thee ?

OED. Thou shalt know by and by,—not yet awhile.

THE. When comes the revelation of thine aid ?

OED. When I am dead, and thou hast buried me.

THE. Thou cravest the last kindness. What's between
Thou dost forget or else neglect.

OED.   Herein
One word conveys the assurance of the whole.

THE. You sum up your petition in brief form.

OED. Look to it. Great issues hang upon this
hour.

THE. Mean'st thou in this the fortune of thy sons
Or mine ?

OED.   I mean the force of their behest
Compelling my removal hence to Thebes.

THE. So thy consent were sought, 'twere fair to yield.

OED. Once I was ready enough. They would not
then.

THE. Wrath is not wisdom in misfortune, man !

OED. Nay, chide not till thou knowest.

THE.   Inform me, then !
I must not speak without just grounds.

OED.   O Theseus,
I am cruelly harassed with wrong heaped on wrong.

THE. Mean'st thou that prime misfortune of thy
birth ?

OED. No. That hath long been rumoured through
the world.

THE. What, then, can be thy grief ? If more than
that,
'Tis more than human.

OED.   Here is my distress :—

I am made an outcast from my native land
By mine own offspring. And return is barred
For ever to the man who slew his sire.

THE. How then should they require thee to go near,
And yet dwell separate ?

OED.   The voice of Heaven
Will drive them to it.

THE.   As fearing what reverse
Prophetically told ?

OED.   Destined defeat
By Athens in the Athenian land.

THE.   What source
Of bitterness 'twixt us and Thebes can rise ?

OED. Dear son of Aegeus, to the Gods alone
Comes never Age nor Death. All else i' the world
Time, the all-subduer, merges in oblivion.
Earth and men's bodies weaken, fail, and perish:
Faith withers, breach of faith springs up and grows.
And neither men nor cities that are friends
Breathe the same spirit with continuing breath.
Love shall be turned to hate, and hate to love
With many hereafter, as with some to-day.
And though, this hour, between great Thebes and thee
No cloud be in the heaven, yet moving Time
Enfolds a countless brood of days to come,
Wherein for a light cause they shall destroy
Your now harmonious league with severing war,
Even where my slumbering form, buried in death,
Coldly shall drink the life-blood of my foes,
If Zeus be Zeus, and his son Phoebus true.
I would not speak aloud of mysteries.
Then let me leave where I began. Preserve
Thine own good faith, and thou shalt never say,
Unless Heaven's promise fail me, that for nought
Athens took Oedipus to dwell with her.

CH. My lord, long since the stranger hath professed
Like augury of blessings to our land.

THE. And who would dare reject his proffered good ?
Whose bond with us of warrior amity
Hath ne'er been sundered,—and to-day he comes

A God-sent suppliant, whose sacred hand
Is rich with gifts for Athens and for me.
In reverent heed whereof I ne'er will scorn
The boon he brings, but plant him in our land.
And if it please our friend to linger here,
Ye shall protect him :—if to go with me
Best likes thee, Oedipus,—ponder, and use
Thy preference. For my course shall join with thine.
  OED. Ye Heavens, reward such excellence!
  THE.   How, then ?
Is it thy choice now to go home with me ?
  OED. Yea, were it lawful.　But in this same spot—
  THE. What wouldst thou do ?　I'll not withstand thy
    will.
  OED. I must have victory o'er my banishers.
  THE. Thy dwelling with us, then, is our great gain ?
  OED. Yes, if thou fail me not, but keep thy word.
  THE. Nay, fear not me !　I will aye be true to thee.
  OED. I will not bind thee, like a knave, with oaths.
  THE. Oaths were no stronger than my simple word.
  OED. What will ye do, then ?
  THE.   What is that thou fearest ?
  OED. They will come hither.
  THE.   Thy guards will see to that.
  OED. Beware, lest, if you leave me—
  THE.   Tell not me,
I know my part.
  OED.   Terror will have me speak.
  THE. Terror and I are strangers.
  OED.   But their threats !
Thou canst not know—
  THE.   I know that none shall force
Thee from this ground against thy will.　Full oft
Have threatening words in wrath been voluble,
Yet, when the mind regained her place again,
The threatened evil vanished.　So to-day
Bold words of boastful meaning have proclaimed
Thy forcible abduction by thy kin.
Yet shall they find (I know it) the voyage from Thebes,
On such a quest, long and scarce navigable.

Whate'er my thought, if Phoebus sent thee forth,
I would bid thee have no fear. And howsoe'er,
My name will shield thee from all injury.

CHORUS.

Friend ! in our land of conquering steeds thou art
        come   I 1
To this Heaven-fostered haunt, Earth's fairest home,
Gleaming Colonos, where the nightingale
In cool green covert warbleth ever clear,
True to the clustering ivy and the dear
    Divine, impenetrable shade,
From wildered boughs and myriad fruitage made,
Sunless at noon, stormless in every gale.
Wood-roving Bacchus there, with mazy round,
And his nymph nurses range the unoffended ground.

And nourished day by day with heavenly dew   I 2
Bright flowers their never-failing bloom renew,
From eldest time Dêo and Cora's crown
Full-flowered narcissus, and the golden beam
Of crocus, while Cephisus' gentle stream
    In runnels fed by sleepless springs
Over the land's broad bosom daily brings
His pregnant waters, never dwindling down.
The quiring Muses love to seek the spot
And Aphroditè's golden car forsakes it not.

Here too a plant, nobler than e'er was known   II 1
On Asian soil, grander than yet hath grown
In Pelops' mighty Dorian isle, unsown,
  Free, self-create, the conquering foeman's fear,
The kind oil-olive, silvery-green,
Chief nourisher of childish life, is seen
To burgeon best in this our mother-land.
No warrior, young, nor aged in command,
    Shall ravage this, or scathe it with the spear ;
    For guardian Zeus' unslumbering eye
    Beholds it everlastingly,
And Athens' grey-eyed Queen, dwelling for ever near.

Yet one more praise mightier than all I tell II 2
O'er this my home, that Ocean loves her well,
    And coursers love her, children of the wave.
To grace these roadways Prince Poseidon first
Framed for the horse, that else had burst
From man's control, the spirit-taming bit.
And the trim bark, rowed by strong arms, doth flit
    O'er briny seas with glancing motion brave.
    Lord of the deep! by that thy glorious gift
Thou hast established our fair town
For ever in supreme renown—
The Sea-nymphs' plashing throng glide not more
        smoothly swift.

ANT. O land exalted thus in blessing and praise,
Now is thy time to prove these brave words true.
OED. What hath befallen, my daughter?
ANT.   Here at hand,
Not unaccompanied, is Creon, father.
OED. Dear aged friends, be it yours now to provide
My safety and the goal of my desire!
CH. It shall be so. Fear nought. I am old and
        weak,
But Athens in her might is ever young.

Enter CREON.

CREON. Noble inhabiters of Attic ground,
I see as 'twere conceived within your eyes
At mine approach some new-engendered fear.
Nay, shrink not, nor let fall one fretful word.
I bring no menace with me, for mine age
Is feeble, and the state whereto I come
Is mighty,—none in Hellas mightier,—
That know I well. But I am sent to bring
By fair persuasion to our Theban plain
The reverend form of him now present here.
Nor came this mission from one single will,
But the commands of all my citizens
Are on me, seeing that it becomes my birth
To mourn his sorrows most of all the state.

Thou, then, poor sufferer, lend thine ear to me
And come. All Cadmus' people rightfully
Invite thee with one voice unto thy home,
I before all,—since I were worst of men,
Were I not pained at thy misfortunes, sir,
—To see thee wandering in the stranger's land
Aged and miserable, unhoused, unfed,
Singly attended by this girl, whose fall
To such a depth of undeservèd woe
I could not have imagined ! Hapless maid !
Evermore caring for thy poor blind head,
Roving in beggary, so young, with no man
To marry her,—a mark for all mischance.
O misery, what deep reproach I have laid
On thee and me and our whole ill-starred race !
But who can hide evil that courts the day ?
Thou, therefore, Oedipus, without constraint,
(By all the Gods of Cadmus' race I pray thee)
Remove this horror from the sight of men
By coming to the ancestral city and home
Of thy great sires,—bidding a kind farewell
To worthiest Athens, as is meet. But Thebes,
Thy native land, yet more deserves thy love.

Oed. Thou unabashed in knavery, who canst frame
For every cause the semblance of a plea
Pranked up with righteous seeming, why again
Would'st thou contrive my ruin, and attempt
To catch me where I most were grieved being caught ?
Beforetime, when my self-procurèd woes
Were plaguing me, and I would fain have rushed
To instant banishment, thou wouldst not then
Grant this indulgence to my keen desire.
But when I had fed my passion to the full,
And all my pleasure was to live at home,
Then 'twas thy cue to expel and banish me,
Nor was this name of kindred then so dear.
Now once again, when thou behold'st this city
And people joined in friendly bands with me,
Thou wouldst drag me from my promised resting-place,
Hiding hard policy with courtly show.

Strange kindness, to love men against their will!
Suppose, when thou wert eager in some suit,
No grace were granted thee, but all denied,
And when thy soul was sated, then the boon
Were offered, when such grace were graceless now;
—Poor satisfaction then were thine, I ween!
Even such a gift thou profferest me to-day,
Kind in pretence, but really full of evil.
These men shall hear me tell thy wickedness.
Thou comest to take me, not unto my home,
But to dwell outlawed at your gate, that so
Your Thebè may come off untouched of harm
From her encounter with Athenian men.
Ye shall not have me thus. But you shall have
My vengeful spirit ever in your land
Abiding for destruction,—and my sons
Shall have this portion in their father's ground,
To die thereon. Know I not things in Thebes
Better than thou? Yea, for 'tis mine to hear
Safer intelligencers,—Zeus himself,
And Phoebus, high interpreter of Heaven.
Thou bring'st a tongue suborned with false pretence,
Sharpened with insolence;—but in shrewd speech
Thou shalt find less of profit than of bane.
This thou wilt ne'er believe. Therefore begone!
Let me live here. For even such life as mine
Were not amiss, might I but have my will.

CR. Which of us twain, believ'st thou, in this talk
Hath more profoundly sinned against thy peace?

OED. If thou prevail'st with these men present here
Even as with me, I shall be well content.

CR. Unhappy man, will not even Time bring forth
One spark of wisdom to redeem thine age?

OED. Thou art a clever talker. But I know
No just man who in every cause abounds
With eloquent speech.

CR.   'Tis not to abound in speech,
When one speaks fitting words in season.

OED.   Oh!
As if thy words were few and seasonable!

CR. Not in the dotard's judgement.

OED.   Get thee gone!
I speak their mind as well—and dog not me
Beleaguering mine appointed dwelling-place!

CR. These men shall witness—for thy word is naught;
And for thy spiteful answer to thy friends,
If once I seize thee—

OED.   Who shall seize on me
Without the will of my protectors here?

CR. Well, short of that, thou shalt have pain, I trow.

OED. What hast thou done, that thou canst threaten
                      thus?

CR. One of thy daughters I have sent in charge.
This other, I myself will quickly take.

OED. Oh, cruel!

CR.   Soon thou'lt have more cause to cry.

OED. Hast thou my child?

CR.   I will have both ere long.

OED. Dear friends, what will ye do? Will ye forsake
                      me?
Will you not drive the offender from your land?

CH. Stranger, depart at once! Thou hast done wrong,
And wrong art doing.

CR. (to attendants). Now then, lead her away
By force, if she refuse to go with you.

ANT. Ah me! unhappy! Whither shall I flee?
What aid of God or mortal can I find?

CH. What dost thou, stranger?

CR.   I will lay no hand
On him, but on my kinswoman.

OED.   Alas!
Lords of Colonos, will ye suffer it?

CH. Thou art transgressing, stranger.

CR.   Nay, I stand
Within my right.

CH.   How so?

CR.   I take mine own.

OED. Athens to aid!

CH.   Stranger, forbear! What dost thou?

Let go, or thou shalt try thy strength with us.

CR. Unhand me!

CH.   Not while this intent is thine.

CR. If you harm me, you will have war with Thebes.

OED. Did I not tell you this would come?

CH.   Release
The maid with speed.

CR.   Command where you have power.

CH. Leave hold, I say!

CR.   Away with her, say I!

CH. Come hither, neighbours, come!
My city suffers violence. Wrongful men
Are hurting her with force. Come hither to me!

ANT. Unhappy, I am dragged away,—O strangers!

OED. Where art thou, O my child?

ANT.   I go away
Against my will.

OED.   Reach forth thy hands, my daughter!

ANT. I cannot.

CR.   Off with her!

OED.   Alas, undone!
                    [*Exit* ANTIGONE, *guarded*

CR. Thou shalt not have these staves henceforth to
                    prop
Thy roaming to and fro. Take thine own way!
Since thou hast chosen to thwart thy nearest kin,—
Beneath whose orders, though a royal man,
I act herein,—and thine own native land.
The time will surely come when thou shalt find
That in this deed and all that thou hast done
In opposition to their friendly will,
Thou hast counselled foolishly against thy peace,
Yielding to anger, thy perpetual bane.   [*Going*

CH. Stranger, stand where thou art!

CR.   Hands off, I say!

CH. Thou shalt not go, till thou restore the maids.

CR. Soon, then, my city shall retain from you
A weightier cause of war. I will lay hands
Not on the maidens only.

Cн.   What wilt thou do?

Cr. Oedipus I will seize and bear away.

Cн. Great Heaven forfend!

Cr.   It shall be done forthwith,
Unless the ruler of this land prevent me.

Oed. O shameless utterance! Wilt thou lay thy
                                      hold
On me?

Cr.   Be silent! Speak no more!

Oed.   No more?
May these dread Goddesses not close my lips
To this one prayer of evil against thee,
Thou villain, who, when I have lost mine eyes,
Bereavest me of all that I had left
To make my darkness light! Therefore I pray,
For this thy wrongful act, may He in heaven
Whose eye sees all things, Helios, give to thee
Slowly to wither in an age like mine!

Cr. Men of this land, bear witness to his rage!

Oed. They see us both, and are aware that I
Repay thee but with words for deeds of wrong.

Cr. No longer will I curb my wrath. Though lonely
And cumbered by mine age, I will bear off
This man!

Oed.   Me miserable!

Cн.   How bold thou art,
If standing here thou think'st to do this thing!

Cr. I do.

Cн.   Then Athens is to me no city.

Cr. Slight men prevail o'er strength in a just cause.

Oed. Hear ye his words?

Cн.   He shall not make them good.
Be witness, Zeus!

Cr.   Zeus knows more things than thou.

Oed. Is not this violence?

Cr.   Violence you must bear.

Cн. Come, chieftain of our land!
Come hither with all speed. They pass the bound.

Enter THESEUS.

THE. Wherefore that shouting ? Daunted by what
            fear
Stayed ye me sacrificing to the God
Who guards this deme Colonos ? Let me know
What cause so hastened my reluctant foot.

OED. Dear friend (I know thy voice addressing us),
One here hath lately done me cruel wrong.
    THE. Who is the wrong-doer, say, and what the
            deed ?
    OED. This Creon, whom thou seest, hath torn away
Two children that were all in all to me.
    THE. Can this be possible ?
    OED.   Thou hear'st the truth.
    THE. Then one of you run to the altar-foot
Hard by, and haste the people from the rite,
Horsemen and footmen at the height of speed
To race unto the parting of the roads
Where travellers from both gorges wont to meet.
Lest there the maidens pass beyond our reach
And I be worsted by this stranger's might
And let him laugh at me. Be swift ! Away !
—For him, were I as wroth as he deserves,
He should not go unpunished from my hand.
But now he shall be ruled by the same law
He thought to enforce. Thou goest not from this
            ground
Till thou hast set these maids in presence here ;
Since by thine act thou hast disgraced both me
And thine own lineage and thy native land,
Who with unlicensed inroad hast assailed
An ancient city, that hath still observed
Justice and equity, and apart from law
Ratifies nothing ; and, being here, hast cast
Authority to the winds, and made thine own
Whate'er thou wouldst, bearing it off perforce,—
Deeming of me forsooth as nothing worth,
And of my city as one enslaved to foes

Or void of manhood. Not of Thebè's will
Come such wild courses. It is not her way
To foster men in sin, nor would she praise
Thy doing, if she knew that thou hast robbed
Me and the gods, dragging poor suppliant wights
From their last refuge at thy will.—I would not,
Had I perchance set foot within thy land,
Even were my cause most righteous, have presumed,
Without consent of him who bore chief sway,
To seize on any man, but would have known
How men should act who tread on foreign soil.
Thou bring'st disgrace on thine own mother-state
All undeservedly, and the lapse of years
Hath left thee agèd, but not wise.—Again
I bid those maids now to be brought with speed,
Unless thou would'st be made a sojourner
In Athens by compulsion. This I speak
Not with my lips alone, but from my will.

CH. Stranger, dost thou perceive ? Thy parentage
Is owned as noble, but thine evil deeds
Are blazoned visibly.

CR.   Great Aegeus' son !
Not as misprising this thy city's strength
In arms, or wisdom in debate, I dared
This capture, but in simple confidence
Thy citizens would not so envy me
My blood-relations, as to harbour them
Against my will,—nor welcome to their hearths
A man incestuous and a parricide,
The proved defiler of his mother's bed.
Such was the mount of Ares that I knew,
Seat of high wisdom, planted in their soil,
That suffers no such lawless runaways
To haunt within the borders of your realm.
Relying on that I laid my hands upon
This quarry ; nor had done so, were it not
That bitterly he cursed myself and mine.
That moved me to requital, since even Age
Still bears resentment, till the power of death
Frees men from anger, as from all annoy.

C. S.   U

Being sovereign here thou wilt do thy pleasure. I,
Though I have justice on my side, am weak
Through being alone. Yet if you meddle with me,
Old as I am, you'll find me dangerous.

    OED. O boldness void of shame! Whom dost thou
        think
Thy obloquy most harms, this agèd head
Or thine, who hast thus let pass thy lips the crimes
I have borne unwittingly. So Heaven was pleased
To wreak some old offence upon our race.
Since in myself you will find no stain of sin
For which such ruinous error 'gainst myself
And mine own house might be the recompense.
Tell me, I pray thee, if a word from Heaven
Came to my father through the oracle
That he should die by his son's hand,—what right
Hast thou to fasten that reproach on me,
The child not yet begotten of my sire,
An unborn nothing, unconceived? Or if,
Born as I was to misery, I encountered
And killed my father in an angry fray,
Nought knowing of what I did or whom I slew,
What reason is't to blame the unwitting deed?
And, oh, thou wretch! art not ashamed to force me
To speak that of my mother, thine own sister,
Which I will speak, for I will not keep silence,
Since thou hast been thus impious with thy tongue.
She was my mother, oh, the bitter word!
Though neither knew it, and having borne me, she
Became the mother of children to her son,
An infamous birth! Yet this I know, thy crime
Of speech against us both is voluntary.
But all involuntary was my deed
In marriage and is this mine utterance now.
No,—that shall not be called a bosom-sin,
Nor shall my name be sullied with the deed,
Thy tongue would brand on me, against my sire.
For answer me one question. If to-day,
Here, now, one struck at thee a murderous stroke,—
At thee, the righteous person,—wouldst thou ask

If such assailant were thy sire, or strike
Forthwith ? Methinks, as one who cares to live,
You would strike before you questioned of the right,
Or reasoned of his kindred whom you slew.
Such was the net that snared me : such the woes
Heaven drew me to fulfil. My father's spirit,
Came he to life, would not gainsay my word.
But thou, to whom, beneath the garb of right,
No matter is too dreadful or too deep
For words, so rail'st on me, in such a presence.
Well thou dost flatter the great name of Theseus,
And Athens in her glory stablished here,
But midst thy fulsome praises thou forgettest
How of all lands that yield the immortal Gods
Just homage of true piety, this land
Is foremost. Yet from hence thou would'st beguile
Me, the aged suppliant. Nay, from hence thou would'st
          drag
Myself with violence, and hast reft away
My children. Wherefore I conjúre these powers,
With solemn invocation and appeal,
To come and take my part, that thou may'st know
What men they are who guard this hallowed realm.

CH. My lord, the stranger deserves well. His fate
Is grievous, but the more demands our aid.

THE. Enough of words. The captors and their prey
Are hasting ;—we, they have wronged, are standing still.

CR. I am powerless here. What dost thou bid me do?

THE. Lead us the way they are gone. I too must be
Thine escort, that if hereabout thou hast
Our maidens, thou mayest show them to my sight.
But if men flee and bear them, we may spare
Superfluous labour. Others hotly urge
That business, whom those robbers shall not boast
Before their Gods to have 'scaped out of this land.
Come, be our guide ! Thou hast and hast not. Fortune
          tune
Hath seized thee seizing on thy prey. So quickly
Passes the gain that 's got by wrongful guile.
Nay, thou shalt have no helper. Well I wot

Thou flew'st not to this pitch of truculent pride
Alone, or unsupported by intrigue ;
But thy bold act hath some confederate here.
This I must look into, nor let great Athens
Prove herself weaker than one single man.
Hast caught my drift ? Or is my voice as vain
Now, as you thought it when you planned this thing ?
    CR. I will gainsay nought of what thou utterest
      here.
But once in Thebes, I too shall know my course.
    THE. Threaten, but go ! Thou, Oedipus, remain
In quietness and perfect trust that I,
If death do not prevent me, will not rest
Till I restore thy children to thy hand.

CHORUS.

Soon shall the wheeling foes   I 1
Clash with the din of brazen-throated War.
    Would I were there to see them close,
    Be the onset near or far !
Whether at Daphnè's gorge to Phoebus dear,
    Or by the torch-lit shore
Where kind maternal powers for evermore
Guard golden mysteries of holy fear
    To nourish mortal souls
Whose voice the seal of silent awe controls
Imprinted by the Eumolpid minister.
    There, on that sacred way,
    Shall the divinest head
Of royal Theseus, rouser of the fray,
And those free maids, in their two squadrons led,
    Meet in the valorous fight
    That conquers for the right.

    Else, by the snow-capped rock,   I 2
Passing to westward, they are drawing nigh
The tract beyond the pasture high
    Where Oea feeds her flock.
The riders ride, the rattling chariots flee
    At racing speed.—'Tis done !

He shall be vanquished.   Our land's chivalry
   Are valiant, valiant every warrior son
      Of Theseus.—On they run ?
Frontlet and bridle glancing to the light,
Forward each steed is straining to the fight,
      Forward each eye and hand
      Of all that mounted band,
Athena's knighthood, champions of her name
And his who doth the mighty waters tame,
      Rhea's son that from of old
      Doth the Earth with seas enfold.

Strive they ?   Or is the battle still to be ?   II 1
      An eager thought in me
Is pleading, ' Soon must they restore
The enduring maid, whose kinsmen vex her sore ! '
To-day shall Zeus perform his will.
The noble cause wins my prophetic skill.
Oh ! had I wings, and like a storm-swift dove
Poised on some aëry cloud might there descry
      The conflict from above,
Scouring the region with mine eye !

Sovran of Heaven, all-seeing Zeus, afford   II 2
      Unto this nation's lord
Puissance to crown the fair emprise,
Thou, and all-knowing Pallas, thy dread child !
Apollo, huntsman of the wild,
—Thou and thy sister, who doth still pursue
Swift many-spotted stags,—arise, arise,
With love we pray you, be our champions true !
      Yea, both together come
To aid our people and our home !

   LEADER OF CH. Ah ! wanderer friend, thou wilt not
            have to accuse
Thy seer of falsehood.   I behold the maids
This way once more in safe protection brought.
   OED. Where ?   Is it true ?   How say you ?
   ANT.   Father, father !
Oh that some God would give thee once to see
The man whose royal virtue brings us hither !

OED. My daughters, are ye there ?

ANT.   Saved by the arm
Of Theseus and his most dear ministers.

OED. Come near me, child, and let your father feel
The treasure he had feared for ever gone.

ANT. Not hard the boon which the heart longs to give.

OED. Where are ye, where ?

ANT.   Together we draw near.

OED. Loved saplings of a solitary tree !

ANT. A father's heart hides all.

OED.   Staves of mine age !

ANT. Forlorn supporters of an ill-starred life !

OED. I have all I love ; nor would the stroke of
          death
Be wholly bitter, with you standing by.
Press close to either side of me, my children ;
Grow to your sire, and ye shall give me rest
From mine else lonely, hapless, wandering life.
And tell your tale as briefly as ye may,
Since at your age short speaking is enough.

ANT. Here is our saviour. He shall tell thee all,
And shorten labour both for us and thee.

OED. Think it not strange, dear friend, that I prolong
The unhoped-for greeting with my children here.
Full well I know, the joy I find in them
Springs from thee only, and from none beside.
Thou, thou alone hast saved them. May the Gods
Fulfil my prayer for thee and for thy land !
Since only in Athens, only here i' the world,
Have I found pious thought and righteous care,
And truth in word and deed. From a full heart
And thankful mind I thus requite thy love,
Knowing all I have is due to none but thee.
Extend to me, I pray thee, thy right hand,
O King, that I may feel thee, and may kiss,
If that be lawful, thy dear head ! And yet
What am I asking ? How can one like me
Desire of thee to touch an outlawed man,
On whose dark life all stains of sin and woe
Are fixed indelibly ? I will not dare—

No, nor allow thee !—None but only they
Who have experience of such woes as mine
May share their wretchedness. Thou, where thou art
Receive my salutation, and henceforth
Continue in thy promised care of me
As true as to this moment thou hast proved.

   THE. I marvel not at all if mere delight
In these thy daughters lengthened thy discourse,
Or led thee to address them before me.
That gives me not the shadow of annoy.
Nor am I careful to adorn my life
With words of praise, but with the light of deeds.
And thou hast proof of this. For I have failed
In nought of all I promised, agèd King !
Here stand I with thy children in full life
Unharmed in aught the foe had threatened them.
And now why vaunt the deeds that won the day,
When these dear maids will tell them in thine ear ?
But let me crave thy counsel on a thing
That crossed me as I came. Small though it seem
When told, 'tis worthy of some wonder, too.
Be it small or great, men should not let things pass.

   OED. What is it, O son of Aegeus ? Let me hear,
I am wholly ignorant herein.

   THE.   We are told
One, not thy townsman, but of kin to thee,
Hath come in unawares, and now is found
Kneeling at great Poseidon's altar, where
I sacrificed, what time ye called me hither.

   OED. What countryman, and wherefore suppliant
        there ?

   THE. One thing alone I know. He craves of thee
Some speech, they say, that will not hold thee long.

   OED. His kneeling there imports no trivial suit.

   THE. All he desires, they tell me, is to come,
Have speech with thee, and go unharmed away.

   OED. Who can he be that kneels for such a boon ?

   THE. Think, if at Argos thou a kinsman hast
Who might desire to obtain so much of thee.

   OED. Dear friend ! Hold there ! No more !

THE.   What troubles thee ?
OED. Ask it not of me !
THE.   What ? Speak plainly forth.
OED. Thy words have shown me who the stranger is.
THE. And who is he that I should say him nay ?
OED. My son, O King,—hateful to me, whose tongue
Least of the world I could endure to hear.

THE. What pain is there in hearing ? Canst thou not
Hear, and refuse to do what thou mislikest ?

OED. My Lord, I have come to loathe his very voice.
I pray thee, urge me not to yield in this.

THE. Think that the God must be considered too;
The right of suppliants may compel thy care.

ANT. Father, give ear, though I be young that speak.
Yield to the scruple of the King, who claims
This reverence for his people's God ; and yield
To us who beg our brother may come near.
Take heart ! He will not force thee from thy will.
What harm can come of hearkening ? Wisdom's ways
Reveal themselves through words. He is thy son :
Whence, were his heartless conduct against thee
Beyond redemption impious, O my sire,
Thy vengeance still would be unnatural.
Oh let him !—Others have had evil sons
And passionate anger, but the warning voice
Of friends hath charmed their mood. Then do not
            thou
Look narrowly upon thy present griefs,
But on those ancient wrongs thou didst endure
From father and from mother. Thence thou wilt learn
That evil passion ever ends in woe.
Thy sightless eyes are no light argument
To warn thee through the feeling of thy loss.
Relent and hear us ! 'Tis a mere disgrace
To beg so long for a just boon. The King
Is kind to thee. Be generous in return.

OED. Child, your dear pleading to your hard request
Hath won me. Let this be as ye desire.
Only, my lord, if he is to come near,
Let no man's power molest my liberty.

THE. I need no repetition, aged friend,
Of that request. Vaunt will I not ; but thou
Be sure, if Heaven protect me, thou art free.

CHORUS.

Who, loving life, hath sought   I 1
     To outlive the appointed span,
Shall be arraigned before my thought
     For an infatuate man.
Since the added years entail
     Much that is bitter ;—joy
Flies out of ken, desire doth fail,
     The longed-for moments cloy.
But when the troublous life,
     Be it less or more, is past,
With power to end the strife
     Comes rescuing Death at last.
Lo ! the dark bridegroom waits ! No festal choir
Shall grace his destined hour, no dance, no lyre !

Far best were ne'er to be ;   I 2
     But, having seen the day,
Next best by far for each to flee
     As swiftly as each may,
Yonder from whence he came :
     For once let Youth be there
With her light fooleries, who shall name
     The unnumbered brood of Care ?
No trial spared, no fall !
     Feuds, battles, murders, rage,
Envy, and last of all,
     Despised, dim, friendless age !
Ay, there all evils, crowded in one room,
Each at his worst of ill, augment the gloom.

Such lot is mine, and round this man of woe,   II
     —As some grey headland of a northward shore
Bears buffets of all wintry winds that blow,—
     New storms of Fate are bursting evermore
          In thundrous billows, borne
          Some from the waning light,

Some through mid-noon, some from the rising
    morn,
    Some from the realm of Night.

ANT. Ah! Who comes here? Sure 'tis the Argive
    man
Approaching hitherward, weeping amain.
And, father, it is he!
    OED.   Whom dost thou mean?
    ANT. The same our thoughts have dwelt on all this
        while,
Polynices. He is here.
    POLYNICES.   What shall I do?
I stand in doubt which first I should lament,
My own misfortune or my father's woe,
Whom here I find an outcast in his age
With you, my sisters, in the stranger land,
Clothed in such raiment, whose inveterate filth
Horridly clings, wasting his reverend form,
While the grey locks upon the eye-reft brow
Wave all unkempt upon the ruffling breeze.
And likewise miserable appears the store
He bears to nourish that time-wasted frame.
Wretch that I am! Too late I learn the truth,
And here give witness to mine own disgrace,
Which is as deep as thy distress. Myself
Declare it. Ask not others of my guilt.
But seeing that Zeus on his almighty throne
Keeps Mercy in all he doth to counsel him,
Thou, too, my father, let her plead with thee!
The evil that is done may yet be healed;
It cannot be augmented. Art thou silent?
O turn not from me, father! Speak but once!
Wilt thou not answer, but with shame dismiss me
Voiceless, nor make known wherefore thou art wroth?
O ye his daughters, one with me in blood,
Say, will not ye endeavour to unlock
The stern lips of our unrelenting sire?
Let him not thus reject in silent scorn
Without response the suppliant of Heaven!

ANT. Thyself, unhappy one, say why thou camest.
Speech ofttimes, as it flows, touching some root
Of pity or joy, or even of hate, hath stirred
The dumb to utterance.

POL.   I will tell my need:—
First claiming for protector the dread God
From whose high altar he who rules this land
Hath brought me under safe-guard of his power,
Scatheless to speak and hear and go my way.
His word, I am well assured, will be made good,
Strangers, by you, and by my sisters twain,
And by our sire.—Now let me name mine errand.
I am banished, father, from our native land,
Because, being elder-born, I claimed to sit
Upon thy sovereign throne. For this offence
Eteocles, thy younger son, exíled me,
Not having won the advantage in debate
Or trial of manhood, but through guileful art
Gaining the people's will. Whereof I deem
Thy Fury the chief author; and thereto
Prophetic voices also testify.
For when I had come to Dorian Argolis,
I raised, through marriage with Adrastus' child,
An army bound in friendly league with me,
Led by the men who in the Apian land
Hold first pre-eminence and honour in war,
With whose aid levying all that mighty host
Of seven battalions, I have deeply sworn
Either to die, or drive from Theban ground
Those who such wrongs have wrought. So far, so well.
But why come hither? Father, to crave thine aid
With earnest supplication for myself
And for my firm allies, who at this hour,
Seven leaders of seven bands embattled there,
Encompass Thebè's plain. Amphiaráus,
Foremost in augury, foremost in war,
First wields his warlike spear. Next, Oeneus' son,
Aetolian Tydeus; then Etéoclus
Of Argive lineage; fourth, Hippomedon,
Sent by his father Tálaüs, and the fifth

Is Capaneus, who brags he will destroy
Thebè with desolating fire. The sixth,
Parthenopaeus, from the Arcadian glen
Comes bravely down, swift Atalanta's child,
Named from his mother's lingering maidenhood
Ere she conceived him. And the seventh am I,
Thy son, or if not thine, but the dire birth
Of evil Destiny, yet named, thy son,
Who lead this dauntless host from Argolis
Against the Theban land. Now one and all
We pray thee on our knees, conjúring thee
As thou dost love these maids and thine own life,
My father, to forgive me, ere I go
To be revenged upon my brother there
Who drave me forth and robbed me of my throne.
If aught in prophecy deserves belief,
'Tis certain, whom thou favourest, those shall win.
Now by the wells whereof our fathers drank
And by the Gods they worshipped, hear our prayer,
Grant this petition : since alike in woe,
Alike in poverty and banishment,
Partakers of one destiny, thou and I
Cringe to the stranger for a dwelling-place.
Whilst he at home, the tyrant, woe is me,
Laughs at us both in soft luxurious pride.
Whose might, so thou wilt favour my design,
I will lightly scatter in one little hour ;
And plant thee in thy Theban palace-home
Near to myself, hurling the usurper forth.
All this with thy consent I shall achieve,
But without thee, I forfeit life and all.

   CH. For his sake who hath brought him, Oedipus,
Say what is meet, and let him go in peace.

   OED. Ay, were it not the lord of all this land
Theseus, that brought him to me and desired
He might hear words from me,—never again
Had these tones fallen upon his ear. But now
That boon is granted him : he shall obtain,
Ere he depart, such utterance of my tongue,
As ne'er shall give him joy ;—ne'er comfort thee,

Villain, who when possessed of the chief power
Which now thy brother holds o'er Theban land,
Didst banish me, thy father, who stand here,
To live in exile, clothed with such attire,
That moves thy tears now that thine own estate
Is fallen into like depth of struggling woe.
But tears are bootless. Howsoe'er I live,
I must endure, and hold thee still my murderer.
'Tis thou hast girt me round with misery,
'Tis thou didst drive me forth, and driven by thee
I beg my bread, a wandering sojourner.
Yea, had these daughters not been born to me
To tend me, I were dead, for all thou hast done.
They have rescued, they have nursed me. They are men,
Not women, in the strength of ministry.
Ye are another's, not my sons.—For this
The eye of Destiny pursues thee still
Eager to light on thee with instant doom
If once that army move toward the town
Of ancient Thebes,—the *town ;* no dearer name,
' City ' or ' Country ' shall beseem thy lip
Till ye both fall, stained with fraternal gore.
Long since I launched that curse against you twain
Which here again I summon to mine aid,
That ye may learn what duty children owe
To a parent, nor account it a light thing
That ye were cruel sons to your blind sire.
These maidens did not so. Wherefore my curse
Prevails against thy prayer for Thebè's throne,
If ancient Zeus, the eternal lawgiver,
Have primal Justice for his counsellor.
Begone, renounced and fatherless for me,
And take with thee, vilest of villanous men,
This imprecation :—Vain be thine attempt
In levying war against thy father's race,
Frustrate be thy return to Argos' vale :
Die foully by a fratricidal hand,
And foully slay him who hath banished thee !
Further, I bid the horror-breathing gloom
Tartárean, of the vault that holds my sire,

To banish thee from that last home: I invoke
The Spirits who haunt this ground, and the fierce God
Who hath filled you both with this unnatural hate.—
Go now with all this in thine ears, and tell
The people of Cadmus and thy firm allies
In whom thou trustest, what inheritance
Oedipus hath divided to his sons.

CH. 'Tis pity for thee, prince, to have come at all:
And now we bid thee go the way thou camest.

POL. Alas! Vain enterprise, and hope undone!
Oh, my poor comrades! To what fatal end
I led you forth from Argos, woe is me!
I may not tell it you,—no, nor return.
In silence I must go to meet my doom.
Daughters of this inexorable sire,
Since now ye have heard his cruel curse on me,
Ah! in Heaven's name, my sisters, do not you
Treat me despitefully, but if, one day,
Our father's execration is fulfilled
And ye shall be restored to Theban ground,
Grace me with funeral honours and a tomb!
So shall this ample praise which ye receive
For filial ministration, in that day
Be more than doubled through your care for me.

ANT. Brother, I beg thee, listen to my prayer!

POL. Dearest Antigone, speak what thou wilt.

ANT. Turn back thy host to Argos with all speed,
And ruin not thyself and Thebè too.

POL. Impossible. If once I shrink for fear,
No longer may I lead them to the war.

ANT. But why renew thy rage? What benefit
Comes to thee from o'erturning thine own land?

POL. 'Tis shameful to remain in banishment,
And let my brother mock my right of birth.

ANT. Then seest thou not how true unto their aim
Our father's prophecies of mutual death
Against you both are sped?

POL.   He speaks his wish.
'Tis not for me to yield.

ANT.   O me, unhappy!

But who that hears the deep oracular sound
Of his dark words, will dare to follow thee ?
  POL. They will not hear of danger from my mouth.
Wise generals tell of vantage, not of bale.
  ANT. Art thou then so resolved, O brother mine ?
  POL. I am.   Retard me not !   I must attend
To my dark enterprise, blasted and foiled
Beforehand by my father's angry curse.
But as for you, Heaven prosper all your way,
If ye will show this kindness in my death,
For nevermore in life shall ye befriend me !
Nay, cling to me no longer.   Fare ye well.
Ye will behold my living form no more.
  ANT. O misery !
  POL.   Bewail me not.
  ANT.   And who
That saw thee hurrying forth to certain death
Would not bewail thee, brother ?
  POL.   If Fate wills,
Why, I must die.
  ANT.   Nay, but be ruled by me.
  POL. Give me not craven counsel.
  ANT.   Woe is me,
To lose thee !
  POL.   Heaven hath power to guide the event
Or thus or otherwise.   Howe'er it prove,
I pray that ye may ne'er encounter ill.
All men may know, ye merit nought but good.
        [*Exit.   The sky is overcast—a storm is threatened*

CHORUS.

New trouble, strange trouble, deep-laden with doom, I 1
From the sight-bereft stranger seems dimly to loom !
      Or peers Fate through the gloom ?
She will move toward her mark or through shining or
              shade ;
Since no purpose of Gods ever idly was made.
Time sees the fulfilment, who lifteth to-day
What was lowly, and trampleth the lofty to clay.
      Thunder !   Heavens !   what a sound !

OED. My children ! Would but some one in the place
Haste hither Theseus, noblest among men !

ANT. Wherefore, my father ? What is thy desire ?

OED. These winged thunders of the Highest will soon
Bear me away to the Unseen. Send quickly !

CHORUS.

Again, yonder crash through the fire-startled air. I 2
Wing'd from Zeus, rushes down, till my thin locks of hair,
      Stiff with fear, upward stare.
My soul shrinks and cowers, for yon gleam from on high
Darts again ! Ne'er in vain hath it leapt from the sky,
But flies forth amain to what task Zeus hath given.
I fear the unknown fatal edict of Heaven !
      Lightning glares all around !

OED. My daughters, the divinely promised end
Here unavoidably descends on me.

ANT. How dost thou know it ? By what certain sign?

OED. I know it perfectly. Let some one go
With speed to bring the lord of Athens hither.

CHORUS.

Great Heaven, how above me, beside me, around, II 1
      Peals redoubled the soul-thrilling sound !
O our God, to this land, to our mother, if aught
Thou wouldst send with some darkness of destiny
      fraught,
Smile gently once more ! With the good let me bear
      What of fortune soe'er,—
Taste no cup, touch no food, the doomed sinner may
      share.
      Zeus, to thee, Lord, I cry !

OED. Is the King coming ? Will he find me alive,
My daughters, and with reason undisturbed ?

ANT. Say wherefore dost thou crave with such desire
The clearness of an undistracted mind ?

OED. I would fully render from a grateful soul
The boon I promised, when I gained my suit.

CHORUS (*looking towards Athens*).

Come, my chief! come with speed! Or, if haply at
    hand,   II 2
    On the height where the curved altars stand,
Thou art hallowing with oxen in sacrifice slain
Yonder shrine of Poseidon, dread lord of the main,
Hie thee hither! Be swift! The blind stranger intends
      To thee, to thy friends,
To thy city, for burdens imposed, just amends.
    Haste thee, King! Hear our cry!

Enter THESEUS.

THE. Why sounds again from hence your joint appeal,
Wherein the stranger's voice is loudly heard?
Is it some lightning-bolt new-fallen from Zeus,
Or cloud-born hail that is come rattling down?
From Heavens so black with storm nought can surprise.

OED. Prince, thou art come to my desire. Some God
Hath happily directed this thy way.

THE. What is befallen? Son of Laius, tell!

OED. My path slopes downward, and before my death
I would confirm to Athens and to thee
My promised boon.

THE.   What sign dost thou perceive
That proves thine end so near?

OED.   The Gods themselves
With herald voices are proclaiming it,
Nought failing of the fore-appointed signs.

THE. What are these tokens, aged monarch, say?

OED. The loud continual thunder, and the darts
That flash in volleys from the unconquered hand.

THE. I may not doubt thee; for thy speech, I feel,
Hath ample witness of prophetic power.
What must I do?

OED.   I will instruct thee now,
Aegeus' great son! in rites that shall remain
An ageless treasure to thy countrymen.
I will presently, with no man guiding me,
Conduct thee to the spot, where I must die.

This is thy secret, not to be revealed
To any one of men, or where 'tis hid
Or whereabout it lies. So through all time
This neighbouring mound shall yield thee mightier aid
Than many a shield and help of alien spears.
More shalt thou learn, too sacred to divulge,
When yonder thou art come thyself alone.
Since to none other of these citizens
Nor even unto the children of my love
May I disclose it. 'Tis for thee to keep
Inviolate while thou livest, and when thy days
Have ending, breathe it to the foremost man
Alone, and he in turn unto the next
Successively. So shalt thou ever hold
Athens unravaged by the dragon brood.
Cities are numberless, and any one
May lightly insult even those who dwell secure.
For the eye of Heaven though late yet surely sees
When, casting off respect, men turn to crime.
Erechtheus' heir! let that be far from thee!
A warning needless to a man so wise!
Now go we—for this leading of the God
Is urgent—to the place, nor loiter more.
This way, my children! follow me! For I
Am now your guide, as ye were mine. Come on!
Nay, touch me not, but leave me of myself
To find the holy sepulchre, wherein
This form must rest beneath Athenian soil.
Come this way! Come! This way are leading me
Guide Hermes and the Queen of realms below.
O Light, all dark to me! In former time
Bright seemed thy shining! Now thy latest ray
Sheds vital influence o'er this frame. I go
To hide the close of my disastrous life
With Hades. Kind Athenian friend, farewell!
May'st thou, thy followers, and this glorious land
Be happy, and in your endless happiness
Remember him who blessed you in his death.

                                        [*Exeunt*

CHORUS.

Prince of the Powers Unseen,   1
  Durst we with prayers adore
Thee and thy viewless Queen,
  Your aid, Aïdôneus, would our lips implore !
By no harsh-sounding doom
    Let him we love descend,
    With calm and cloudless end,
  In deep Plutonian dwelling evermore
To abide among the people of the tomb !
Long worn with many an undeservèd woe,
Just Gods will give thee glory there below.

Dread Forms, who haunt this floor,   2
  And thou, the Unconquered Beast,
  That hugely liest at rest
By the dim-shining adamantine door,
—Still from thy cavernous lair
    Gnarling, so legends tell,
    A tameless guard of Hell,—
Mayest thou this once thy vigilance forbear,
And leave large room for him now entering there.
Hear us, great Son of Darkness and the Deep ;
On thee we call, God of the dreamless sleep !

Enter Messenger.

Mess. Athenian citizens, my briefest tale
Were to say singly, Oedipus is gone ;
But to describe the scene enacted yonder
Craves no brief speech, nor was the action brief.
  Ch. Then he is gone ! Poor man !
  Mess.   Know it once for all,
He hath left eternally the light of day.
  Ch. Poor soul ! What ? Ended he with peace divine?
  Mess. Ay, there is the main marvel. How he moved
From hence, thou knowest, for thou too wert here,
And saw'st that of his friends none guided him,
But he they loved was leader to them all.
Now, when he came to the steep pavement, rooted
        x 2

With adamant foundation deep in Earth,
On one of many paths he took his stand
Near the stone basin, where Peirithoüs
And Theseus graved their everlasting league.
There, opposite the mass of Laurian ore,
Turned from the hollow pear-tree and the tomb
Of marble, he sate down, and straight undid
His travel-soiled attire, then called aloud
On both his children, and bade some one fetch
Pure water from a running stream. And they,
Hasting together to the neighbouring hill
Of green Demeter, goddess of the Spring,
Brought back their sire's commission speedily,
And bathed, and clothed him with the sacred robe.
When he was satisfied, and nothing now
Remained undone of all he bade them do,
The God of darkness thundered, and the maids
Stood horror-stricken on hearing ; then together
Fell at their father's knees and wept and wailed
Loudly and long with beating of the breast.
He, when that sound of sorrow pierced his ear,
Caressed them in his arms and said :—' My daughters,
From this day forth you have no more a father.
All that was mine is ended, and no longer
Shall ye continue your hard ministry
Of labour for my life.—And yet, though hard,
Not unendurable, since all the toil
Was rendered light through love, which ye can never
Receive on earth so richly, as from him
Bereaved of whom ye now shall live forlorn.'
Such was the talk, mingled with sobs and crying,
As each clung fast to each. But when they came
To an end of weeping and those sounds were stilled,
First all was silent ; then a sudden voice
Hurried him onward, making each man's hair
Bristle on end with force of instant fear.
Now here, now there, not once but oftentimes,
A God called loudly, ' Oedipus, Oedipus !
Why thus delay our going ? This long while
We are stayed for and thou tarriest. Come away ! '

He, when he knew the summons of the God,
Gave word for royal Theseus to go near;
And when he came, said: 'Friend for ever kind,
Reach thy right hand, I pray thee (that first pledge)
To these my children :—daughters, yours to him !—
And give thy sacred word that thou wilt never
Betray these willingly : but still perform
All that thou mayest with true thought for their good.'
He, with grand calmness like his noble self,
Promised on oath to keep this friendly bond.
And when he had done so, Oedipus forthwith
Stroking his children with his helpless hands
Spake thus :—'My daughters, you must steel your
        hearts
To noble firmness, and depart from hence,
Nor ask to see or hear forbidden things.
Go, go at once ! Theseus alone must stay
Sole rightful witness of these mysteries.'
Those accents were the last we all might hear.
Then, following the two maids, with checkless tears
And groans we took our way. But by and by,
At distance looking round, we saw,—not him,
Who was not there,—but Theseus all alone
Holding his hand before his eyes, as if
Some apparition unendurable
Had dazed his vision. In a little while,
We marked him making reverence in one prayer
To the Earth, and to the home of Gods on high.
But by what fate He perished, mortal man,
Save Theseus, none can say. No lightning-flash
From heaven, no tempest rising from the deep,
Caused his departure in that hour, but either
Some messenger from heaven, or, from beneath,
The lower part of Earth, where comes no pain,
Opening kindly to receive him in.
Not to be mourned, nor with a tearful end
Of sickness was he taken from the Earth,
But wondrously, beyond recorded fate.
If any deem my words unwise, I care not
In that man's judgement to be counted wise.

CH. Where are those maidens and their escort ? Say.
MESS. They are not far off, but here.   The voice of
      weeping
Betokens all too plainly their approach.

ANT. Alas !
How manifold the inheritance of woe
Drawn from the troubled fountain of our birth !
Indelible, ineradicable grief !
For him erewhile
We had labour infinite and unrelieved,
And now in his last hour we have to tell
Of sights and sorrows beyond thought.
     CH.   How then ?
ANT. Friends, ye might understand.
     CH.   Speak.   Is he gone ?
ANT. Gone !   Even as heart could wish, had wishes
      power.
How else, when neither war, nor the wide sea
Encountered him, but viewless realms enwrapt him,
Wafted away to some mysterious doom ?
Whence on our hearts a horror of night is fallen.
Woe 's me !   For whither wandering shall we find
Hard livelihood, by land or over sea ?
ISM. I know not.   Let dark Hades take me off
To lie in death with mine age-honoured sire !
Death were far better than my life to be.
    CH. Noblest of maidens, ye must learn to bear
Meekly the sending of the Gods.   Be not
On fire with grief.   Your state is well assured.
    ANT. If to be thus is well, then may one long
For evil to return.   Things nowise dear
Were dear to me, whiles I had him to embrace.
O father ! loved one ! that art wearing now
The eternal robe of darkness underground,
Old as thou wert, think not this maid and I
Will cease from loving thee !
     CH.   He met his doom.
    ANT. He met the doom he longed for.
     CH.   How was that ?

ANT. In the strange land where he desired to die
He died. He rests in shadow undisturbed;
Nor hath he left a tearless funeral.
For these mine eyes, father, unceasingly
Mourn thee with weeping, nor can I subdue
This ever-mounting sorrow for thy loss.
Ah me! Would thou hadst not desired to die
Here among strangers, but alone with thee
There, in the desert, I had seen thee die!

ISM. Unhappy me! What destiny, dear girl,
Awaits us both, bereaved and fatherless?

CH. His end was fortunate. He rests in peace.
Dear maidens, then desist from your complaint.
Sorrow is swift to overtake us all.

ANT. Thither again, dear girl, let us go speedily!

ISM. Say, for what end?

ANT.   Desire possesses me—

ISM. Whereof?

ANT. To see the darksome dwelling-place—

ISM. Of whom?

ANT.   Woe is me! Of him, our sire!

ISM.   But how
Can this be lawful? Seest thou not?

ANT.   How say'st thou?
Why this remonstrance?

ISM.   Seest thou not, again,
He hath no grave and no man buried him.

ANT. Take me but where he lies. Then slay me there.

ISM. Ah! woe is me, doubly unfortunate,
Forlorn and destitute, whither henceforth
For wretched comfort must we go?

CH.   Fear nought,
Dear maidens!

ISM.   Where shall we find refuge?

CH.   Here,
Long since, your refuge is secure.

ANT.   How so?

CH. No harm shall touch you.

ANT.   I know that.

CH.   What then
Further engrosseth thee ?

ANT.   How to get home
I know not.

CH.   Seek not for it.

ANT.   Weariness
O'erweighs me.

CH.   Hath it not before oppressed thee ?

ANT. Before, it vexed me ; now it overwhelms.

CH. A mighty sea of misery is your lot.

ANT. Woe is me ! O Zeus ! And whither must we go ?
Unto what doom doth my Fate drive me now ?

CH. Children, lament no longer. 'Tis not well
To mourn 'mongst those with whom the honoured dead
Hath left the heirloom of his benison.

Enter THESEUS.

ANT. Theseus, behold us falling at thy feet.

THE. What boon, my children, are ye bent to obtain?

ANT. Our eyes would see our father's burial-place.

THE. 'Tis not permitted to go near that spot.

ANT. O Athens' sovereign lord, what hast thou said ?

THE. Dear children, 'twas your father's spoken will
That no man should approach his resting-place,
Nor human voice should ever violate
The mystery of the tomb wherein he lies.
He promised, if I truly kept this word,
My land would evermore be free from harm.
The power which no man may transgress and live,
The oath of Zeus, bore witness to our troth.

ANT. His wishes are enough. Then, pray thee, send
An escort to convey us to our home,
Primeval Thebes, if so we may prevent
The death that menaces our brethren there.

THE. That will I ; and in all that I may do
To prosper you and solace him beneath,—
Who even now passes to eternity,—
I must not falter. Come, lament no more.
His destiny hath found a perfect end.

NOTES

SOME PROPER NAMES

AIDONEUS, Hades or Pluto.
ARES, The War-God, a destructive Power.
DEO, Demeter.
ERINYES, the Furies.
HELIOS, The Sun-God.
RHEA, the Mother of the Gods.
THEBE, the town of Thebes personified.

ANTIGONE.

P. 6, l. 126. *The serpent.* The dragon, the emblem of Thebes.

l. 130. *Idly caparisoned.* Reading ὑπεροπλίαις.

P. 7, l. 140. *Self-harnessed helper.* An allusion to the σειραφόρος, or side trace-horse, in a chariot-race.

P. 13, l. 342. *Children of the steed.* Mules are so-called by Homer.

P. 30, l. 955. *Dryas' hasty son.* Lycurgus. See Homer, *Iliad*, vi.

l. 971. *Phineus' two sons.* Idothea, the second wife of Phineus, persecuted his two sons by Cleopatra, a daughter of Boreas, whom he had repudiated and immured. The Argonauts saw them in the condition here described.

P. 31, l. 1120. *The all-gathering bosom wide.* The plain of Eleusis, where mysteries were held in honour of Dêo or Demeter.

P. 39, l. 1301. Reading *ὀξυθήκτῳ . . . περὶ*ξίφει.

l. 1303. *The glorious bed of buried Megareus.* Megareus, son of Creon and Eurydice, sacrificed himself for Thebes by falling into a deep cave called the Dragon's Lair.

AIAS.

P. 48, l. 172. *Her blood-stained temple.* In some of her temples Artemis was worshipped with sacrifices of bulls, and, according to an old tradition, also with human sacrifices.

P. 49, l. 190. *The brood of Sisyphus.* Amongst his enemies, Odysseus was reputed to be the offspring of Sisyphus and not of Laertes.

P. 59, l. 574. *Named of the shield.* Eurysakes means Broadshield.

P. 71, l. 1011. *Who smiles no more.* Compare a fragment of the *Teucer* of Sophocles (519, Nauck),

'How vain then, O my son,
How vain was my delight in thy proud fame,
While I supposed thee living ! The fell Fury
From her dark shroud beguiled me with sweet lies.'

KING OEDIPUS.

P. 86, l. 36. *That stern songstress.* The Sphinx. See also ' minstrel hound.'

P. 96, l. 402. *Will hunt Pollution forth.* The party cry of ' driving out the pollution ' was raised against the Alcmaeonidae and other families in Athens, who were supposed to lie under a traditional curse.

P. 99, l. 525. *Who durst declare it.* Τοῦ πρὸς δ᾽ ἐφάνθη. Though the emphatic order of words is unusual, this seems more forcible than the v. r. τοὔπος δ᾽ ἐφάνθη.

P. 102, l. 625. [CR. *You'll ne'er relent nor listen to my plea.*] A line has here been lost in the original.

P. 113, l. 1025. *Your purchase or your child ?* Oedipus is not to be supposed to have weighed the import of the Corinthian shepherd's words, ' Nor I nor he,' &c., *supra.*

P. 128. l. 1526. *His envied fortune mounted beaming.* Reading ἐν ζήλῳ πολιτῶν (with 2 MSS.) and ἐπιφλέγων from my conjecture.

ELECTRA.

P. 131, l. 6. *The wolf-slaying God.* Apollo Lyceius, from *Lycos,* a wolf.

P. 140, l. 363. *Ne'er be it mine,* &c. Reading τοὐμὲ μὴ *λυποῦν μόνον* | βόσκημα.

P. 143, l. 451. *That lingers on my brow.* A somewhat forced interpretation of τήνδε λιπαρῇ τρίχα. Possibly τήνδ' ἀλάμπρυντον τρίχα : 'And this—unkempt and poor —yet give it to him.'

P. 144, l. 504. *Chariot course of Pelops, full of toil.* Pelops won his bride Hippodameia by bribing Myrtilus, his charioteer ; whom, in order to conceal his fault, he flung into the sea.

P. 150, l. 722. *That pulled the side-rope.* See on Ant., p. 7, l. 140.

l. 151. *In letting loose again the left-hand rein.* The near horse (see above) knows his business, and, when the slackening of the rein shows that the goal is cleared, makes eagerly for the direct downward course. But if he is let go an instant too soon, he brings the car into contact with the stone.

l. 746. *Caught in the reins.* In an ancient chariot-race, the reins were often passed round the body of the charioteer, so as to give more purchase. See this described in the *Hippolytus* of Euripides.

P. 154, l. 837. *One in a woman's toils | was tangled.* Amphiaraüs, betrayed by Eriphyle for a necklace.

P. 160, l. 1085. *Through homeless misery.* I read αἰῶν' ἄοικον for αἰῶνα κοινόν of the MSS.

l. 1086. *Purging the sin and shame.* I read καθαγνίσασα for the impossible καθοπλίσασα.

P. 172, l. 1478. Thou hast been talking, &c. Otherwise, reading with the MSS. ζῶν τοῖς θανοῦσιν οὕνεκ' ἀντανδᾷς ἴσα, *At point to die, thou art talking with the dead.*

TRACHINIAN MAIDENS.

P. 180, l. 104. *Bride of battle-wooing.* 'Dêanira' signifies ' Cause of strife to heroes.'

P. 185, l. 303. *Ne'er may see thee.* The Spartan captives from Pylos had lately been at Athens, and some of them were reputed descendants of Hyllus, the son of Dêanira.

P. 195, l. 654. *Frees him for ever.* His last contest brings his final deliverance.

P. 201, l. 860. *From Love's dread minister.* i. e. from Aphrodite, working through the concealed and silent Iole.

PHILOCTETES.

P. 222, l. 194. *Through Chrysa's cruel sting.* Chrysa was an island near the Troad, sacred to a goddess of the name. Her precinct was guarded by a serpent, whose bite, from which Philoctetes suffered, was incurable. See below, p. 254, l. 1327.

P. 226, l. 344. *The fosterer of my sire.* Phoenix, the tutor of Achilles.

P. 227, l. 351. *For I ne'er | Had seen him.* The legend which makes Achilles go to Troy from Scyros is probably ignored.

l. 384. *Vile offset of an evil tree.* Alluding to the supposed birth of Odysseus. See on Ai., l. 190, p. 60.

P. 230, l. 489. *Of old Chalcodon.* One of the former generation, a friend and neighbour of Poeas the father of Philoctetes.

P. 237, l. 729. *Of him, whose home is in the skies.* Heracles, imagined as transfigured on Mount Oeta.

P. 254, l. 1328. *The sky-roofed fold.* The open precinct that was sacred to the goddess, merely surrounded by a wall. See above, note on p. 222, l. 194.

P. 255, l. 1333. *Phoebus' child.* Asclepius.

OEDIPUS AT COLONOS.

P. 265, l. 158. *Mingles with draughts,* &c. Where libations are mixed of water and honey.

P. 288, l. 888. *The God.* Poseidon. See above, p. 282, l. 55.

P. 306, l. 1525. *neighbouring.* γειτονῶν (the participle), l. 1534. *The dragon-brood.* The Cadmeian race at Thebes, sprung from the dragon's teeth sown by Cadmus.

N.B.—For other questionable points the student is referred to the small edition of *Sophocles,* by Campbell and Abbott (2 vols., Clarendon Press, 1900).

Oxford: HORACE HART, Printer to the University.

WORKS BY THE

REV. LEWIS CAMPBELL,

HON. LL.D., GLASGOW; HON. D.LITT., OXFORD,
Emeritus Professor of Greek in the University of St. Andrews.

I. WRITINGS.

1. Tragic Drama in Aeschylus, Sophocles, and Shakespeare. Smith, Elder & Co. 1904.

2. A Guide to Greek Tragedy. Rivingtons. 1891.

3. Religion in Greek Literature. Longmans. 1898.

4. Plato's Republic, in Murray's Home and School Library. 1902.

5. Life of James Clerk Maxwell (with W. Garnett). Macmillan (second edition). 1884.

6. Life of Benjamin Jowett (with E. Abbott). Murray. 1897.

7. The Christian Ideal (Sermons). Macmillan. 1877.

8. Nationalization of the Old English Universities. Chapman & Hall. 1900.

II. EDITIONS.

1. Plato's Theaetetus. Clarendon Press (second edition). 1883.

2. Plato's Sophistes and Politicus. Clarendon Press. 1867.

3. Plato's Republic (with B. Jowett). Clarendon Press. 1894.

4. Sophocles, Plays and Fragments. Clarendon Press. 1879–81.

5. Sophocles, seven Plays in smaller edition (with E. Abbott). Clarendon Press. 1886.

6. Aeschylus, in Macmillan's Parnassus Series. 1897.

7. Jowett's Epistles of St. Paul. Third edition, abridged. Murray. 1895.

8. Jowett's Theological Essays (Selected), with Introduction. Clarendon Press. 1906.

9. T. Campbell's Poems (Selection), with Introduction, Golden Treasury Series. Macmillan. 1904.

10. Letters of B. Jowett (with E. Abbott). Murray. 1898.

III. TRANSLATIONS.

1. Aeschylus, in English Verse. Kegan Paul. 1900.

2. Sophocles, in English Verse. Murray. 1883.

The World's Classics

THE best recommendation of **The World's Classics** is the books themselves, which have earned unstinted praise from critics and all classes of the public. Some two million copies have been sold, and of the volumes already published nearly one-half have gone into a second, third, fourth, fifth, sixth, seventh, eighth, ninth, or tenth impression. It is only possible to give so much for the money when large sales are certain. The clearness of the type, the quality of the paper, the size of the page, the printing, and the binding—from the cheapest to the best—cannot fail to commend themselves to all who love good literature presented in worthy form. That a high standard is insisted upon is proved by the list of books already published and of those on the eve of publication. A great feature is the brief critical introductions written by leading authorities of the day. The volumes of The World's Classics are obtainable, bound in cloth and leather, as given on page 1; and special attention is directed to the sultan-red limp leather style for presentation.

The **Pocket Edition** is printed on **thin opaque paper,** by means of which the bulk is greatly reduced.

January, 1919.

LIST OF THE SERIES

The figures in parentheses denote the number of the book in the series

Aeschylus. The Seven Plays. Translated by LEWIS CAMPBELL. (117)

Ainsworth (W. Harrison). The Tower of London. (162)

A Kempis (Thomas). Of the Imitation of Christ. (49)

Aristophanes. Frere's translation of the Acharnians, Knights, Birds. and Frogs. Introduction by W. W. MERRY. (134)

Arnold (Matthew). Poems. Intro. by Sir A. T. QUILLER-COUCH. (85)

Aurelius (Marcus). The Thoughts. A new translation by JOHN JACKSON. (60)

Austen (Jane). Emma. Introduction by E. V. LUCAS. (129)

Bacon. The Advancement of Learning, and the New Atlantis. Introduction by Professor CASE. (93)
    Essays. (24)

Barham. The Ingoldsby Legends. (9)

Barrow (Sir John). The Mutiny of the Bounty. Introduction by Admiral Sir CYPRIAN BRIDGE. (195)

Betham-Edwards (M.) The Lord of the Harvest. Introduction by FREDERIC HARRISON. (194)

Blackmore (R. D.). Lorna Doone. Intro. by T. H. WARREN. (171)

Borrow. The Bible in Spain. (75)
    Lavengro. (66)
    The Romany Rye. (73)

Brontë Sisters.
    Charlotte Brontë. Jane Eyre. (1)
        Shirley. (14)
        Villette. (47)
        The Professor, and the Poems of Charlotte, Emily, and Anne Brontë. Introduction by THEODORE WATTS-DUNTON. (78)
    Emily Brontë. Wuthering Heights. (10)
    Anne Brontë. Agnes Grey. (141)
        The Tenant of Wildfell Hall. (67)

Brown (Dr. John). Horae Subsecivae. Intro. by AUSTIN DOBSON. (118)

Browning (Elizabeth Barrett). Poems: A Selection. (176)

Browning (Robert). Poems and Plays, 1833-1842. (58)
    Poems, 1842-1864. (137)

Buckle. The History of Civilization in England. 3 vols. (41, 48, 53)

Bunyan. The Pilgrim's Progress. (12)

Burke. Works. 6 vols.
    Vol. I. General Introduction by Judge WILLIS and Preface by F. W. RAFFETY. (71)
    Vols. II, IV, V, VI. Prefaces by F. W. RAFFETY. (81, 112-114)
    Vol. III. Preface by F. H. WILLIS. (111)

List of the Series—*continued*

List of the Series—*continued*

List of the Series—*continued*

List of the Series—*continued*

List of the Series—*continued*

Smollett. Travels through France and Italy. Introduction by THOMAS SECCOMBE. (90)

Sophocles. The Seven Plays. Trans. LEWIS CAMPBELL. (116)

Southey (Robert). Letters. Selected, with an Introduction and Notes, by MAURICE H. FITZGERALD. (169)

Sterne. Tristram Shandy. (40)

Swift. Gulliver's Travels. (20)

Taylor (Meadows). Confessions of a Thug. (207)

Tennyson (Lord). Poems. (3)

Thackeray. Book of Snobs, Sketches and Travels in London, &c. (50)
Henry Esmond. (28)
Pendennis. Introduction by EDMUND GOSSE. 2 vols. (91, 92)

Thoreau. Walden. Introduction by THEODORE WATTS-DUNTON. (68)

Tolstoy. Essays and Letters. Translated by AYLMER MAUDE. (46)
Twenty-three Tales. Translated by L. and A. MAUDE. (72)
The Cossacks. Translated by L. and A. MAUDE (2 8)
Resurrection. Trans. L. MAUDE. Intro. A. MAUDE. (209)
Anna Karenina. Trans. AYLMER MAUDE. 2 vols. (210, 211)

Trollope. The Three Clerks. Intro. by W. TEIGNMOUTH SHORE. (140)
The Warden. (217)

Virgil. Translated by DRYDEN. (37)

Watts-Dunton (Theodore). Aylwin. (52)

Wells (Charles). Joseph and his Brethren. With an Introduction by ALGERNON CHARLES SWINBURNE, and a Note on Rossetti and Charles Wells by THEODORE WATTS-DUNTON. (143)

White (Gilbert). The Natural History of Selborne. (22)

Whittier. Poems. A Selection. (188)

Wordsworth. Poems: A Selection. (189)

Other Volumes in Preparation.

HUMPHREY MILFORD
OXFORD UNIVERSITY PRESS
LONDON, EDINBURGH, GLASGOW
NEW YORK, TORONTO, MELBOURNE, BOMBAY
CAPE TOWN, & SHANGHAI